Praise for *Core Light Healing*

"I've been a fan of Barbara Brennan's work for over 25 years—she has touched thousands with her healing gift. In Core Light Healing, *Barbara has created the essential healing guide—a fascinating read for anyone seeking to understand the role that energy plays in mental, physical, and spiritual health and to free themselves from destructive patterns and suppressed trauma that prevent them from living their very best life."*

— James Van Praagh, *New York Times* best-selling author of *The Power of Love*

"Books like Core Light Healing *show up in your life—like people you love—as acts of destiny! Barbara Ann Brennan is a NASA-trained physicist and an extraordinary mystic. She's here to take you on a mind-altering, heart-opening journey into the cosmos and your divine nature. Let's go!"*

— Robert Holden, author of *Holy Shift!* and *Life Loves You*

"To know Barbara Brenna is to know her 'core light healing' work. She is a delightful person, fellow-teacher, and friend. She lives the life of spirit and brings the 'magic' and discipline of the healer to everything she does. We've known Barbara for over 40 years. When we first met, she was a brainy blond NASA scientist. Not long after, she revealed herself on deeper levels as she entered another world—the world of the heart and healing."

— Bert and Moira Shaw, co-founders of The 50/50 Work and authors of *Bully Big Mouth*

Praise for *Hands of Light*

"This book is a must for all aspiring healers and health-care givers, an inspiration to all who want to understand the true human being."

— Elisabeth Kübler-Ross

"Barbara Brennan's work is mind opening. Her concepts of the role disease plays and how healing is achieved certainly fit in with my experience."

— Bernie S. Siegel, M.D., author of *Love, Medicine and Miracles*

Praise for *Light Emerging*

"All we need for healing is light and love, and Barbara Brennan understands this so clearly. Light Emerging takes us to new depths of healing knowledge. I highly recommend it!"

— Louise Hay

"Barbara Brennan is a pioneer in the interface between science and the healing arts. Her book is filled with deep knowledge and wisdom springing from direct experience and practice. It is destined to become a classic."

— Kyriacos C. Markides, author of *Fire in the Heart*

"Barbara Brennan is that rare and vital combination of scientist, healer, and teacher. Her book is a powerful tool for all of us to live at the new norm of optimum wellness"

— Barbara Marx Hubbard, author of *The Revelation*

"Having personally experienced Barbara Brennan's healing gifts, I am honored to endorse her book. She combines the research methods of her extensive scientific background with her intuitive powers and her inherent wisdom. Modern 'medicine' is thereby enlarged and made human by this remarkable union."

— Rollo May, Ph.D., author of *Love & Will* and *The Cry for Myth*

CORE LIGHT
HEALING

ALSO BY BARBARA ANN BRENNAN

Hands of Light

Light Emerging

✛ ✛ ✛

CORE LIGHT HEALING

My Personal Journey and Advanced Healing Concepts for Creating the Life You Long to Live

BARBARA ANN BRENNAN

Illustrated by Aurelien Pumayana Floret and Bona Yu

HAY HOUSE, INC.
Carlsbad, California • New York City
London • Sydney • Johannesburg
Vancouver • New Delhi

Published and distributed in the United States by: Hay House, Inc.: www.hayhouse
.com® • *Published and distributed in Australia by:* Hay House Australia Pty. Ltd.: www
.hayhouse.com.au • *Published and distributed in the United Kingdom by:* Hay House UK,
Ltd.: www.hayhouse.co.uk • *Published and distributed in the Republic of South Africa
by:* Hay House SA (Pty), Ltd.: www.hayhouse.co.za • *Distributed in Canada by:* Raincoast
Books: www.raincoast.com • *Published in India by:* Hay House Publishers India: www
.hayhouse.co.in

Senior editor: Lisa VanOstrand • *Editor:* Stuart Adams • *Indexer:* Jay Kreider
Cover design: Aurelien Pumayana Floret • *Interior design:* Riann Bender
Illustration consultants: Lisa VanOstrand and Denise Mollo
Illustrations and diagrams: Aurelien Pumayana Floret and Bona Yu

Cataloging-in-Publication Data is on file at the Library of Congress

Tradepaper ISBN: 978-1-4019-5419-2

10 9 8 7 6 5 4 3 2 1
1st edition, July 2017

Printed in the United States of America

CONTENTS

ACKNOWLEDGMENTS

I have the deepest gratitude for all those who believe in me and my work. My spiritual guides have been a big part of my life and were instrumental in the message that is being delivered in *Core Light Healing*. I am forever grateful to my husband, Eli Wilner, who had the wisdom and strength to see me walk this glorious journey.

I give special thanks to all my loyal and dedicated office employees: to Diane Dodge, whose vision and skillful leadership carried this book from conception to fruition; to Stuart Adams, who worked with such care, dedication, and skill from the beginning draft to the completed book; to Denise Mollo, who brilliantly managed the project and provided invaluable insight as an illustration consultant and editorial advisor. The staff at the Barbara Brennan School of Healing has always supported me, and I am eternally grateful.

I give a heartfelt thanks to Lisa VanOstrand for her assistance in making this book a reality, and to the illustrators Aurelien Pumayana Floret and Bona Yu for their roles in creating such beautiful illustrations.

EDITOR'S FOREWORD

I believe Barbara Brennan could easily be regarded as the most influential hands-on healer and clairvoyant of the 21st century. Her work is clearly visionary and groundbreaking. Barbara Brennan's theories of the human energy field (HEF) are still widely quoted. In fact, her theories of the HEF have been adapted and woven into the overall narrative of the field of energy healing. They have served to be instrumental in informing and guiding many of the more recently created energy healing modalities. Other aspects of her work, such as the importance of clear intentionality, have also proven to be far-reaching. I have no doubt her school, workshops, books, students, and overall sphere of influence have touched thousands, if not millions, of lives all over the world.

People were clearly fascinated by Barbara's life stories. They wanted to know about her childhood, her healing abilities, and the unseen world of psychic phenomena that she was able to see and experience. These subjects were often the material of frequent questions from her students and lecture audiences. Barbara channeled material ranging from personal to global issues and on a wide variety of topics, including but not limited to: health, healing, psychology, spirituality, angels, and demons. No subject that could be of service to another was considered off-limits.

Now for the first time, the reader is able to hear Barbara's life story in her own words. Some of the material may feel dated and perhaps even old-fashioned. This might be expected, considering Barbara Brennan grew up in the 1940s and on a Wisconsin farm. She often shared that until she went away to college, she never saw much—except

cows—as she grew up. Barbara experienced childhood in a time when spanking was still a common form of punishment by most parents. She matured in a time when, no doubt, things were considerably different from today's world. However, from both a global and personal perspective, the message Barbara delivers is timeless. From a global perspective, mankind faces the same struggles today as in the past. From a personal perspective, as human beings we all desire to live meaningful lives and to maximize our creative potential.

Core Light Healing is a book that gives an account of a life that focuses on the phenomena that have made Barbara Brennan different from others in the healing field. Barbara's thoughts as she works through those differences and her struggles to come to terms with both aspects of herself—scientist and healer—are evident throughout the book. Many of us desire to see, feel, and experience the unseen world; this can come as a simple expression of longing to have contact with a deceased relative. And herein lies one of Barbara's greatest gifts: her ability to create a bridge between the seen and the unseen worlds and to allow the reader to walk through those worlds with her.

Core Light Healing is about the creative process to manifest the life of your dreams!

In Part I, Barbara Brennan reviews the configuration of the Human Energy Consciousness System (HECS). She then goes on to describe the creative process as it flows through the HECS. When the creative pulse is unblocked, we are able to manifest our longing. Unfortunately, we all have blocks that stop the creative flow. The blocks are where we have stopped our energy due to wounding and traumas that have occurred in childhood. These blocks prevent us from creating what we want and lead us in a vicious cycle of repetitive patterns. Barbara guides us through the steps to release these blocks. When the blocks are released, the creative energy is now free to flow, and the end result is not only the physical manifestation of our heart's longing but also more core essence, more core light.

The groundbreaking *Hands of Light* introduced readers to the far-reaching effects of the HEF as a vehicle for our experience of reality. In much the same way, Part II of *Core Light Healing* takes the reader on an unprecedented journey of the fourth, or astral, level of the HEF, illuminating this mysterious and often misunderstood world and its profound effects on us, our relationships, and humanity. The fourth level is the bridge between the three-dimensional physical world and the higher spiritual worlds. The fourth level contains everything from objects to beings to thought-forms. This is the level of relationship, and as such we are always co-creating with the inhabitants of the fourth level through the law of "like attracts like." This level is also known as the astral world. Since the fourth level does not exist in three-dimensional reality, this level is not visible to the naked eye. Yet from time immemorial, different cultures have described and had access to this world.

Part II begins with a description of how high sense perception works and how to perceive the levels of the HECS. Before we can understand the fourth level, we must first perceive it! Barbara then gives a detailed explanation of the fourth level and how it functions differently from the physical world. Barbara offers plenty of examples from her own healing practice, including her experiences of working with various objects and beings, visiting the lower realms of the fourth level, and her encounters with black magic.

Barbara defines the blocks in the fourth level that stop the creative process as "time capsules" that have potentially occurred through multiple lifetimes. She describes the process of releasing this blocked creative energy through time capsule healings. She explains how the HECS is affected through the process of death and traveling through the astral body.

Because the fourth level is a level of relationship, we find there various types of cords. These cords serve to invisibly transmit information, usually between two people. For example, we create genetic cords to our birth parents and then relational cords to people with whom we have personal connections. These cords can either be healthy or carry distortions that will interfere with our creative process. Ancestral roots, which are damaged genetic cords, connect us to our ancestors and carry false belief systems that are perpetuated through multiple generations. Barbara Brennan gives detailed explanations on healing genetic and relational, as well as ancestral, root cords.

Also included is channeled poetry from her guide, Heyoan, which further elucidates and integrates the concepts presented throughout the book. Finally, each chapter ends with questions to encourage the reader to further explore and work with the material presented in that chapter. Enjoy the journey as we travel from self-exploration to a guided walk through the interface between the physical and spiritual worlds. At the end of the journey is a greater understanding of how *you* are the creator of your own life!

Lisa VanOstrand
BBSH Graduate 1995
BBSH A&P Department Head
Former Dean of BBSH Advanced Studies

LIST OF FIGURES

INTRODUCTION

Tools for Living in the 21st Century

You stand with one foot
in the physically based reality,
and the other in the
spiritually based reality.

What is between,
is the solid ground of your core.

— H E Y O A N

In my first book, *Hands of Light: A Guide to Healing Through the Human Energy Field*, I focused primarily on the structure and function of the first seven levels of the human energy field, its relationship to the human body, and its use in hands-on healing. *Hands of Light* offers a clearer understanding of how and why hands-on healing works.

In my second book, *Light Emerging: The Journey of Personal Healing*, I focused on clarifying our healing process with which we create our lives. Our healing process moves through our Human Energy Consciousness System (HECS), which is composed of four dimensions: our physical body, our human energy field, our hara, and our core essence.

In this third book, *Core Light Healing: My Personal Journey and Advanced Healing Concepts for Creating the Life You Long to Live*, I describe how to create the life you long to live by learning to understand, heal, release, and utilize your creative life energies that arise out of your core essence in the core of your being. To do so means to learn

to recognize and become familiar with the deeper parts of your being. This includes your inner goodness as well as your inner darkness. To release your creative core energies, you need to learn to honor your soul's longing, the deeper source of light, love, and life within you. This source of creativity within you may be far more powerful than you can imagine. Learning to accept that it is there, and to be with it, will change your life forever. Every living creature on the earth, and most likely everywhere else in the cosmos, has an inner core light, or core essence, that is unique to each. *It, in fact, is you!*

I invite you to take this journey with me.
It will be your journey.
Each individual's journey is unique
as well as personal.

Let yourself be who you are.
Who you are is divine.
Let this essence of self that is light
shine throughout your body, your field,
your four dimensions, and your life.

Let it shine into the universe; it is infinite.
It will carry you to and through your life
beyond your most wonderful longing.

It will carry you into your life,
the one that you have dreamed of
as long as you can remember!
Come with me into the most brilliant,
honorable you!

The you that you have not yet dreamed possible!
It is the one you have longed for all your life!

My Path, My Life

Here is a little of my story to give an example of the path I traveled that took me to where I am now. To learn to honor the past is to honor one's life lessons, no matter what they may have been. So here goes my brief history.

I was born in Oklahoma in a shack on a large wheat farm. The umbilical cord was wrapped around my neck and I was blue. No doctor was in attendance. My mother told me that they didn't know if I would survive because I made no sound at birth. But then, as my mother loved to tell me, "You started making lots of noise and you haven't stopped yet!" Of course, I believed her. She didn't have a dishonest bone in her body.

Shortly after I was born, my parents moved us to another state, then from one house to another. It seemed that we moved every two years or so.

At a young age, I constantly questioned everything about reality, to the annoyance of everyone around me. I just never understood the reality that others seemed to have. It seemed to be all about rules: what not to say, what not to do, how not to behave, and what to believe, even if it was ridiculous. People never seemed to be honest about what they really thought or felt. They just pretended that they felt like they were supposed to feel. I did not think like other people thought. I definitely was not interested in being like everyone else— even in high school! I was more interested in not being like the other girls. We were supposed to study home economics. I wanted to study physics and math. But then the whole high school voted for me to be homecoming queen! I knew that I would be the one, but I had no idea why. I didn't even have a boyfriend. As homecoming queen, I had to ask a boy to go to the homecoming dance with me. I was way too shy. So finally, I asked the football player I was supposed to ask. I didn't even know him, and had never even said as much as a "hi" to him before! He said yes. We didn't even know how to talk to each other since we didn't know each other at all. I was very embarrassed because my mother had made my dress. Everyone else had beautiful formal gowns their parents had bought for them. I could hardly wait till it was over.

The University of Wisconsin–Madison

Since my parents had no money to pay for college, I started to work at the age of twelve. I worked for the neighbors in their garden and babysitting. I continued to work through high school, car hopping at Howard's A&W Root Beer Stand. After that, I was a waitress, then later a hostess, in a nice restaurant. Halfway through college, I had to drop out for a semester to earn money. To do so, I worked in a door factory from midnight to dawn. I used a hammer to pound together the cracks in the veneers of door fronts after they came out of a big slicing machine. This was probably the worst job I ever had. After earning enough money, I switched from a state college to the University of Wisconsin (UW) in Madison.

Later, in my first research job at UW, I worked on a research barge going back and forth across Lake Mendota, measuring the moisture content and temperature of the air above the lake. As air blows across the lake, it absorbs water vapor. This experiment was to find out how much the moisture in the air increases as it blew across.

I earned my BS degree in physics from the physics department, and then my MS degree from the meteorology department at UW. In the meteorology department, I focused on the physics of the upper atmosphere, rather than learning how to predict the weather. My master's thesis work was to design and build the omnidirectional infrared radiometer that was flown on the Tiros III satellite, the third satellite the U.S. launched. Dr. Verner Suomi was my major professor. He was on President John F. Kennedy's Science Advisory Board.

NASA Goddard Space Flight Center

My first job after college was as a NASA research physicist at Goddard Space Flight Center. This was very early in NASA's days. I worked on remote sensing instruments that flew on the Nimbus 2 satellite. I built them, tested them, and also calibrated them, both in the lab before flight and also when they were in flight on the satellites.

The instrument, called the medium-resolution infrared radiometer, or MRIR for short, was flown on the Nimbus 2 satellite. The MRIR measured radiation from the earth in five different wavelength bands, ranging from the ultraviolet through the visible to the infrared ranges of the electromagnetic spectrum. I worked on the data from these instruments, and wrote and published papers about the information we learned.

When there was trouble interpreting the satellite data, we used a Convair 990 aircraft (named *Galileo*) to verify the data. I was "principal investigator" for the MRIR airplane measurements taken to verify the MRIR satellite data. We flew as high as possible, directly under the Nimbus 2 satellite as it passed overhead. We did this for all kinds of different earth surfaces, such as the highly concentrated saltwater basin of the Salton Sea in Southern California, the extremely dry desert called the Salar de Atacama in Argentina, the thick green jungles at the headwaters of the Amazon called the Rio Negro, the Arctic ice caps, the cold Antarctic Ross ice shelf, in storms in both the Atlantic and the Pacific Oceans over several different ocean wave heights, and over many types of cloud formations. All of this was to measure the differences in both the reflected and radiated light from different earth surfaces, at different altitudes, to calibrate the effects of the atmosphere on the radiation coming from the earth. We needed all these measurements to compare to the satellite data. Between expeditions, I would work on the

data to create ways to correct the satellite data that was modified by the atmosphere. I loved my job at Goddard. I still miss it to this day.

Several years later, while I was still doing research at Goddard, things in America where changing, especially in the Washington, D.C., area where I was living. Women's liberation and race riots were making big headlines in Washington and affecting the whole country. Since I was a physicist, I hadn't thought about women's liberation. But then I realized that the job I had was very unusual for women at that time. In fact, I was the only woman physicist in my division for several years, until Mary Tobin was hired. Then we were the only two female scientists in our division. I presume there were more women at Goddard, but not in our division.

At that time, I lived in a part of Washington, D.C., that was a mostly black community. Having been raised in Wisconsin, and having started working early in life, I had just never thought about race or sexual orientation. I was not familiar with the injustices with which black and gay people were treated. Some of our co-workers at Goddard were black. Mary and I thought nothing of renting a car and riding around with our platonic co-working friends to see the sights wherever our expeditions took us. However, one day when we were flying out of a southern U.S. city, our two friends refused to go with us.

We were shocked and couldn't figure out why they were so mad at us! We didn't know what we had done wrong. They then reminded us that they were black men, and that we were in the southern United States. It was too dangerous. We were shocked that simply riding around in a car with our colleagues would be dangerous. This woke me up to what was going on in the country. I got involved!

I supported equal rights for all. I even joined the women's rights movement and marched for equal pay for women. I did this even though I had always been respected in my profession and earned pay equal to that of my male colleagues at NASA. I found out that many women in the U.S. were underpaid. It was a real wake-up call for me.

I began to think of other issues in life. With all the social issues arising in D.C., I started to change.

I became interested in inner space and psychological processes. I began taking weekend workshops in bioenergetics. I liked it so much that I started training to be a bioenergetic therapist at the Institute of Psychophysical Synthesis in Washington, D.C.

The Institute for Psychophysical Synthesis

I trained full-time (40 hours/week) for two years in body psychotherapy in Washington, D.C., at the Institute for Psychophysical Synthesis. During this time, I learned to perceive the human energy fields (HEFs). One of the people who ran the training group I joined was blind from cataracts at the time. But she could clearly see and describe the flow of energy through the bodies of the students in the group. So I decided to observe how she was "seeing," and copy what she was doing. To my surprise, it worked! Once I learned to copy what she did, I could also see what she described. At first I was stunned by what I was "seeing," since at that time I had never heard of such a thing.

I continued to hone my skills by methodically observing how my HEF functioned when I used my high sense perception (HSP) to observe the HEF of my clients. HSP is simply a way to receive information through the use of the natural built-in senses that we already have but most people simply do not acknowledge, much less know how to use. So they simply do not develop the ability to do so. I coined the term *high sense perception* because at that time the words *psychic* or *clairvoyant* implied weird stuff. I learned a lot from these simple observations. And I chose not to mention what I was seeing to others for several years.

I was very surprised about how systematically and logically the HEF functioned. I noticed how similar the human energy field and the natural earth energy fields I measured with the MRIR at Goddard appeared to be. Yet this was different; the instrument was in my own head. What a surprise

that was! It even functioned like the MRIR in some ways. So I simply proceeded to develop and fine-tune my ability to perceive the HEF by making more observations of the phenomenon with my HSP. I used my HSP to observe the HEF phenomenon within and between people. I watched the HEF interactions as people went through personal psychological processes while I was in training to become a bioenergetic therapist. I continued this practice of observation when I became a therapist and group leader. I learned a lot about people's energetic habitual defense systems that eventually cause their physical health issues.

I was amazed at how much information was available through HSP. The person's thoughts, feelings, and movements all showed in the HEF before they happened in the physical world.

To clarify how HSP worked, I observed my own HEF at the same time as I observed my clients' HEF by switching focus from the other to myself very quickly. My observations revealed that an enormous amount of detailed information is contained in these natural bioenergy fields. This includes information about the client's health, causes of absence of health, the relationship between mental and emotional functioning, how the HEF's functioning affects the physical body's health, as well as the client's life choices and the lifestyle that results from those choices. I wrote about this in *Hands of Light*.

In *Light Emerging*, I focused on the process of healing through our four dimensions, or HECS—the physical body, the human energy field, the hara, and the core essence. I also included how human interactions can be understood from the perspective of our four dimensions. I first learned about these four dimensions from the channeling I did when teaching healing.

New ideas take some time to get used to, especially ones that affect us personally. Sometimes religious doctrines are used to stop the new ideas from catching on! Science has freed us from many of the old ways. For years the church taught that the earth was the center of the universe. The earth was the realm of man and the realms of heaven were in the sky on clear spheres rotating around

Earth. Yet science has not had an easy birthing. When Galileo looked more closely through his telescope and saw that the earth was not the center of the universe, he was considered a heretic and locked up by the church. Many years later, when Pasteur tried to teach his germ theory of disease, people ridiculed him, saying, "How could something that is so tiny that I can't even see it kill me?" Now it is accepted as common knowledge. We have learned to trust science. Science has drastically changed our views of reality. The idea of action at a distance and the concept of a force field are needed to explain observable natural phenomena such as gravity and electromagnetism. Someone had to think of that, and along came Isaac Newton and James Clerk Maxwell. Their work scientifically proved one did not have to physically touch something to affect it.

Science surprises us as it challenges our old beliefs. Now we look out into the universe and see other possible worlds. There is water on Mars! Is there life on it? Yep, we found it—microorganisms (not the little green men of our fantasies). More recently, with the Cassini probe, it has been discovered that there is more water in interstellar space than on the earth. Wow, that's a new one! The reason to look for water is that it is intimately associated with biological life (as we know it so far).

So why do we not assume that life, even intelligent life, is everywhere, rather than rare? Yes, we need to prove it, yet why the negative assumption? Why not say, "Life must come in many forms! Life is probably everywhere! Let's try to find it in its many surprising forms!" It is only a matter of time before science finds life throughout the universe. We are just beginning to look.

Someday, with the help of science, we will develop instruments to find and measure the energy consciousness fields that are (*from my perspective*) an intimate part of life. Yet in order to research something, one must become curious about observed phenomena. Then one must have some ideas about what one is observing and what to look for.

It is even better to have some personal experiences that spark the curiosity to find the right questions. Then questions can be asked through observations. Questions lead to more questions and eventually to some hypothesis to check out. Then one can eventually postulate a theory, check the theory with experimental evidence, and eventually, with hard work, prove or disprove it. There is always more on the horizon.

I loved that NASA job and respected the dedicated scientists with whom I worked. We were some of the first who were privileged to be part of that early exploration.

But as the 1970s began, and times changed, I became more interested in *inner* space. I began focusing on inner space to discover what within me needed healing and development. I had personal process sessions to explore my inner reality, how it developed, and how my childhood experiences affected my experience of reality. I explored the choices I had made in personal relationships, and changed them if they were not healthy for me. The exploration of my "inner space" became so interesting that I decided to study it formally. So I resigned from my research position at Goddard. In the required formal resignation form, I had to fill out my reason for resigning. I wrote down the words from a popular song called "The Great Mandala," which talked about taking one's place on the wheel of life as it turns through one's brief moment in time.

My favorite boss at Goddard, Dr. Bill Nordberg, who was born in the remote mountains of Austria, was always lighthearted and kind. I always respected and enjoyed working with him. After reading my resignation form, he called me into his office and asked in a jovial tone:

"Barbara! What's a Mandala?!!!"

We both had a good laugh!

✛ ✛ ✛

Core Energetics

I studied several types of body-centered psychology in Washington, D.C., in a curriculum developed by James Cox, D.Th., at the Institute for Psychophysical Synthesis—later called the Community of the Whole Person—and developed a practice in it. Then, to learn more, I studied bioenergetics with John Pierrakos, M.D., who co-founded the Bioenergetics Institute in New York City with Dr. Al Lowen. Dr. Lowen is the author of the popular book *Language of the Body*, as well as other books.

It was during that training that I started seeing colors and forms throughout the interior and around the body. As I continued to observe this "light-like" phenomenon, I became curious about how this new (for me) phenomenon was related to what was already familiar from my research work both in graduate school at the University of Wisconsin and at Goddard Space Flight Center.

It was only later that I found out that the phenomenon was discussed in esoteric literature and made to be mysterious. It was called the *aura*, a term I have never liked. There was an "aura" of specialness around those who could perceive the aura. I never considered it to be mysterious. It is not. I simply observe another natural phenomenon that is actually quite similar to what I had measured at NASA. There is only one major difference. This phenomenon is intimately associated with life and directly related to life experience. The big problem is that, from what I know now, this phenomenon has never actually been measured well. I think that this is because there are additional measurements needed to understand it, such as a clearer understanding of consciousness and the conscious experience of life. Are there ways to measure it? Such a study, then, would become a marriage of the science of physics, neurology, and psychology, and possibly something new that no one knows yet. Until then, I will make do with what I have to offer about this wonderful phenomenon from which we can learn a great deal about ourselves and the living world of which we are a part.

For lack of any scientific equipment to observe or measure the phenomenon, I used my ability to observe it with HSP. By using HSP, I was led to many more questions and observations. I was surprised over and over again with what I observed. It was not at all what I expected, and I soon learned to let go of many preconceived ideas that I had about the phenomenon. I was shy, embarrassed, and afraid, and for many years I kept it secret.

We are in the infancy stage of exploring the life energy fields. Science has not yet really worked on this subject. Very little if any research at all has been done. So until science moves forward, I will rely on my HSP to gather information about the life energy fields and their intimate role in our personal lives as well as life itself.

In the spirit of the search, join me in this great exploration that is just beginning. I hope this book will help you become more curious about the life energy fields all around and in you. More people are experiencing them every day. More people are interested every day. Why? Because they can help us understand many life experiences that cannot be explained within the presently accepted (and limited) paradigm of what it means to be alive in a physical body.

I would like to start with the hypothesis that our life and physical bodies are full of energy. Well, we already know that; it has been measured. There are magnetic fields and electric currents running through the body everywhere. Yes, the coarser ones are easier to measure; even acupuncture meridians can be measured. Many of those who measure them assume that the energy fluctuations measured from the body are solely generated within and by the body. But are they all? What if there are finer ones that are more difficult to measure? What if some fields are from the body and others are not? What if the others that are subtler are actually a priori (or before) the physical body?

Why assume that energy bodies do not exist at all, when for centuries human beings have been describing their experiences and perceptions of them in the languages and conceptual forms of their cultures? Why assume that they do not exist before and after the body, as also has been described by many cultures, without bothering to try to measure them?

When the apple fell on Newton's head, he got the idea of gravity because he saw what happened. It made him curious. That is what happened to me. I began to see things. I became curious. I began looking for the phenomena. The more I looked, the more I saw, the more I began to carefully observe. I wrote about this in *Hands of Light*, experiencing the energy fields surrounding everything in nature—trees, plants, animals—and I referred to those fields as life energy fields. (I referred to the ones that surrounded humans as human energy fields.) Therefore, for myself, after years of observations, the life energy fields became a normal part of the natural world. They function as part of it—a very important part of it. Someday this will be a normal part of modern life, perhaps in this 21st century. It has been common knowledge for centuries for many native peoples all over the earth. Soon we will develop the instruments to measure it, like anything else we have been curious about.

So I hope this book will, at least, make you curious.

Curiosity

*Curiosity leads to observation
that leads to investigation
that leads to discovery
that leads to understanding
that leads to applications
that then improve our lives!*

When I became curious, I started observing the phenomena. I asked myself many questions and then explored this new world of energy consciousness whenever I could. With each answer, I took a further step into the unknown. Each answer led to more difficult questions that challenged our present, generally accepted worldview. Do life energy fields exist? Are they associated with how we live our lives, with the state of our health, with how we create our lives, with our death? How? Do they exist beyond what we identify as physical life? Is there life beyond the physical? Is it or will it be our life? What is heaven from a more modern-day view? What is hell? Is there a more satisfactory way to describe them, given how we see the universe now, compared to when the major present-day religions were birthed? Can we find a way to understand these things that is more applicable to how we experience our lives now? How could such information help us create healthier, happier lives in which we have the power to re-create our lives the way we want them to be? What, then, dear reader, is meaningful to you? What does life mean to you? What is the life you long to live? This book is about how to re-create your life (and your health) into the life of your dreams by understanding and then utilizing your life energy fields, which are, after all,

Actually You!

PART I

HEALING OUR BLOCKS AND RELEASING OUR CREATIVE ENERGY

*"When the time is ripe for change, change is natural.
It unfolds from within and it makes us freer to re-create our
life according to our life's purpose."*

— BARBARA BRENNAN

OUR HUMAN ENERGY CONSCIOUSNESS SYSTEM

Love exists before life.
Love is the breath of life
before the first breath was taken
in spiritual or physical form.

Love is before light.
The ground of your being is nothingness,
or no-thing-ness.

Love arises out of the void as the creative force.

— HEYOAN

To get to Core Light Healing, it is first necessary to study the Human Energy Consciousness System (HECS), to know its structure and how it functions. I have described this in detail in my first two books, *Hands of Light* and *Light Emerging.* I will briefly review it again and include new information.

Moving beyond the Physical World of Three Dimensions

It all started when I was a child, growing up on a farm in Wisconsin. My first entries into the realities beyond the physical went unrecognized for many years. I didn't realize I was entering spaces of life experience that were beyond the normal three dimensions of the physical world we are all used to. Because I lived on a farm, I was intimately aware of the existence of cycles of life.

There was the seasonal crop planting, the spring birth of baby animals, the fall harvest, and so on. The natural world seemed to flow in unending cycles of life, each cycle unique and essential to all the others.

I tried to walk through the woods with my eyes closed, trying to "see" or "feel" the trees before running into them. I got confused because I felt the trees long before I got very close to them. So I assumed that I couldn't do it at all. I assumed that I was impatient and just couldn't keep my eyes closed long enough to reach the trees. The trees always felt a lot bigger and closer than they were. I couldn't figure it out. But I kept trying!

In the summer, when I tried to see the trees with my eyes closed, they looked like large green envelopes of light. In the fall, the envelopes turned red. As fall turned to winter, a great deal of activity occurred as the green was drawn inward, and sparkling, misty clouds wafted off. Winter brought a clear quiet envelope with a slight shimmer. It was something like looking into a drop of water, but without water's natural magnification qualities due to its higher density than air.

In the spring, the envelopes around the trees burst into activity again, drawing in bright points of light from the air around the envelope. Winter's clear shimmery envelope drew up green light from deep within its interior, changing the color of the tree's envelope from its clear winter stillness to the burst of spring-colored green.

After a while I got used to seeing it with my eyes open, and just assumed everyone did. It was nothing special to me. I could see if the trees were happy or sad (from a child's perspective), thirsty or hungry, sick or healthy.

I knew the four winds and what they brought to the land as they exchanged places at different times of the year. I sat silently in the woods without moving to see how many little animals would walk across my feet. I silently talked to the animals. I considered them my friends. I was especially fond of toads and turtles. I found a way to keep a toad sitting on my nose for a long time. We just gazed into each other's eyes. What is it like to be you? I would ponder. They remained silent. They were just being, well, toads.

The natural world that surrounded me was constantly changing, evolving, and reorganizing. I watched for clues of how it happened. The changes were rhythmic, natural, and always occurred first with the movement of light and energy around and through everything. Then the physical phenomena would follow. Of course, I didn't know it was light and energy. It was just a natural flow of life, not separated from anything else. I saw that these cycles exist everywhere—within, around, between, and in association with everything.

As I continued my observations as an adult, I realized that the energy consciousness phenomena always preceded the physical. That is

important! I thought that perhaps energy flow organizes form. But how does it do this? Is it a kind of natural energy that also contains some form of coding or intelligence, or even some kind of unknown consciousness? If so, then the energy fields I observed must have some kind of consciousness. When I realized this, more questions arose. Why don't most scientists deal with this intimate relationship of life? Why is consciousness usually separated from the study of how the world works, including anatomy and physiology? Why has such an unspoken assumption of division been so firmly held for so long?[1]

After studying the seemingly unexplainable phenomena for many years, I began to realize that since these energy fields appear to be part of life, that life experience in the energy consciousness world would not necessarily be exactly like life in the physical world. It would function naturally in an energy consciousness world, and the physics that would govern such a world would be different from the physics that govern the physical world. It would be life beyond the physical reality, yet at the same time be intimately connected with physical reality.

Such experiences and the wisdom gained from them provide a wonderful map with which to navigate into the 21st century. Humankind is taking its first baby steps from living in a physical, psychological, and mental orientation of self and the world to living with a greater awareness of energy consciousness and how it creates and influences our world. This movement takes us into a vast uncharted territory of the experience of being alive, or "aliveness," as I prefer to call it. It requires letting go of most of our basic assumptions about "the way things are."

The Human Energy Consciousness System (HECS)

I would like to introduce you to the system I have developed from my experiences over the

---

1   It is only a matter of time before science finds and measures the life energy consciousness fields throughout all of the natural world that are an intimate part of life. Many are trying. So until that happens, I will rely on my high sense perception to gather information about the life energy fields and their intimate role in our personal lives.

last forty years of observing the human energy consciousness phenomenon. I call this system the Human Energy Consciousness System, or HECS for short. In this chapter, I will review both the HECS and the human energy field, or HEF. It is important to note that in the many years I have been observing and learning about the HEF, it became apparent that the energies that make up this field are, in essence, consciousness. And because of this important distinction, the addition of the word *consciousness* to the Human Energy Consciousness System has been incorporated throughout this book to remind you that energy is consciousness.

I will then go on to describe how our creative process through the HECS works and its extreme importance in all aspects of our life. I will discuss why it is so important to understand how this process works, so that we can create not only optimum health but also the life we long to live. I cannot overemphasize the importance of learning to utilize this creative life process. It empowers us to understand and to regulate our creativity in order to accomplish our personally chosen life goals while living the life we want. Once we understand the effect of energy consciousness on our physical reality, it can release great powers of creativity within us as we learn new ways of being and doing.

After reviewing the HECS in this chapter, I will then provide more information about the HECS and the HEF, which is essential to understand how we function in the energy consciousness realities that are associated with the four aspects or dimensions of the HECS as well as each level of the HEF.

The structure of the Human Energy Consciousness System is quite simple. There are four major aspects or dimensions of the HECS. The four dimensions are the core star, the hara, the human energy field, and the physical body. I see these four aspects as different "dimensions" of our being. I use the word *dimensions* for lack of a better term. Each dimension is distinctly different from the others and functions completely differently.

The Core Star

The deepest dimension of our being is the core dimension in which the core star exists. The core star dimension is our natural divine source of life; it is the source of life within us. Both in the center of the core star and at its outer perimeter that stretches out infinitely is what I call the "black velvet void." (See Figure 1–1.) **The black velvet void is teeming with un-manifest life. It is full of unimaginable power; it is the source of all manifestation. This undifferentiated life exists within and all around us.** It is the foundation of all that is normally called life, on all levels we know, including these four dimensions. When I perceive it with HSP, it is in constant motion, yet it is still. It is un-manifest, yet I experience more life there than in any of the four dimensions of the manifested levels of our being.

From my perspective, there is a relationship between this black velvet void, teeming with un-manifest life, and the quantum mechanics concept of zero point field. Since the black velvet void and the zero point field are the sources of all manifestation, I believe they are one and the same. One is understood from the perspective of direct spiritual experience, and the other from the perspective of quantum physics. On the personal spiritual level, we tap into it with a clear intention to create life, what we want in life, and our awakening. From the point of view of physics, we hope to expand our understanding of the physical world, develop equipment that will solve our energy problems, measure and heal our HECS, and physically take us to the stars.

It is possible through deep meditation to directly experience the black velvet void within the core star. The direct experience of this infinite boundless life is quite wonderful. It is the source within us and within every cell of our bodies out of which we build our Human Energy Consciousness System, our bodies, and our lives. A key point about the black velvet void is that it seems to have all the characteristics of the spiritual "void" referred to by many of the world's sages. My use of the term Human Energy Consciousness System (HECS) can be considered to include all the manifestations of life, material and beyond the material. This would include what is called the "void," the level of consciousness of no thoughts and no self. But there is a catch! No thoughts and no self do not exclude the experience of aliveness or awareness.

Moving out from this central area of no-thing-ness is the creation of light, the edge of creation from no-thing-ness into the manifestation of light. The core star light is the first manifestation out of the void and into individuality. It appears as a bright point of light that radiates out from us in all directions.

It is pure light, but not necessarily composed of colors as we normally perceive them. (See Figure 1–2.) This light is different for each individual living creature on earth. It is the sum total of all that we have become, in our most refined level of being, through our many experiences in our many incarnations through many millennia. The essence radiated from this place within us is unique. It is the distilled essence of all the higher principles that we have imbibed, digested, learned, and become. It is beyond dimensions, yet it is holographic and appears in the center of each physical cell of our body, in the cell's nucleus, and in our DNA. The core star is the opposite of a black hole. It spews out manifest life!

The following is a description from Heyoan of the connection between the black velvet void and core essence:

There is no disconnection
from the void of the core essence
to all else within your life.
The surging of your life force
and its manifestations
comes from this deep apparent emptiness.

You can find this deep, black, velvet void
within the center of every cell,
within every cell's nucleus,
within the DNA,
always surrounded by the
supernova explosion of core essence.

The Hara

The next dimension in which we exist is the hara. The core star dimension is the foundation for the hara. **The hara dimension is experienced as intention or purpose. The hara plays a major part in successfully incarnating—as well as clarifying—one's life purpose and intention to incarnate. The hara also plays a role in our moment-to-moment intentionality, as you will see in later chapters.**

The hara consists of a main vertical tube of light in the centerline of the body. There are two additional tubes that are in the center of the arms and legs. As the hara is the foundation for the HEF (the HEF is described below), it connects not only with the seven main chakras in the center of the body, but also with some of the minor chakras that are located in the arms and hands as well as the legs and feet (see Figure 1–3).

When healthy, the hara extends from about three and one-half to four feet above the head all the way down into the center of the earth.

At the top of the hara is a small upside-down funnel where it enters other dimensions that reach toward the Godhead. As previously discussed in *Hands of Light* and *Light Emerging*, this point is where the hara line originates; I refer to it as the individuation point (ID point). It represents our first individuation out of the core star dimension into this incarnation, and through it we have our direct connection to the Godhead.

The soul seat is located in the area of the upper chest bone (the manubrium). It appears as a soft pulsating light of various pink, lavender, and white colors. This light carries our souls' longing for what we want to accomplish in this lifetime. This longing leads us through our life.

The main power center in the hara appears as a hollow sphere. It is called the tan tien. It is located in the hara about two to three inches below the navel, depending on how tall you are (see Figure 1–4). When the tan tien is healthy, it is a sphere containing the powerful energy of intention. The tan tien has the capacity to hold enormous amounts of power; it becomes filled with power through meditation and exercise. Advanced healers know how to regulate the energy flows in the hara tube from the tan tien to the minor hand chakras to release energy for healing. Martial artists are also able to regulate and utilize this power of the tan tien in their practices (see Appendix). It is the power of clear intention.

Heyoan gave an example of such power when he said that

The tan tien holds the one note
with which you draw your physical body
up into manifestation
from your mother the earth.

The lower end of the hara below the tan tien, when healthy, goes deep down all the way into the center of the earth. When it does this, we are very grounded and in alignment with our purpose for incarnation in this present life on earth.

The Human Energy Field (HEF)

The hara dimension is the foundation for the HEF, and must exist before the HEF can come into existence. Many readers will recognize what I call the HEF as the auric field or the energy body, and these terms can be used interchangeably.

Description of the Basic HEF Structure: The HEF consists of many levels, or "frequency ranges" of energy. The most well-known of these levels are the first seven. Please note that the HEF has many more levels than the seven that are mentioned here. Each of the seven frequency ranges has a specific function related to our life process. The HEF is not layered like an onion. The frequency range of each level goes all the way through and extends from the physical body. Each consecutive level of higher frequency range extends further out from the body. The health and specific nature of each level is very important when studying the creative force through the HEF levels because it is who we are, and through it we create not only how we experience life, but also many aspects of our life itself.

Throughout this book, we will be looking at the HEF from several different perspectives that all influence the creative process. From one perspective, levels one through three of the HEF correspond to three-dimensional reality. Level four is the bridge between the physical world and the nonphysical world, and is highly influenced by our thoughts and emotions. Levels five through seven are the spiritual world.

Another perspective of the HEF is based on whether the level is associated with reason, will, or emotion. In the HEF dimension, time is no longer linear, but is an innate aspect of each energy consciousness experience. Since our energy consciousness can be divided into the three aspects of our life experience, all energy consciousness in the HEF "dimension" is experienced as either reason, will, or emotion.

In this book, I will be using the terms *emotion* and *feelings* somewhat interchangeably but also in different contexts. In the case of reason, will, and emotion, as you will see in Chapter 3, we have a tendency to favor one or two of these aspects of ourselves more than the other(s). This tendency creates distortions in our HECS to some degree. For example, is it more important to you to understand things logically (reason), do you prefer to feel them (emotion), or do you like to get things done (will)? I use the term *feelings* to denote the general sense of the unstructured levels of the fields and their associated chakras. For example, level two and the second chakra are related to feelings. Any imbalance in reason, will, or emotion shows directly in the levels of the field that correspond to our reason (the third level and seventh levels), will (the first and fifth levels of the HEF), and feelings (the second, fourth, and sixth levels).

I will also make a distinction between emotions and feelings in our interactions with others. In this context, emotions are reactions to a situation from the past and will cause a distortion in our HECS, whereas feelings are responses to a situation in the present moment.

To balance these three aspects, according to my guide Heyoan, is part of the work of

The sacred healing path
of spiraling into one's core essence.

It is a path of gathering the pieces of yourself
that are scattered throughout time and
space and bringing them into the wholeness
of the sacred now within you.

Another view of the HEF is to look at whether the level is structured or unstructured. The HEF is composed of alternating structured (odd-numbered) and unstructured (even-numbered) levels.

The Structured Levels of the HEF: The first, third, fifth, and seventh levels are composed of structured lines of light with bright particles flowing through them. The first level is structured as blue lines of light. It is the energy consciousness of our personal will. It also gives rise to the structure of our physical body. The third level is structured as yellow lines of light. It is the energy consciousness of our rational mind that we use in the physical world. The fifth level corresponds to the divine will within us and is a template for the first. It looks more like the negative of a photograph—where one would expect lines of light, there is empty space; where one would expect empty space, there is an opaque dark blue color. The seventh level is composed of very strong gold lines of light. It corresponds to our higher or divine mind.

The lines of light exist around and through all the parts of the body. They essentially outline (in three dimensions) all the various parts of the body, including the interior of the body, such as limbs, organs, and cells, as well as the interior of the cells. Therefore, on each structured level of the field, one can see a three-dimensional view, both the outside and the inside of any part of the body. This view is composed of the lines of light of that level (blue lines on the first level, yellow lines on the third level, and gold lines on the seventh). What I mean by this is that if you look at any part of the body, say on the first level of the field, you will see it as a three-dimensional composition of blue lines of light: the organs look like organs composed of lines of blue light with "particles" of light flowing through them.

Understanding and learning to perceive this is very important in the use of advanced healing skills. These lines become damaged in the field long before any disease sets in. The lines also become damaged when we are injured. This is easy to see. By restructuring the broken, frayed, or twisted lines with Brennan Healing Science skills, the injured or diseased organ returns to health more rapidly than it otherwise would if the lines were not restructured. How much and how long a client's body can maintain the restructuring work done by a Brennan Healing Science Practitioner depends on many things, such as the state of health of the client's body and HEF, the amount of energy the client's HEF can handle, the client's readiness to change, the client's self-care, the ability of the healer, etc. Several restructuring sessions are usually, but not always, needed. With each restructuring, the client takes quantum leaps ahead in his return to health. These advanced techniques also work very well with normal health care given by the medical profession.

The Unstructured Levels of the HEF: The multicolored unstructured levels of diffuse light that are sandwiched between the monocolored lines of light are feeling levels. They can be considered to be composed of bioplasma that is the substance of our feelings. The second level is like colored clouds of light and carries our feelings about ourselves. The fourth is denser than clouds and is thick colored fluid, like gelatin before it hardens. It is the bioplasma that carries our feelings about others. I have written extensively about how this works between people in *Light Emerging*. The sixth level is composed of beautiful amorphous beams of diffuse light radiating out from our bodies in all directions. It is the bioplasma of our higher divine feelings. (See Figures 1–5 through 1–12 for colored pictures of each level of the HEF. See Figure 1–13 for all seven levels of the HEF.)

The Seven Chakras: Within the HEF are energy centers called chakras. In the Hindu tradition the chakras are seen as flowers with petals, yet the name chakra means wheel. To me they look like cone-shaped vortices that spin clockwise if healthy. A clockwise spin draws the energy consciousness, or bioplasma, into the HEF. **Each chakra exists on each level of the field and is composed of the same type of energy consciousness of that level.** This means that:

1. The chakras on the first level of the field are composed of blue lines of light with particles of light flowing through them, just like the rest of the first level of the HEF.

2. On the second level, the chakras are composed of diffuse colored clouds of light that swirl in the direction the energy particles in the structured lines are moving.

3. On the third level, the chakras are composed of finer lines of light that are colored yellow. They also have fine particles of light flowing through them, but they are smaller than the ones on the first level. These lines of light appear to scintillate.

4. On the fourth level of the field, the chakras are composed of multicolored bioplasma that is thicker and heavier than that of the second level.

5. On the fifth level, the chakras are like the negative of a photograph that provides the blueprint, so to speak, for the first level.

6. On the sixth level, the chakras simply radiate beautiful iridescent light of many beautiful colors.

7. On the seventh level, the chakras are composed of very strong gold lines of light, just like the rest of the seventh level.

As you can see from the above list, the color of each chakra will vary according to the specific HEF level you are on.

The energy consciousness taken in by each chakra on each structured level is sent throughout the HEF on that level along the lines of light that lead to all parts of the body. The energy consciousness taken in by the chakra on the unstructured levels of the field also follow the flow of the lines of light of the structured levels, but flow more like bioplasma. All the energy consciousness taken in by the chakras on all levels of the HEF flow to each limb, each organ, as well as each cell. Thus all parts of the physical body receive energy consciousness from each chakra on each level of the HEF. The HEF and physical body work together as an intricate system of bioenergy consciousness and physical living flesh. You might think of the HEF as another, more subtle electrical system of the body that is more finely tuned to our thoughts, will, and feelings than to the systems one studies in anatomy and physiology.

The chakras have three major functions:

1. To take energy consciousness into each level of the energy bodies from the universal energy consciousness field (UEF) or ambient bioplasmic fields all around us.

2. To serve as sensory organs for senses corresponding to the HEF that are beyond what is considered to be normal in the physical world (high sense perception). Thus they are doorways to other realities that serve us in our physical lives, through sudden ideas that just pop up, hunches, feelings of something being right or wrong, or the feeling that something is going to happen.

3. To govern the level of the HEF to which they correspond (first chakra corresponds to the base note of the first level, the second to the base note of the second, and so on). This becomes a very useful tool for HSPs to learn to distinguish between different levels of the field for sensing them in a very precise way in order to restructure them.

Figure 1–14 (side view with chakras) shows the seven major chakras and vertical power current system (VPC). **The vertical power current is the main power current running vertically along the spine into which the hearts or roots of the seven chakras are imbedded. The main tube of the hara is also located inside the vertical power current.**

The vertical power current is seen as beautiful, luminous, entwined ropes of light that spiral and pulse up and down the center of the body.

The first **chakra** is located between the legs, where it enters the physical body in the perineum. Its tip is seated in the sacral-coccyx joint.

The **second chakra** enters the body in the pelvic area above the pubic bone on the front of the body and into the center of the sacral area on the back of the body. Its tip is in the center of the body, at the center of the sacrum.

The **third chakra** enters in the solar plexus on the front and in the diaphragmatic hinge in the back. Its tip is deep inside the body just in front of the physical spine.

The **fourth chakra** is located in the center of the body at the front and back of the heart. It is not located to the left side like the physical heart is.

The **fifth chakra** is located at the front and back of the center of the throat.

The **sixth chakra** is located in the center of the forehead and opposite it on the back of the head. The tips ideally sit in the center of the third ventricle.

The seventh or **crown chakra** sits on the top center of the head. Ideally, its tip joins the tips of the sixth chakra in the third ventricle in the brain.

Each chakra is composed of several smaller vortices that are neatly set inside the overall cone shape. The first chakra has only four vortices, while the crown is said to have one thousand. As one ascends up the chakras, they become smaller and it becomes more difficult to count the number of vortices. Different ancient traditions give different numbers of "petals" for each chakra. Figure 1–15 gives the number of smaller vortices or petals that are used in the Hindu tradition.

Figure 1–15
The Number of Vortices in Each Major Chakra

CHAKRA	NUMBER OF SMALL VORTICES
7–Crown	972 Violet-White
6–Head	96 Indigo
5–Throat	16 Blue
4–Heart	12 Green
3–Solar Plexus	10 Yellow
2–Sacral	6 Orange
1–Base	4 Red

Notice that the chakras are paired. The seventh is paired with the first, and the second, third, fourth, fifth, and sixth are paired on the front and back of the body. The smaller vortices within each chakra are also paired front and back with each other. This is very important in the healing skill of restructuring the chakras on each level of the field, as damage to a chakra or small vortex of a chakra will affect the functioning of its pair on the other side of the physical body. The vortices of each chakra on each level metabolize a different frequency of energy consciousness. The energy consciousness is then brought to the areas, organs, and cells of the body that utilize it for healthy functioning.

The Chakras and the Metabolism of HECS Bioplasma and HSP: Chakras metabolize HEF bioplasma. Since chakras are charged, they attract charged energy consciousness, or energetic bioplasma, into them from the surrounding biofield, or universal energy field (UEF). Chakras are cone-shaped structures that also pull bioplasma/energy consciousness into their centers by spinning, much like a tornado pulls things into it. This HECS bioplasma nurtures the human energy field and also carries information about the surrounding UEF.

The chakras are also perceptual centers that sense through high sense perception (HSP). When functioning properly, they give us the ability to perceive the world beyond our normal sensory perception. We can sense in a much broader range of perceptions. This is discussed further in Chapter 6 on Practical HSP.

Because of these extremely important functions, our chakras play a major role in our life processes. Any distortion in a chakra will cause more effect than a distortion in other parts of the HEF. I will discuss the general types of distortions found in chakras, and will give specific examples of distortions in the solar plexus chakra and their effects in Chapter 3.

A note regarding bioplasma: there are four states of matter—solids, liquids, gases, and plasmas—of which we are made. Plasmas are groups of charged particles, or ions. (Interstellar space is full of them.) Since the particles in plasma carry a charge, they are affected by electromagnetic fields. It appears to me that the HEF, as well as the hara and core star, are composed of bioplasma.

This bioplasma of the HEF is directly associated with consciousness. Bioplasma contains energy consciousness. Most humans are unaware of their energy consciousness and cannot sense it. Or, if they do, they refer to their experience of being sensitive as "intuition," or "having a feeling" that they "know something," or "should do something," like leave a certain location to go to another place, or "go home right now."

Keep in mind, there are also other types of plasmas in the physical body as well, such as blood plasma, or the interstitial fluids that are also sometimes referred to as plasmas. For our discussion here, we are referring to the bioplasma of the HEF.

The Physical Body

The physical body is the last of the four aspects of our being. The HEF is the foundation and the unfolding pattern or template for the physical body, coming into existence before the physical body. The physical body is nested in the HEF, and is completely dependent on the three deeper dimensions as well for its origin, its life, its growth, its shape, and its health.

All other aspects of the three dimensions listed above exist within and throughout the physical body. The physical body cannot exist without them. This is true of all life-forms in the physical world. Each cell, including everything in the cell, has a core star and a hara. Each has a purpose for its life.

Figure 1–16 shows all four of the dimensions of the HECS.

Chapter 1 Self-Review: Some Exercises to Sense Your HEF and HECS

1. Try to sense the levels of your HEF. People who do more physical activities are better at sensing the lower levels first. If you tend to be a feeling person, try focusing on the second level. If you hold love above all things, focus on the fourth level first. If you tend to surrender to God's will, focus on the fifth level first, although it may be the hardest to sense. Those who spend a lot of time meditating can sometimes sense the sixth or seventh level more easily. If your meditations focus on feeling bliss or spiritual ecstasy, try to sense the sixth level first. If your meditations focus on stillness and divine mind, try sensing the seventh level first. Use the information in this chapter to help guide you. Feel, see, hear, know, and sense the level of your field you choose.

2. Can you relate each level of the HEF to your life experience? This is getting to recognize yourself in the levels of your HEF.

3. Sense yourself as each of the four dimensions of your HECS. Notice which aspect of yourself is easiest to sense, and which is hardest. Practice.

Chapter 2

OUR CREATIVE PROCESS THROUGH OUR HUMAN ENERGY CONSCIOUSNESS SYSTEM

Humanity has the gift of co-creation,
the gift of free will
and the gift of your physical body
and your energy-consciousness system,
including intentionality and core essence.

You have the tools to become conscious co-creators.

— HEYOAN

The Creative Pulse of Life through the HECS

(Note: the terms Creative Process and Creative Pulse are used interchangeably within this chapter.) After teaching me about the four dimensions or aspects of our being, Heyoan proceeded to channel information about the creative process through the four dimensions. At first I assumed he was talking about the creative process of visualization to get what you want in your life, i.e., the process of materialization. However, it turned out to be much more than that.

Heyoan taught that our incarnation process itself is an act of creation. In addition, incarnation is a way to open more creative possibilities for ourselves as well as for others around us, for in incarnation, we learn a great deal about ourselves. Heyoan says that the creative process of incarnation begins long before what we call incarnation, as well as long before conception.

According to Heyoan, the creative process originates deep inside the center of the core star, in the black velvet void that is teeming with powerful, undifferentiated, un-manifested life. **In our creative process, we *ignite* the black velvet void of undifferentiated life within us by merging into it with our *longing to create*.**

Success can only be accomplished with our clear intention that is aligned with our longing *and with the intention of the Creator*.

The gift of incarnation is to create. Each of us is born with a longing to create. Each individual's longing is unique and very specific. This is both the purpose and reason to incarnate. When we create in this way, we develop and expand the expression of our individuated divine essence in our core light. It becomes more brilliant with each such creation.

The creative process then upwells from our core into the dimension of the hara line and is transmuted into our creative intention, or purpose, in the hara. Hara then holds this intention in place to keep our creative process flowing up into our next dimension, the HEF. In doing so it is transmuted into the three aspects of the HEF—reason, will, and emotion—with which we then create our physical lives.

How the Relationship between Aspects of the HECS Gives Rise to the Idea of Dimensions

As explained in Chapter 1, each aspect of the HECS appears to be nested in the other. Each appears to arise out of and be dependent upon the one it is nested in for its existence. Moving out from the central area of nothingness, or no-thing-ness, that is teeming with life, the black velvet void gradually becomes light. This light, which is the point of our origin, our core star, influences our hara because it is the foundation of the hara. The hara is the foundation of the HEF and influences it. The HEF is the foundation of our physical body and influences it. There is no direct connection between them, yet they do influence each other as if through different dimensions. The influence seems to move as if they upwell from the deeper, more fundamental aspect of ourselves into the next manifested dimension, in a manner that is more like a *transmutation of influence* into the next dimension, rather than a *direct flow or transmission of a substance*. Thus there is a major transmutation in the influence of the creative pulse of life as it upwells through each dimension.

Let's examine what this transmutation means in practical terms.

Overview of the Creative Process as It Manifests through the HEF

The core star is composed of *individuated divine essence*. As the essence of the core star upwells into hara, it is transmuted into *intention* in the hara dimension, thus *essence becomes intention*. As intention is transmuted into each level of the HEF, it is expressed as the *energy consciousness of reason, will,* and *emotion*, according to the level of the field. As the energy consciousness of the HEF upwells into the physical world, it is transmuted into *living flesh*. Thus we are composed of all four of these "dimensions."

How the Creative Process Manifests through the Core Star and Hara Dimensions

Your creative process is initiated in your core. It draws up creative energy from the black velvet void. The creative energy is first individualized as it moves through the core star as core essence. It then upwells into the hara dimension and moves through your intention to create whatever it is you long to create. When your hara line is completely aligned and centered inside you, you experience effortless intention. In such moments, you have no resistance to the flow of creative life through you. See Figure 2–1, which shows an aligned hara line. As the creative force moves into your hara dimension, it ignites your magnificent longing in your soul seat. Some may call it your magnificent obsession. What that is for you may not yet be clear to you. What do you yearn for? What life do you want to live? Remove any personal taboos you have about it. At least allow yourself the fantasy. Let the fantasy develop into a mature vision of what it is. Let yourself long for it. Begin your creation; *it is what you took birth for*. Practice feeling it, seeing it, knowing its details, and then let it grow. Let it become something that surprises you. Here is what Heyoan said about longing:

You are co-creators of all that you long for.
Simply by your knowing that you long for it,
you can be absolutely sure
that you have already begun its creation.

All of your sweet longings
are actually creations that you initiated
some time ago,
creations that are already in process of coming true.
You are their creator.

Experience the powerful creative force in your tan tien. Experience your connection to Father God and Goddess Mother Earth at each of the far ends of the hara line.

If your hara is healthy and therefore balanced in all the aspects as mentioned above, your creative force flows through all in a balanced way, and thus proceeds down toward the physical world via the next dimension, your HEF.

The Creative Pulse through the HEF

Your creative force then upwells from your hara dimension into your HEF dimension. Note in Figure 2–1 the connection between the hara and the HEF; the main tube of the hara is located inside the vertical power current of the HEF. In the HEF, it manifests first in the highest levels of your HEF and proceeds to cascade down from the higher to the lower levels on its way to physical manifestation.

While moving through each HEF level, it takes on the nature of each level—reason, will, or emotion—and the state of our evolutionary development of that level, such as the degree of understanding and clarity for the reason levels, the degree of our ability to align our personal will with divine will on the will levels, and the evolutionary development of our ability to choose love in all life circumstances on the unstructured feeling levels.

To become aware of it, you must be able to sense each level of your field as the creative pulse of life moves through it. The following is an explanation of how the creative life pulse moves through each level of the HEF:

The Creative Pulse in the Seventh Level of the HEF

The seventh level of the HEF is the manifestation or functioning of our higher or divine mind. When your creative life pulse moves through your seventh level, it is experienced as a sense of divine wisdom. If you are aware of it in the seventh level of your HEF, you may feel your creation is divinely inspired.

The Creative Pulse in the Sixth Level of the HEF

While moving through the sixth level, the creative life pulse expresses your feelings about divinity. In this level, you feel the creative force so strongly that no matter what you may have to go through you feel your creation will be great. Faith is the creative life force coming through the sixth level of the field. Many people may also have the experience of divine ecstasy for their creation in this level.

The Creative Pulse in the Fifth Level of the HEF

While moving through the fifth level, the creative pulse of life expresses as your free will, and is influenced by the state of development of your ability to understand and choose to align with divine will. If you are aware of it in the fifth level, you will experience a perfect pattern of divine precision as your creation unfolds.

The Creative Pulse in the Fourth Level of the HEF

While moving through the fourth level, the creative pulse of life expresses as your loving feelings about others, and is influenced by the state of development of your ability to love others in relationship. If you become aware of it in the fourth level, you will experience a loving relationship with your creation that supports your creative process.

The fourth level is the level before physical manifestation. Levels one, two, and three take place in three-dimensional reality. The fourth level is where all your interactions take place with others; it is therefore the level of relationship. And because it is the level before physical reality, it contains both the seen and unseen realities. Thus your relationship with everyone

in your physical world and also with everything else in this reality will have a tremendous effect on your creative process. Fourth-level reality will be explored in great detail in Part II.

The Creative Pulse in the Third Level of the HEF

While moving through the third level, the creative pulse of life expresses your thoughts and mental understanding. This level is influenced by the state of development of your human mind. If you are aware of it in the third level, you will have the necessary mental acumen to bring your creation into physical reality.

The Creative Pulse in the Second Level of the HEF

While moving through the second level, the creative pulse of life expresses your feelings about yourself, and is influenced by your state of self-love. Self-love must be recognized, acknowledged, understood, and cultivated as a necessary skill to live a healthy way of life. If you are aware of it in the second level of your HEF, you will feel personal pleasure in creating it in your life and gain a better and more loving opinion of yourself.

The Creative Pulse in the First Level of the HEF

While moving through the first level, your creative pulse of life is expressed as your physical feelings, sensations, and will to be incarnated at this time. Your creative pulse is influenced by the state of the energetic template of your physical body. If you are aware of it in the first level, you will feel the physical will to accomplish your creative acts. You will also feel pleasure in your body and your life in the physical world as your creation comes close to materialization.

The Creative Pulse as It Manifests in the Physical World

The creative process is then precipitated into our physical body and the physical world. It is expressed in our actions in the physical world and is influenced by the state of our physical health. Our physical bodies need appreciation and loving care as well as recognition for their spectacular intricacy and innate beauty. Taking care of our physical body is an agreement we have made for the gift of the incarnation process. It is the vehicle through which we manifest our creations into the physical world.

The creative process is also influenced by the conditions of our lives, which are the result of our creative process over time. Recognizing, understanding, and learning to improve the condition of our lives—physically, emotionally, mentally, and relationally—is required to do this.

Further Clarification on the Pulse of Life

When Heyoan was teaching me about the creative pulse of life, he did it in phases. First he taught me the creative process as described previously in this chapter. So naturally, I thought the final phase was the materialized product, which could be a state of superb health, a painting, one's income tax, a relationship.

But then Heyoan said,

No, that is only halfway through the creative process!

"What do you mean?" I asked.

Heyoan proceeded to teach me the rest of the creative process as it reversed directions and proceeded into the deeper levels of one's being—into the deeper levels of the HECS just described above but in reverse. (See the following section on the Four Phases of the Creative Pulse of Life.) It finally completed its creation in a brighter light in the core star.

Then Heyoan proclaimed,

The final "product," if you will, of the creative pulse of life is more individuated core essence!

"What is that?" I asked.

The individuated core essence is the individuated divine within each being. It is both universal and individual.

"How can that be?"

The core essence of the core star exists beyond the physical and energetic dimensions you are used to. It does not depend on the usual space coordinates, within which you limit yourselves for a while in incarnation, with the purpose of focused learning.

Core essence is not limited in that way. It can be uniquely individual as an expression of your individual core qualities, and is also part of all beings, manifest and un-manifest.

Incarnation is a result of the intent to individualize, in an organized form of manifestation, for the purpose of creating more individualized core essence, which can then be experienced as luminous emptiness without losing self, without getting lost in undifferentiated divine wholeness.

To do this, you must first learn how to become a co-creator with the divine. Thus you must first learn how the divine creates. You must ask, "How does the divine create through me, a manifestation of the divine?" Here is the answer:

*The divine universe
is a reciprocating universe.
It is benign.
It responds to your flowing creative current
by becoming co-creator with you.*

*If you stop your flowing creative current,
the universe simply waits for you
to allow it to flow again.*

Cause and Effect

The above Heyoan quote means that the divine does not make us do anything, or become something personally. God does not punish us personally for doing or not doing something. Instead, the divine universe simply waits for us to initiate creativity in our lives. Then it responds, in kind, to all our thoughts, desires, and actions (including the negative ones). This is simply called cause and effect.

While many people refer to cause and effect over lifetimes as karma, this term can have a negative connotation—as if it were punishment, especially when we take it personally. But it isn't God directing punishment. **Cause and effect is simply how the universe functions. If we don't** **get the effect (outcome) we want, we just don't know how to create it yet.** It takes more learning until we know how to do it. Such an understanding includes learning a lot about ourselves and how we function, as well as replacing our erroneous dualistic concepts about reality with clear unified (or holistic, if you prefer) concepts that help us understand how the world actually works. The more we learn about this, the better we will be able to accomplish our life's longing.

The Four Phases of the Creative Pulse of Life

The creative process has four phases. I referred to these phases in my previous book, *Light Emerging*, as stasis, expansion, stasis, and contraction. There is always a moment of stasis, followed by a wave of expansion, then another moment of status, ended by a wave of contraction. This is then followed by another moment of stasis, after which another wave of expansion begins. All living beings follow this creative pulse of life. Note that in some situations, like a healing, the creative pulse starts with expansion, followed by stasis, contraction, and then stasis. Regardless of where you start in the creative pulse, these four phases are always involved and follow one another like a wave going in and out.

The First Phase of the Creative Pulse of Life: First is the stillness of the empty black void deep within the core star from which all creation arises. This is a point of stasis.

The Second Phase of the Creative Pulse of Life: In the second phase we follow the creative pulse of life arising in the core star and upwelling through hara, the HEF, and then into the physical. From this expansion out of the core, the essence of who you are expresses itself through the dimensions of intention (haric level) and personality (HEF or auric level), and then your creation manifests into the physical world.

The Third Phase of the Creative Pulse of Life: After reaching the physical, the creative pulse goes into a static mode of rest. It is the stasis at the end of our expansion. Here we pause for self-observation as we reflect on our creation. As Heyoan reminded us, this is really only the midpoint of the creative process.

The Fourth Phase of the Creative Pulse of Life: After self-observation, the creative pulse of life contracts inward from the physical world into the auric down into the Haric level, and then back into the Core. It is deep within the Core that we reach the final stage of the creative pulse of life. Often there can be a resistance to this phase, but it is important to remember that we need to give equal time and attention to the contraction phase of the creative pulse, as well as to the silent void of the deep inner stasis phase that will follow. As the creative pulse returns through the four dimensions and back into our core star, it brings all that has been learned and created back into the individual self. Thus, the final result of the creative pulse of life is to create more divine core essence. Then we again move into the deep inner stasis of the silent void until our next creative pulse arises.

Life Pulses

The creative pulse of life
is not just one pulse. It is infinite pulses of
infinite phases,
frequencies, and sizes, all
stemming out of the core essence.

It arises from not only the core star,
but out of every cell of your body,
out of every part of every cell,
the DNA, the elements, and the atoms.

Life expands, creates,
goes into stasis, reflects,
contracts, distills the knowledge,
and brings conscious awareness to the center of
your being.
There are many phases
on this creative wave of life.
Each individual pulsates in many different
expansion and contraction phases
around different aspects of life.
Some long, others short.
Some fast, others slow.
All life pulses are universal.
Each life pulse permeates everything.

Your every action, your every phrase,
reaches the great expanse of the universe.
All are synchronized
in the great symphony of life.

The Results of a Clear Creative Process through the HECS

If your hara and HEF are clear, charged, and balanced in the area of a particular longing, you will be able to easily manifest it. In fact, you already do this on a daily basis. You create so easily in the areas you are clear in that you don't even notice it. To you it is nothing.

But to your friends it is amazing!

They will ask you, "How can you do that?"

You might answer, "Oh, it's nothing, it just comes naturally."

On the other hand, you will say the same thing about your friends' talents. These are core talents. They come directly from the core essence that you or your friends have created in life experiences, whether or not they are this incarnation, or any incarnation, for that matter. In these areas of your being, the creative current precipitates directly down from your core unimpeded. You have no blocks or unhealed wounds. When I say area, I refer to your physical, emotional, mental, and spiritual state of being in any particular aspect of your life, such as health, career, or relationships.

Now let's take a look at how the creative process functions through an ideal, clear, unblocked HEF. I have never seen an HEF that is completely clear in all areas. This includes the many spiritual leaders and gurus that I have seen over the years. However, our fields do tend to be clear in certain areas of our lives. In these areas, we are able to create unimpeded. In Figure 2–2, the arrows pointing down through the HEF depict the clear, unimpeded creative process into the physical world when our HEF is unblocked. These are the areas of our lives in which things just come naturally. If we choose to create something, it works. No problem! Usually, we don't think anything of it. We don't even concentrate on it. We just do it. It simply flows down through the levels, expressing the nature of each level, as it creates that aspect of our creative endeavor. We call these things talents. Each person is different from the other.

Every one has many such talents. What are yours? Many of us have been taught, as I was, not to mention our talents or good aspects, for fear that it means we are egotistical. This is just plain unhealthy. Usually, we don't notice the areas of our lives that work easily that are a result of our talents. Yet our talents are more than just talents. They are the areas of our being through which our core essence shines through fully. They are the areas of our being in which we just naturally express our developed core essence. Ultimately they are the areas of our being in which higher principles are expressed.

For example, a friend of mine, with whom I have worked for many years, has the ability to be in a state of deep supportive consideration with whomever she is in communication. This is an expression of the higher principle of divine love. Another friend has the ability to be deeply present, even in the physical cells of another person. She can do this no matter what their emotional or physical condition is, even if it is the dying process. This is an expression of divine will and divine love. Another friend is passionate about integrity and principles and can clarify them in confusing situations. This is an expression of divine truth. Another can quietly and calmly lead a group of disagreeing people into agreement. This is an expression of divine truth and will. Another is a serious educator and always focuses on making sure students are led to successful completion (another expression of divine truth and will).

Another is honest to the T (divine truth); another is the most organized person I have met (divine will). All of these people have followed their sacred longings, worked and studied to develop their talents, through which their core essence shines beautifully in these things that they love.

Chapter 2 Self-Review: Some Questions to Ask Yourself about Your HECS and Your Creative Process

1. Trace your creative process through the levels of your HEF. Try as best you can to sense them using the information in this chapter. Feel, see, sense it. First travel back into your history to find something that you really wanted and then finally were able to create in your life. Note the personal process you went through as it came through the aspect of each level of your field: higher mind, will, and feeling; then through loving relationship; and then down through personal/human mind, will, and feeling.

2. Now trace your creative process through the four phases of the creative pulse: stasis, expansion, stasis, and contraction.

3. Relate each creative experience to the creative force of love as it moves through you.

Chapter 3

HEALING THE BLOCKED CREATIVE PROCESS

*This exploration can be seen as work
to open the flow of creative energies through you,
to discover and understand how they are blocked
and then to open them for the purpose of learning and clarifying co-creation.*

*You are here to become consciously aware of your purpose,
which is co-creation with the divine.
You do not study to find what is wrong,
or what is bad in you,
or what is objectionable.*

You are here to learn and clarify your personal co-creative process with the divine.

— HEYOAN

In the last chapter, I described the clear creative process and showed that the final result of our creative pulse (and creation for that matter) is divine core essence, or more core light. How we experience our lives and our health depends on how well formed, clear, and balanced are the four dimensions of our being, including each level of the HEF. Each of the four dimensions has a great influence on the creative pulse as it moves through each dimension. Since the deeper dimensions are the foundation of those above, their influence is stronger, like the foundation of a building. Any disturbances in the deeper dimensions will affect all those that rest upon them.

The work of healing must include all aspects of our four dimensions. This includes not only the hara and the HEF but also the specific aspects of each: the state of the three aspects of the hara, as well as its placement, alignment, and connection to the earth; the health and balance of the levels of the HEF; and, last but not least, how well we can be present with and honor our life pulse each moment as we create our lives with it. To do this, it is important to thoroughly understand our four dimensions and how they can become blocked. We must become consciously present in each dimension as well as knowingly sense the dimensions as the creative process flows through them.

The Blocked or Distorted Creative Process

Sometimes our creative force encounters interference during the creative process as it cascades down through the four dimensions. These are the areas of work for us in this lifetime. **In other words, in any area where there is interference with the creative process, personal growth is required.** Such areas in one's self are not hard to find. What have you always wanted but still have not been able to manifest in your life? Any distortion in any area of your hara or HEF will interfere with your creative process.

Distortion in the Hara: If there is distortion in your hara, you will split your creative force according to that distortion. This is called split intentions. You have split your creative force into two opposing directions that then cancel each other out to the degree they are imbalanced. If they are directly opposed to each other, and of equal power, then nothing is created. You have reached a stalemate within yourself! You are at cross purposes with yourself and can't get anything done in that particular creative endeavor.

Intention is very different from will. By clarifying what it means and how you use it, intention becomes a good tool for centering, stabilizing, and self-empowering from within. One way to use intention is to measure your degree of balance between the three aspects of your psyche: reason, will, and emotion. In Chapter 2, I discussed reason, will, and emotion as one way of viewing the HECS. If all three are balanced, then you have achieved centering, or clear intention, which is the intention to become whole, to move away from the self-identity of your duality and into wholeness. You are in sync with the universe and you are simply living life as it is, with no resistance. You can then create life from the experience and perspective of wholeness. If the three are not balanced, the will aspect moves your hara line more to the back and the emotion aspect moves your hara line more to the front.

When you are out of sync, feeling resistance, and trying to force the world to do what you want, your hara line is shifted to the back of your body. This then interferes with our creative force and splits it in two. The feeling aspect of our creative energies is decreased and separated from our will aspect. This is known as willfulness.

According to Heyoan, what most of humanity calls will is actually a distortion of will. It is a "forcing current," and is one of the most common ways we interfere with the creative process. Figure 3–1 shows a common example of how the HEF becomes imbalanced during a forcing current. The hara line and the vertical power current (VPC) shift to the back; this shift causes the chakras on the back of the body to become very large. In this configuration, the individual becomes openly aggressive and forces life and others to obey the commands of their ego. It is this distorted configuration that initiated humanity's misconception of will. We use our "will" (or so we call it) to distort our field and manipulate others/the world/God to do what we want, when we want. But it is not true will. It is a forcing current that imbalances our HEF and interferes with our ability to create what we want to have in our lives.

There are many less obvious ways to force life to give us what we want. We can become the poor, emotional underdog, in which our VPC and hara line are displaced forward (Figure 3–2), or we can become the one who is submissive but then stabs the other in the back (Figure 3–3), with the hara and VPC moved forward on the lower half, and toward the back on the upper half. The hara and VPC can also be displaced to either side of the body. This results in overactivity when they are on the right, and underactivity when they are on the left. Of course, there are many more hara/VPC distortions as well. HEF distortions will be explained in the next section.

To summarize, whenever your intention is split, your creative current splits. The creative energies go in opposite directions. They oppose each other, and our original intention to create is blocked. If one side of your split intention is stronger, the resultant weakened creative force will go in the direction of the stronger intent. But it may not have enough energy to manifest your intent, or if it does, your manifestation will be weak, incomplete, unsatisfactory, and not completely what you visualized. You will not be able to completely create what you consciously intended until you are able to establish a strong, clear intention and a complete aligned hara line for that particular purpose. To heal such a split takes a lot of self-exploration and self-discovery to become aware of the two opposing forces and to figure out how those two opposing forces prevent your original creation. The cause of your split intention is your habitual negative beliefs in your child consciousness, which will be described later in this chapter and in Chapter 4. Once you understand your split and heal it, you can then redirect your creative purpose and energies for your original creation. That original purpose may have been from the perspective of a child. It takes a few weeks to let it mature into adulthood. After that maturation occurs, your original intention will apply to your adult life and to your adult creations.

What Blocks Are Like in the HEF and Where They Are Located

In the following sections we will explore what blocks are and how they disturb the creative process as it moves through the HEF. I will discuss how blocks interfere with the creative process and show unhealthy movement of blocks through the HEF and the damage that ensues. Later, I will show a healing approach to remove blocks from the HEF.

What is popularly referred to as a block is dark accumulated energy consciousness. This accumulation occurs only in the second and fourth levels of the field, the unstructured and the feeling aspects of the HEF. It accumulates because one or more of the structured levels containing the reason and will aspects (one, three, five, and seven) that guide the flow of energy through the field has become disfigured. Technically, a block includes any disfigured structured level and any weakened and/or undercharged unstructured level, as well as the dark accumulated energy in the unstructured levels of the field. Usually, all these types of disturbances will occur in any one block. A block may or may not

run through all the first seven levels of the field, and can be located anywhere in the HEF. Blocks usually affect two to three levels of the field. However, in very serious cases they can run through all the first seven levels of the HEF. In such a case the individual with these blocks is very ill.

Disturbances in the Structured Levels of the HEF: All your creations need a clear flow of the creative force through all the aspects of your HEF in order to be complete and whole. For example, if the reason-oriented levels of your field, three and seven, are more developed, this may result in the energy of the HEF to become displaced upward, toward the head. In this case, we create a defense as the smart manipulator.

Disfigurations in the structured levels (one, three, five, and seven), as well as the chakras in those levels, will appear as rips, tears, entanglements, or distortions of the lines of light. Such disturbances in the structured levels distort, change, divert, and completely stop or leak out your creative energy as it attempts to move through these levels of your HEF down into the physical world to manifest in physical reality. If there are tears in the chakras they will not be able to metabolize the creative energies needed to manifest your creations.

Disturbances in the Unstructured Levels of the HEF: Disfigurations in the unstructured levels of the HEF will also create disturbances in the flow of the creative force. Level two is our feeling experience of self, our ability to have healthy self-love. Level four is our feeling experience for others in relationship and our ability to love in relationships of all kinds, as well as giving and receiving in healthy ways. The disfigurations of levels two and four come in the form of blocks that are composed of accumulated dark energy consciousness of various muddy colors, such as green-brown or dark red. The blocks are the stagnated energy consciousness of various unresolved emotional experiences. Blocks are also found in the chakras in the unstructured levels of two and four. It is this type of block that can completely stop the creative force and absorb its energy. When located in a chakra on these levels, this type of block stops the intake of the energy consciousness through the chakra that is needed to charge these levels of the field to make them strong and healthy.

Level six corresponds to our spiritual feelings and our ability to experience divine spiritual love and ecstasy. Disturbances in level six of the HEF usually appear as weakness or absence of energy consciousness rather than darkness and stagnation. This is because most people do not spend a lot of their time in life in the experience of spiritual divine love. I have not seen any discoloration of any level above level four.

The Substance of Belief: The unstructured levels not only relate to held stagnant dualistic belief systems, but actually are the substance of dualistic belief systems. This is because the unstructured levels have the capacity to hold strong emotions and feelings. Thus the healing process must include not only clearing the field, but also learning new holistic concepts to replace the old, obsolete, dualistic ones. **Dualistic concepts are all based on splitting things into two contrasting halves (black or white, man or woman) or opposing halves (good versus bad, you versus me—even either/or can be seen that way).**

Holistic concepts support and promote deep healing, and prevent the creation of blocks caused by living dualistically. Learning to live holistically means living in, consciously creating, as well as responding to the universe and life in an entirely different way. Thus one builds a strong foundation for one's life based on holistic principles and concepts that support integration into a newly organized inner experience of life in a benign abundant universe.

Each level of the HEF corresponds to a specific part of our reality and is related to specific holistic concepts that correspond to the function(s) of that level. Until the blocks in all the levels of the field and chakras are dealt with and cleared, the creative process cannot continue to move through these HEF levels in a completely clear, unimpeded way. Therefore, studying holistic principles and concepts is an essential part of healing the disfigured levels of the HEF.

Dualistic Reality and Holistic Reality

Since the HEF levels are composed of personal will (level one), feelings about yourself (level two), reason (level three), feelings in relationships (level four), the divine will within you (level five), feelings about the divine (level six), and the divine mind within you (level seven), any disfiguration in any of these levels will cause a lack or weakness of that aspect of yourself and your creations. As a result, you will also have dualistic rather than holistic concepts about all these aspects of your being and your life. If they are disfigured, so are your belief systems. If you have dualistic belief systems, your hara and HEF will be disfigured. In other words,

Disfigurations of the hara and HEF are signatures of the dualisms we live in, because the HEF and hara are inseparable from our experience of reality.

Holistic reality becomes clear to us as the disfigurations of the HEF and hara are healed.

Unfortunately, our outmoded dualistic ideas have been taught for thousands of years. They are no longer applicable for healthy life in the 21st century. Moving out from under the agony of suppression and punishment that is inherent in the split realities of dualism is our mandate for the 21st century. Our idea that *the world is made up of opposing halves* is the cause of many problems. It creates a lot of confusion when it is extended into our belief systems.

During the 21st century, more and more cultures will come into close contact with one another through globalization and modernization. There is a need for a new understanding of what the divine means. These new concepts will need to be holistic and integrated into the levels of the HEF that connect to the divine. Divine mind, divine love, and divine will need an entirely different understanding that is based on tolerance and mutual respect.

On the more personal level, the old ideas and ways of limiting love must be released to allow us to love unconditionally. This requires an entirely new understanding of what love is that is essential to living in the modern world. The old belief systems about others who are different and the way the world works must be replaced with open-minded communication and discovery. We need to understand and actively enter this global community with love and respect. Part of this process will be letting go of preconceived ideas about others who are different from us.

In holistic reality, each individual is self-responsible to the core. As I mentioned previously, learning holistic concepts and replacing the old dualistic ones is a very important part of the healing process. I will present these holistic concepts throughout this book. Most of them are defined in Chapters 5 and 19.

We All Have Disfigured Haras and Blocks in Our HEFs: The truth is that the human condition at this stage of our human evolution has a long way to go before a holistic society is created. I have never seen a completely clear and balanced HEF or hara that remains balanced and clear all the time. Everyone has personal healing work to do. Healing work includes learning to understand and develop higher core principles with yourself to live by, as well as healing the hara and HEF.

To summarize, our undeveloped understanding of the world—our unconscious dualistic belief systems and lack of knowledge of the true holistic way the universe actually operates—prevents us from having a clear creative process. So not only do we need to learn what our blocks are and then clear them, we also must learn new holistic principles to support our creative life force. These holistic principles must replace the dualistic ones we have been unconsciously living by. Later in this chapter, I will explain in more detail about dualistic belief systems and the harm they cause to our creative pulse.

Blocks in the HEF simply weaken, distort, or divert the creative process, so that what you create is not really exactly what you expected to be the outcome. How far your outcome is from what you wanted depends on the strength and degree of dualistic split in the blocks. To understand this,

we must first understand the nature of a block. To clear it, you will be challenged to learn new concepts.

The So-Called Inner Child: Here is a simple concept to start with. It confronts a popular form of therapy called inner child work used in process groups around the world:

Don't take care of your inner child!
Your inner child does not exist!
You created a label called "inner child."

NEW CONCEPTS

Inner child = unevolved consciousness
Blocks contain trapped unevolved consciousness.
The real work is to release and reeducate
your unevolved consciousness
that is trapped inside the block.

In other words, there isn't a child inside you. Just let that notion go! The last thing you want to do is spend the rest of your life coddling or rocking your block to sleep! You need to open the block up and release its trapped unevolved consciousness, educate it, and help that unevolved consciousness evolve into a holistic state. You also need to develop a positive adult ego to do this with if you haven't already.

Let me make more sense of this. Let's explore the following questions: How is a block created? Where in the HEF are blocks located and why? What holds a block in place? What is the relationship between our blocks and our wounds? Why don't blocks just go away? How do blocks affect our creative process and therefore our lives? Why do they re-create the vicious cycles of negative behaviors and experiences in our lives? How do we break our vicious cycles? And, of course, how do we heal our blocks?

The Process of Creating Blocks in Our HEF: We create a block when we experience something that frightens us. It could be a simple accident, or it could be that another person treated us in a negative way. A very simple example of this would be the following: You are five years old. Your mother is setting the table for a dinner party. She has her good china and crystal out and is carefully placing it. You take a crystal stem glass and move toward the table. You trip and fall. The crystal breaks and you are so startled that you begin to cry. Your mother swirls around with a loud gasp and stares at you in shock and disbelief. For a brief moment, scenes of how hard she worked to earn enough money to finally buy her favorite crystal run through her mind uncontrolled. She is also upset that she will now have to clean this mess up before her dinner party. Her anger rises and she shouts for you to be quiet and stop crying! Then she is afraid that you hurt yourself. She catches her reactions and calms down, but it is too late. The second you fell, you held your breath. Your good feelings of lovingly helping your mother have vanished. You are dazed and terrified. From that moment on, you will be nervous and more careful about crying and expressing your feelings when you are scared. Your feelings about helping will be slightly tainted with reservation. That is a simple case. The next time a similar incident happens, more energy consciousness will be added to the block and you will be even more wary about helping someone. Everyone's life through childhood is full of much more complicated, repeated negative experiences. In Chapter 4, I will describe the process of creating blocks through the womb and beyond.

The more painful and frequent the experience, the stronger the block that is created. Since all families have repeated negative dynamics, all children growing in them will create blocks in their fields. This is true for everyone.

How a Block Is Created in the HEF: There is a very simple way that blocks are created energetically. As soon as we are startled or feel fear, there is one thing we do first without thinking about it. In fact, it happens so fast that it is impossible to stop because it is a physiological response. The first thing we do is to take a sudden in-breath and hold it. Here is the chain of events that occurs:

We take a sudden in-breath and hold it.

Our alerted body goes into the fight-flight response.

The HEF fight-flight reaction is different. As soon as we hold our breath, the normal energy flow of the HEF is interrupted and the energy consciousness of our thoughts split off from our energy consciousness of our feelings. In other words, we energetically separate the energy of our feelings from the energy of our thoughts. This is an actual event in the energy consciousness of the HEF.

Our feeling energies freeze, and our mind energy becomes more active and alert. Thus, we have split ourselves into duality.

Our mind is set up to look out for any situation similar to the painful ones of childhood.

This split between mind and feelings remains in separation until we put it back together again. It takes healing and personal growth work to do this.

Thus, from that moment on, our blocks will serve to impede our creative flow of life force. In other words, the block creates a split as our creative flow moves through our field on its way into physical manifestation.

Without the energy of feelings that fuels our creations, our creations cannot be completed and we are not successful, because

Our mind determines
what is created.

Our feelings fuel
the process of creation.

Our will determines
the pattern or form of the creation.

Without all three in sync,
our creation remains incomplete!

Why Blocks Don't Go Away, but Keep Getting Stronger: Blocks don't just go away, because they can't. They do not have the fuel to change until we add more energy consciousness to them.

The energy consciousness in the block stays split in a lower energy state until enough energy consciousness is added into the system to bring the feelings and mind back together.

If the above doesn't make sense to you, just remember a painful experience from childhood. That is not hard to do. Just remember the time something painful happened to you when you were a child and couldn't do anything about it.

Remember it? Got it?
Good.
Are you crying?

Since you can remember it without having the feelings that you had then, it means your feelings are not flowing. The feelings from the memory are still blocked.

Since you are remembering it, your mental energy is still flowing.

You have not blocked your mental energy from the memory.

Right? Got it?

It is as simple as that.

The block will stay there until enough energy consciousness reenters that block to unlock the feelings so that they may flow again, allowing the mental and feeling energies to come back together. Rarely does this happen naturally. The norm is the opposite.

We are often taught that it is inappropriate for us to have feelings when they flow naturally. We are taught from a very early age to suppress them. Each time a feeling is evoked, it is suppressed. We are very creative in how we suppress our feelings. The more feelings we suppress, the more energy consciousness of a lower frequency accumulates around the feelings. Thus blocks accumulate dense, dark energy in the second and fourth levels. On the second it becomes dark clouds; on the fourth it becomes thick, gooey mucous. Over time, as the block grows in strength, it becomes more complicated and grows in layers.

In addition to this, similar traumas accumulate in the same region of the body and come together around an archetype. Thus our blocks grow into more complicated disturbances in the field. The flow of energy consciousness in our HEF flows around the block. We become very sensitive to particular situations that evoke a flow of energy that may disturb the block enough to release the feelings within it, so we avoid those situations in our life. In fact, we create entire lifestyles that help hold our blocks in place.

The Anatomy of a Block: Let's look at the details of a block from the perspective of Figure 3–4, which is a diagram of the anatomy of a block. A block has several layers; each layer helps hold the block in place. On the outside layer is the outer defense. It is a strong outer layer that we don't let most people through. This outer defense helps us behave correctly according to our family lifestyle and the cultural norms in which we grow and mature.

As adults, our irrational thinking and unresolved emotions come out when we can't avoid certain ideas and emotional energies that are like the ones we had trouble with as children. Any "outer" situation that is similar to an unresolved childhood experience can evoke irrational or emotional behavior from us if the situation is strong enough to get through our outer defense. This irrational/emotional energy has been left unresolved. It is the leftover defense of the child that we once were when we tried to defend ourselves but could not. Thus, when it does come out, it is not grown up. When we do it as adults (and eventually stop irrationally defending having acted that way), we admit (to those we trust) that it was not really about the situation we are in right now.

As children we had no power to change our basic situation. Yes, young children do learn how to manipulate parents. But children's lives are controlled by their parents. Young children are completely powerless to change certain aspects of their situations. Most adults will do anything not to feel powerless, thus we can see why there is resistance to going deep inside these inner places we all have. Upon deeper contemplation, it appears that

A lot of the fear adults in therapy have
about sinking into early childhood pain
is the dread of the experience
of total powerlessness.

The Child Consciousness

Located inside the block is what the Pathwork Lectures call the "child consciousness." **Our unevolved child consciousness inside our blocks is expressed as irrational emotional reactions to defend against feeling the painful events of our childhood that are buried beneath it.**

As adults, these reactions are expressions of confusion about reality from the consciousness of the child that we were when we created the blocks within us. Essentially, we react emotionally from our unevolved child consciousness. **The developmental level of our child consciousness is at the level of a child who, with its undeveloped intellect, experiences the world in extreme opposites.** The conclusions of the child consciousness about the world are simply not the truth. In a child's mind, the world and the people and things in it are either good or bad. It is one or the other.

Children generalize conclusions and apply them to everyone. For example, in the case of a father that yells at or hits a child, the child may conclude that all men are like its father. Its conclusion about reality is simply that "all men are cruel." The child will then develop behaviors toward men according to this *conclusion*. They will probably have negative feelings about men, such as anger and fear. When the child becomes an adult, their behavior toward men may provoke cruelty from men who have such tendencies.

Images: These erroneous conclusions have a very big effect on our lives and function to distort our creative process. **Conclusions about reality, such as those above, come together to make a picture or *image* of how reality is. This image is frozen in the past. Over time, this frozen image about reality becomes unconscious. But the emotional/irrational reactions that stem from it still function to keep us from going deep inside our block to feel the true pain from early childhood, when we were helpless to do anything about our situation.**

Our Wounds: Wounds are composed of unevolved energy consciousness that was blocked, taken out of the now and off the creative pulse of life, and then held stagnant in that past time frame when it happened. Essentially, that portion of a person's being has stayed the age he was when he was not strong enough to handle the incident when it occurred without blocking the flow of energy and his system's reaction to it.

Another reason wounds remain in place is that they are held there, because the energy consciousness in the wound is split between feelings and memory, as described earlier. Since these energies are split, they do not have the power to release themselves. The only way to heal them is to bring them back together into wholeness. To do this, the healer introduces more energy consciousness into the wound. This activates the energy consciousness, brings it to the client's conscious awareness, and the childhood experience completes itself as it comes out of the frozen state and back into life.

Once the healer brings the wound to the client's conscious awareness, then and only then do we get to the true pain held in the original wound with its "inconvenient feelings." It is only in sinking into this true deep pain held in the original wound that the wound can be healed. The true pain inside the wound may last only a few moments, or perhaps for the whole healing session. With the pain come many revelations for the client. They continue to be uncovered for several weeks after the wound is released. These are revelations about how one has lived one's life under the constraints of the image, including choices, avoidances, unnecessary self-placed limitations, lack of self-nurturance, issues with authorities, and other unhealthy behaviors. There are two big differences now, however, from that time when the wound was made. During the healing, the healer is present with the client in a loving, accepting state, and is not punishing. Also, the client can now, as an adult, change the present situation that he/she has created due to the image and blocked creative energy. It takes time, understanding, and practice, but it will happen.

Types of energy consciousness introduced into the wound by the healer during a healing session would be those that most support the healing of the image in the wound. They are the energies of higher principles and states of being, such as unconditional love, truth, wisdom, trust, and courage, depending on the nature of the wound. Unconditional love works for everything.

This type of healing releases our original core creative energy from deep inside the wound. It has been trapped there since we stopped the flow of our energy at the time the block was created in early childhood. This portion of our creative force has been trapped inside, unable to move or create anything since then. This is an important key to re-creating our lives. We have been lacking that creative energy since we created the block. We have many blocks that keep our creative energies stagnant. We are unable to use these energies to create what we want in our lives. In fact, the blocks and our emotional/irrational defenses of our blocks create what we don't want by virtue of the negative images we have about life. Let's look at how this happens.

How Blocks Affect Our Creative Process and Our Lives

Figure 3–5 shows what happens to our creative process when it is affected by blocks in the field. Look at your life. What is it that you have been trying to create, perhaps for years?

Listen to yourself when you say things like, "Why does this always happen to me?" or "Oh no! Not again, here it goes again," or "I knew that was going to happen to me again!" These are clues to let you know that deep inside the wound, inside your unevolved or child consciousness, you carry the belief that this is the way the world works. Each time it happens to you again, your erroneous belief deep in your child consciousness is confirmed. It isn't that the world is what your child consciousness believes it to be. It is because you have blocked your creative energies and you cannot create what you long for. Once you have released the block by going through the defense and feeling your original childhood pain, you then will regain your original creative energies, no longer locked inside the block, to use for your creative desires. It is then a matter of reeducating

your child consciousness, so that it can grow up and learn how to function in the real world.

Recycling a Block in the HEF: Once the block is ignited by energy impinging upon it, it starts to move. Energy can come from either the inside or outside of the client to ignite an emotional reaction from the block. Usually, in daily life, the blocks we hold around our pain are strong enough to hold our outer defense in place, as was shown in Figure 3–4. However, there are certain things that upset us enough to elicit a reaction. This happens when the incoming energy consciousness is strong enough to get through our outer defense. It then hits the next line of defense and ignites an emotional reaction (ER). The ER then charges and splits the client's field, which then cycles through the negative reaction. This negative reaction becomes habitual. Once it is habitual, it becomes a repeated pattern of behavior that causes a lot of trouble in one's life. This repeated pattern is called a vicious cycle (VC). The concepts of emotional reactions and the vicious cycle were originally described in the Pathwork Lectures channeled by Eva Pierrakos. Bert and Moira Shaw, developers of the 50/50 Work, clarified and simplified these concepts into the idea of the original wound holding "inconvenient feelings." In my work, I added the human energy field dynamics of what happens in the HEF to hold a block in place, the energy exchanges during the expression of an ER, and how to learn to energetically redirect and transmute an ER, healing the vicious cycle by energetically working with the underlying causes of the ER and the wound configurations in the HEF. The psychodynamics of a vicious cycle are explored in greater detail in the next chapter. Let's take a look at what happens in the energy field when an ER is ignited and cycles through the field.

Figure 3–6(a) shows a block in a client's solar plexus that is very dark and compressed. Figure 3–6(b) shows the block beginning to move up the vertical power current. As the energy begins to move up the vertical power current, the block will begin to cycle more. Figure 3–6(c) shows the block in a full-blown cycle. At this point, the person has usually completely succumbed to the influence of the dualistic view of the reality held in the block. After some time of being caught in the vicious recycling of emotional reactions and irrational thoughts that may or may not be acted out (meaning directed at another person), the block settles down and returns to its normal resting place in the field (Figure 3–6[d]). Unfortunately, each time such a recycling occurs, more negative/dualistic energy consciousness is added to it, and it becomes a little more compacted and a little more habitual.

Clearing a Block from the HEF to Free the Creative Force

Now let's look at what happens when a healer clears a block like the block shown in Figure 3–6(a). Figure 3–7(a) shows what occurs in a healing session when the healer begins to run energy into the block. The first thing that happens is that the block begins to expand. This may at first disturb the healer, as it looks like the block is getting bigger. However, in just a few more minutes, the healer will see that the block is simply expanding a little as it loosens. As the process continues and the field is more energized by the healer, the client experiences early childhood feelings, and the split currents of mental and emotional energy begin to join back together. Figure 3–7(b) shows the block well on its way up the vertical power current (VPC) as it is being released. As the block continues to travel up through the chakras and levels of the field, the healer helps the client integrate the unblocked energy consciousness into the higher levels of the HEF (Figure 3–7[c]). The healer does this by continuing to carefully run energy into the field at higher levels during the expansion phase of the life pulse.

Once the healing is completed, much of the blocked energy that has been held in the past (at the age of the client when the block was created) is now being reintegrated into the whole HEF in the present time frame. It joins the creative pulse of life in client's life in the now. While trapped inside the block, the child consciousness couldn't grow up. Now it is free to do so. It will take several weeks to grow up. During that time, the client's positive adult ego will have the job of reeducating the unevolved child consciousness so that it can grow into balanced holistic adulthood.

Remember that all blocks are dualistic; they were originally created by separating the mental memory from the feeling experience of a painful life situation. As soon as that split is made, the block is created and it has less energy than the surrounding HEF. That is why blocks are not easy to clear by oneself. New integrated energy must be carefully run into the block to give it enough energy to integrate the feelings with the memory. Such healings need to be done with tender loving care and the unbroken focus and presence of the healer.

The healer and client have freed the trapped part of the client's creative force, with its original positive intent, into the client's creative processes of the moment. Whatever creative longing that was blocked now has the chance to be created. In addition to that, the positive attributes that we usually assign only to children are also now freed and integrated into the field in the here and now. The client experiences wonder, exuberance, simple pleasure, joy, excitement about life, and simple love and trust, now, here, unthwarted by useless negative self-control. Also, the client feels relief as the experience of having fear is greatly reduced in the client's life. In Chapter 14, you will see that blocked energy coagulates into what I call time capsules.

Note that Figure 3–7(b) also shows that a small part of the block is completely released from the field as it moves up through the vertical power current. This is the transformed and cleaned energy that had accumulated in the fourth level of the HEF as mucous. It is transformed by virtue of the fact that it has moved up through the VPC.

In addition to the natural flow that occurs up the vertical power current, there are also other ways to remove the mucous and transform it. During a healing like the one just described, healers can also scoop out the mucous with their energy hands and transform it into a higher frequency and release it into the light. Brennan

Healing Science Practitioners never just scoop it out and throw it on the floor without transforming it. Others will walk through it and absorb it into their fields. If one wishes to scoop it out, clean it, transform it into earth energy, and put it deep into the earth, that is also okay. (Figure 2–2 shows the clear creative process that is once again restored through the Brennan Healing Science method.)

Releasing Your Creative Energy to Re-create Your Life

Let's take a look at what happened inside the block when it was released. Figure 3–8 is another diagram showing the anatomy of a block; this time, the block is being released. Remember that the energies of our thoughts and feelings are split inside the block. The client will also have fear of feeling the pain. The choice is to simply surrender to the natural flow of feelings, which is, in this case, the client's pain. Notice that once enough positive supportive energy with the intent to heal has been poured into the block, the split intentions with opposing creative energies inside the block once again come together as one with the positive intent to create. This then releases the entire block, including defenses, painful feelings, and the original creative energies of the core.

Whatever the client's presenting complaint is about, this process will release the original creative energies, held in the block perhaps for lifetimes, into the client's field in order to re-create the client's life in a way that was originally intended.

This is why, as some people complain, it is necessary to feel the pain. It isn't that the healer just wants the client to feel the pain: the pain in the wound contains the trapped original core creative energies that are necessary to free the client's life to create what the client wants. They are the precise energies missing from life that the client needs to re-create in the way that is wanted. It is necessary to recognize the image around the trapped creative energies, and how that image keeps the client's life trapped, so the client can be educated. The results are well worth it.

Chapter 3 Self-Review: Some Questions to Ask Yourself about Your Blocked Creative Process

1. What are the things that you want most in life that you have not been able to create?

2. How does this relate to your childhood experiences?

3. What simplistic dualistic reality does your unevolved child consciousness believe in?

Chapter 4

UNTANGLING YOUR LIFE

The vicious cycle of defense is simple,
but wishes to appear extremely complicated.
In your vicious cycle,
you can recite over and again your many life stories
that tell how terrible things have been,
how the patterns of life repeat,
how life is doing you wrong.

You can repeatedly recite many different ways and incidents to prove it all.
Your vicious cycles are simply defense camouflaged as life.
They are just regurgitated, undigested,
unassimilated experiences.

Yet
life is always moving into the unknown.
Each moment is new and different from the last.
It is the process of constant co-creation.

— HEYOAN

Another Way to View Your Blocks

The work of dissolving your illusions and untangling your life is probably the hardest thing you will ever do. It takes time, effort, and dedication, but it is well worth it. You will learn things you didn't even know were there to learn. Your life will change into the life you want. Once you are committed, you will receive all the help you need. At times, it may not seem like it, but in the long run, you will understand. With each step you take on your spiral healing path into your core, you will grow a little more into the beautiful being of light that you are. More pieces of your life will come together. You will see things from the broader, more integrated perspective, like a hologram including the whole of all aspects of your life.

33

An Overview of the Three Essential Steps of This Work

1. The first step is to untangle our blocks, which are created based on dualistic energy, beliefs, and defenses. These blocks underlie the habitual cycles of pain that we create for ourselves.

2. The second is to replace the internalized, negative voices of what is called our superego with a wise, kind, loving adult ego. We criticize ourselves with our superegos rather than encourage ourselves to simply learn a better way of being and doing.

3. The third aspect, presented in the next chapter, is to reeducate ourselves about our dualistic concepts and beliefs, and replace them with realistic, balanced concepts that become a firm foundation upon which to build a new life. I call these concepts *unitive concepts*.

Entangling Your Life through the Creation of Blocks

Life's Preconditions: In the last chapter, I discussed how our blocks are created when something frightens us. Now I will explain how our blocks are created as we progress through life. You come into life with certain preconditions in yourself and in your HECS. We can call these preconditions "tendencies."

The Creation of Blocks in the Womb:

You incarnate into a physical form with preconditioned tendencies. You are connected to your physical body through its ongoing development inside the womb. From the very moment of conception, you begin being impacted by your world. Your tendencies will affect how you react to these impacts. Your entire world is the womb and physical body of your mother; you are impacted by everything that she is experiencing.

You can hear the sounds inside and around her: heartbeat, physiological responses, and biochemical processes. At a certain stage in your growth in the womb, you begin to see. I have seen a video taken of a fetus inside the womb into which an amniocentesis needle is inserted. As the needle was inserted, the fetus turned its head, looked at the needle, and grabbed the needle with its hand. Dr. David Chamberlain, author of *Babies Remember Birth*, who has studied babies in the womb for years, has many such stories. He observed that twins play games with each other in the womb. One story I particularly like was of twins that liked to kiss each other through the membranes of their individual fetal sacs. After they were born and grew enough to play in the backyard, they played the same kissing game through the freshly washed sheets that were hung out to dry. Another great book on babies in the womb is *The Secret Life of the Unborn Child* by Thomas Verny with John Kelly.

The Creation of Blocks Shortly after Birth:

At birth, the baby's HEF is exposed to the UEF outside the mother's HEF for the first time. The baby's field tenses with each experience. The baby's energetic field grows through life, and with each impact from the "outside" field—the UEF—the baby tenses, adds more color and form, and then relaxes. The baby's field is also impacted by the HEF of each member of the immediate family.

When the little child perceives pain in the child's parents, the first response is to make the pain go away, to heal it. The little child has not developed much of a defense system. The child loves the parents and wants to help them. Growing up, the child becomes more impacted by the distortions in the family.

The Creation of Blocks during Childhood and Beyond:

As children grow, they learn defense patterns to stop the pain that has impacted them from very early on. Also, as children grow they become more active and reach out more through curiosity. By the time children are two or three they have been told no some 60,000 times.

Defense systems begin setting in to not only protect against the direct impact of painful experiences, but also to manipulate the world to get what they want. The types of defense systems that children create are the ones that work in the family structure in which they each grow up. Children learn how to be according to family traditions that are usually unconscious; i.e., whatever works is what they learn to do. Unfortunately all defense systems are dualistic.

And unfortunately this means children will need to split their energy consciousness.

Thus children become dualistic, and for each painful experience, the pain becomes compressed deep inside the wound. The wound is covered in the defense and becomes a block in the energy field. Recurring painful experiences join together according to "like attracts like." Blocks and defenses get stronger as life continues. The HEF's defense gets stronger and the HEF becomes more distorted. We develop "vicious cycles" through which we recirculate our pain by re-creating similar painful experiences that then bring about more blocks in the field. For example, children who feel abandoned may continue to attract situations as adults in which they are abandoned. Children who have been abused may attract adult situations in which they are abused or treated badly. You can probably think of some of your own personal examples from childhood. The underlying dualistic belief system may be something like, "I am bad."

The Vicious Cycle of Hopelessness, Despair, and Self-Disempowerment

As previously noted in Chapter 3, the origin of the material about vicious cycles, including the concept of emotional reactions that are associated with them, is in the Pathwork Lectures channeled by Eva Pierrakos.

Entanglements: Blocks create entanglements that result in vicious cycles of re-created pain that then keep us trapped, unable to create what we want in our lives. Here I present some simple basic ideas about vicious cycles. We all create vicious cycles of painful experiences in our lives because we are not whole. Our lack of self-knowledge, lack of self-love, and misunderstanding of how the universe/divine creates through us results in our suffering. We all suffer from our misconceptions and erroneous belief systems about reality upon which we create our lives. We then add more suffering by defending against feeling the original pain of our early childhood wounds. We actually suffer more from our defense than from the real pain in the early wounds themselves. **We repeatedly re-create vicious cycles of pain that perpetually keep us from creating the life we want. This type of pain is called "hard pain" because we pull away, tense up, and resist feeling the original pain and hopelessness of our wounds.** Knowing the steps around the vicious cycles helps us understand the psychological states we go through when we get caught in them. With this understanding we can find ways to break our vicious cycles and learn how to create the lives we want.

First, I will discuss the steps of the vicious cycle. Then in the next section, I will discuss how to break and release the vicious cycle to re-create your life.

The Structure of the Vicious Cycle

Our state of being varies day to day. Sometimes we are more centered into our core and live in a greater degree of wholeness; other times we are more separate from our core and wholeness. One can look at this outer defense as a kind of homeostasis, or more accurately, our state of *imbalanced homeostasis*. I use these words because we all are on a path of healing into our cores and into our wholeness. All of us are imbalanced in some way, yet can live our lives with a lot of love. It is as simple as this:

*If you are in a physical body,
you've got work to do.*

Looking at how we live our lives from a broader view, we can see that even our lifestyle is part of our imbalanced homeostasis. To a certain extent, we all tend to avoid situations that frighten and challenge us. Our imbalanced homeostasis is the condition in which we generally live our lives. It is simply the human condition at present.

As shown in the diagram in Figure 4–1, the vicious cycle is the psychological loop you get caught in when defending your wound. In it, you cycle around the wound and never heal it. You just add more hard pain to the block. There are four major steps around the vicious cycle that are easily recognizable:

Step 1 = First line of defense = your imbalanced homeostasis

Step 2 = Second line of defense = your emotional and irrational reactions

Step 3 = Third line of defense = your hard pain that you keep re-creating in your life

Step 4 = Return to imbalanced homeostasis

Let's look at these steps in detail:

Step 1 of the Vicious Cycle: Energy impacts your HECS system. It can be from outside or inside your HECS:

1. Outside your HECS—from someone else, such as your significant other, a friend, your boss, someone who says or does something that evokes your defense system

2. Inside your HECS—from things such as bad dreams, accidental self-injury, illness, or just having a bad day, origin unknown

This energy input breaks through your first level of defense and disrupts your normal imbalanced homeostasis.

Step 2 of the Vicious Cycle: The energy, having broken through the first line of defense around your wound, impacts the next level of defense, which will manifest as either an emotional reaction (ER) or an irrational reaction (IR). Both are dualistic and part of your defense system.

A Word about Our Reactions versus Our Responses to Life: In order to clarify human behavior in terms of reactions or responses to life, we use the terms *rational responses* and *feeling responses* to refer to our being in reality given the present life situation. When we are in reality about a present situation in life, we have rational and feeling responses to it. In other words, our energy consciousness is flowing freely. It is not split or blocked.

On the other hand, we use the terms *emotional reactions (ER)* and *irrational reactions (IR)* to refer to our not being in reality about the present life situation. When we are not in reality about a present life situation, we react to it with irrational and emotional reactions. In this case, we have fallen back into our past and are acting as if the past were now. We have activated the second layer of our defense system, blocking and splitting our energy consciousness, and we are in duality. Moreover, all emotional reactions are irrational and all irrational reactions are emotional. Therefore, I have abbreviated our reactions to simplify communication, and call them **ER/IRs**.

Our ER/IRs are based on the belief system of the unevolved child consciousness and are acting as if the past were now. Two main points about an ER/IR:

1. They are dualistic, i.e., the feeling energy is separated from the mental energy.

2. They do not take self-responsibility. They blame and demand from the other.

Figure 4–2 is a point-by-point description of the major aspects of an ER/IR. It gives the anatomy of an ER/IR. It is helpful to determine if you are having one.

FIGURE 4–2

ANATOMY OF AN ER/IR

1. An ER/IR can be ignited internally or externally.

2. An ER/IR has nothing to do with the "present situation" in the "external" world.

3. The person, situation, or event onto whom/which the ER/IR is being transferred is seen as the cause of an ER/IR.

4. An ER/IR is not objective.

5. It is impossible to have an objective communication with a person who is flooded with an ER/IR.

6. Directly expressing an ER/IR toward the person one is blaming for its cause can wound that person.

7. Using the statement "listen to the grain of truth in what I am saying" while expressing an ER/IR toward the person it is blamed on is making the other person responsible to figure out what one's grain of truth is while wounding them.

Step 3 of the Vicious Cycle: If you continue in the blame and demand, you will go into your hard pain, which is both powerless and hopeless. It is powerless and hopeless because you have given your creative power to create your life over to the other. Thus you have made yourself powerless by abdicating your free will and your creative force to the other who you are trying to make responsible for your life. You say to yourself, "Oh no! Here it goes again, I knew that would happen!" That is why it is hopeless. No matter how hard you try to blame the other for your life, no matter how hard you demand that they give it to you, it will not and cannot work. You will feel the hopelessness of the situation. But it isn't *the* situation, it is *your* situation, because you are the one who is holding it in place, not *them*. You cannot change your life by making them change. You are the one who must change.

Step 4 of the Vicious Cycle: If you don't learn that you are the one who must change and learn how to do it, then, after a painful interaction or a fight with your significant other and

after adding more pain to your wound, you settle down your ER/IRs and once again go back to Step 1 of the vicious cycle, your imbalanced homeostasis. Unfortunately, this strengthens the energetic pathway of your reaction in your HEF. The energy consciousness of your vicious cycle is strengthened, making it easier and more likely to happen again, since we are creatures of habit. The more we repeat our vicious cycle reaction, the more likely we will slip into it again.

Breaking the Vicious Cycle

It is very difficult to break the vicious cycle in the beginning. You are going into the unknown, and it requires surrendering to your fear of the unknown and to feeling the helplessness and powerlessness that you have spent your whole life defending against. By breaking it you move into the freedom of a creative, loving life. It does take courage to face the terror of the unknown and fear of pain. Yet once into the pain, everything changes.

Once having learned and become accustomed to the process of breaking your vicious cycles, the outcomes are magnificent. We release our creative love energy, which is trapped inside the wound that is also trapped inside the block. By breaking each vicious cycle, we create a new way of life, a way of life of spiraling into our core. With each spiral, more creative love energy is released. **With each spiral, we learn to trust the process of surrendering into the "soft pain" of old wounds. With each spiral, we learn to deal with our fears that block our path inward toward our core. Each of us can make the choice: minutes of going into the terror and feeling the soft pain, or lifetimes of re-creating the hard pain, hopelessness, and self-disempowerment, and the inability to create a healthy, fulfilled life.**

It takes understanding, effort, faith, and dedicated practice to break the vicious cycle, but the more you do it, the easier it gets. Figure 4–3 shows the breaking of the vicious cycle when confronted with a situation that triggers our defense. In this figure, there is a conscious choice to spiral inward to release the pain of old wounds rather than reacting to the trigger with an ER/IR.

There are specific steps to break the vicious cycle. Now let's take a more detailed look at what we can do at each of these steps.

Steps to Break the Vicious Cycle:

1. The first step is to align your intention for healing and learn to recognize that you are having an ER/IR. Learning to recognize that one is in an ER/IR and learning to handle it is essential to personal growth.

   Some keys to remember this are:

   a. Your focus is external on the other person, not internal on yourself and on your internal process that is the actual cause of your situation. Learning to handle an ER/IR means learning to direct one's intention inward rather than outward. You must isolate the energy of an ER/IR from the person an ER/IR is about.

   b. You are in blame and demand that the other changes in some way.

   c. You have given over your power. You believe that if they change, your life will get fixed. It only gets fixed when you change.

   d. Your vicious cycle will continue until you change and take responsibility for your life.

2. The person having an ER/IR is responsible to take care of it. Recognize that you are expressing unevolved child consciousness through your ER/IR.

3. A key to breaking any habitual vicious cycle that you circle around with your significant other is to never try to continue the engagement when you are in an ER/IR. It rarely works. Muster your strength to admit that you are in an ER/IR and simply stop it. Disconnect from the communication. Find or set up a way of signaling the other ahead of time. Then disconnect and leave. It is very important to set this up ahead of time and make a joint agreement with your significant other, so that your significant other is reassured, and the situation does not get blown out of proportion as arguments tend to do. This takes practice. The more you practice, the better. You will get to the point that you can do this *before* going into the ER/IR. For example, if you are about to have an ER/IR, say so, or agree on what words would work for both of you, such as:

   a. "I'm about to have an ER. I need to leave now, but I will be back!"

   b. "I'm having an ER. I need some space; see you later."

   c. "I need some time to center."

This saves you from creating more pain, both in yourself and your significant other, by not saying things that you wish you hadn't said. This is why it is important beforehand to speak to your loved one and set up some mutually agreeable ways to stop the cycle.

4. There are a couple of other key things to learn to do when in an argument. This will take some practice and active agreement with your partner, but it is worth it:

a. First, never block the doorway, as it could bring up issues of entrapment and frighten your partner.

b. Don't pick anything up. This can also frighten your partner, as he/she may also be in unevolved consciousness and automatically make a negative assumption from early childhood about what you will do with what you picked up.

c. Whatever it is you are trying to get in that moment, give it up. Convince yourself you will speak about it when you are both more centered and grounded.

d. If hurtful things are said to you, let yourself feel the early pain they bring up. If you said something hurtful, let yourself see the hurt you have inflicted. Apologize to yourself and your partner. What early pain were you defending when you said it? Acknowledge to your partner that it was your unevolved consciousness speaking and forgive yourself.

e. This process helps you develop a loving adult ego with which to make life choices such as these.

5. When you do stop the cycle of outward focus on the other and turn inward, if you are in an appropriate situation and can give yourself time to go into a deep healing, then you can choose to do so. If not, you can use your adult ego to simply disconnect from the entangled ER/IR situation and choose to do something else for a while. This also takes skill and practice in order to not act out another ER. If you do have the time and space for self-healing, here's what you can do. Direct your focus down into the origin of the problem, which are the dualistic energies inside the wound. As you sink into the pain inside the wound and the dualistic energies come together, the pain will be soft because it is a step into wholeness. Directing one's attention internally and feeling the fear, anger, hurt, etc., of the pain in the wound is healing. It is the young, early pain in which you really were helpless to change the situation. At the time you were a child, it was devastating. Now you can tolerate feeling the helplessness. It is a relief to simply be in what was, acknowledge the truth of it, feel love for yourself, and release the pain that has been held deep inside, perhaps for many lifetimes.

6. With the pain, you release the original creative intent, and your core creative energies can now become active in re-creating your life. Your field will begin to glow with new core energies. You will immediately feel younger. Your skin will be more vibrant. This integration of core energies takes some time. It is a continuing process.

7. During this experience and afterward for several weeks, you will also have more realizations about your image, your belief systems, why you have acted in the way you have in your defense, and what the truth really is.

8. It takes some time to educate the child consciousness that has now been released into your field and your life.

9. Developing a positive adult ego is also important for the task of educating the child consciousness that has been released. To do this, it is necessary to first recognize your child consciousness's version of an adult ego. It is called your superego. It is the child's version of its understanding of why the adult authority in their life keeps telling them **no or "you are bad!"** So the superego is a negative ego. It is a negative authority that is not nice to you at all. Why? Think about when you were six or seven years old and you wanted to run out and play, or you saw the ocean for the first time and you ran as fast as you could into it. Think about how it feels to a six- or seven-year-old who is screamed at by his parents when they try to stop him from hurting himself as he lunges toward the ocean. Or when a parent insists to their hurt child that they stop crying. The parent's voice is loud, stern, angry, and afraid all at the same time. It says things like, "Who do you think you are?" "Behave yourself and do what you are supposed to do." "Be practical; don't take chances." "Crybaby!" or "Boys don't cry."

Now, be that child you were in a similar situation. What are the words you say to yourself? What is the energy that you are experiencing like? How do you now say the words to yourself each time you reprimand yourself for something you did do, didn't do, or wanted to do? What do you hear and feel? It's not a nice voice, is it? So you are most likely now treating yourself worse than your parents did! It is important to learn to recognize your superego that keeps you in line. Here is what Heyoan has said about the superego:

Your Superego

*Your superego is just your self-internalized voice
from your childhood authorities' fear.
You created your superego as a child
when you thought and understood reality as a child.
Thus your superego
is only as old as you were when you created it.*

*Your superego tries to keep you safe in a world
that your childhood authorities saw as dangerous.
You have taken on those voices
and created a superego for yourself
that supposedly regulates you in a helpful way.*

*Reconsider that conclusion!
What does your internalized negative authority
of your immature child consciousness
say to you?
Notice how often it uses negative self-judgments!*

*Self-judgment is the resistance
to your simple soft pain
of regretting your moment's choice
to fly from unity.*

*Learn to recognize the language
of the superego.
It is a language of duality.*

*Your superego is the part that judges you!
It is the part that does not accept
your painful experiences in this lifetime.
It does not accept your mistakes,
and points each one of them out to you.
It doesn't even respect
your learning process
or give you time and space to learn.*

*Consider the possibility
that this entire construct
of critical authority within you
is not needed.*

*Your superego has convinced you
that you need to be reprimanded*

in order to behave well.
You don't really believe that, do you?

Rather than reprimand yourself,
consider that whatever your concern,
it is related to a personal need
that you have not yet learned to fulfill.
Your superego blocks your learning
by reprimanding you into imbalance.

Heyoan's Homework to Explore Your Superego

- *What role does your superego play in your imbalance?*

- *How are you reprimanding yourself into imbalance?*

- *What are your personal needs that you have not yet learned to fulfill?*

- *How do your unmet needs relate to your superego's reprimands?*

Developing a Positive Adult Ego to Handle Your Authority Issues

Since superegos are our internalized critical voice and are a response to authority from our child consciousness, it is important to replace your superego with a positive, or adult, ego. Developing an adult ego is necessary for your personal health and well-being. An adult ego is that of a balanced, mature, kind, and loving adult. The adult ego is kind, loving, clear, and strong. With it you can set practical, achievable goals and boundaries that are aligned with your life's purpose. It regulates your free will choices with which you live your life. To develop a positive adult ego, a good model is very useful. Choose a person who has been steadfastly kind, clear, and firm, and observe how they handle their interactions with others, especially with those who are subordinates. Observe how they do it and practice what they do. You can even ask them how they do it, or what kind authorities they had in their life as they grew up that helped them develop it.

Truthfulness, kindness, gentle firmness, and personal regard for the self and the other are important. Observe how you respond in situations, especially with regard to authority.

1. *How do you react or respond to an authority?*

2. *Observe yourself in situations in which you find it hard to be nice to yourself.*

3. *Do you also find it hard to be nice to others in the same type of situation?*

If so, you are probably caught in a negative belief and are traveling through the vicious cycle around an old wound. Explore this vicious cycle. Search for your wound that is related to the situation. Surrender into your pain and feel it. In feeling your pain, you will get clear on how the authority in your early years treated you in a way similar to how you now treat yourself and others. How does your negative inner authority keep you from feeling the soft early pain in your wound? Now try another way:

Practice being kind to yourself in life situations
that bring up your fear from your early wounding.

It is most important to understand what a positive inner authority does for you, and thus, how to develop a positive adult ego. Here are some of the things Heyoan has said about how authority is mishandled on earth:

Authority and Free Will

In your earthly world,
authority is mishandled a great deal
as you can see anywhere on the planet.

In some areas there is severe punishment
for disobeying "authority."
Of course one would rage against it
when it interferes with your God-given rights of
free will.

Your use of free will
is distorted by your authority issues.
Consider the authority within you
that regulates your free will.

How do you choose to use your free will?
Does your inner authority regulate
your free will in a kind and gentle way
with yourself?

Do you have an understanding authority within you
that allows you time and space
to center into yourself
to find out what your truth is?

Do you have a kind and loving authority within you
that allows you to live in ecstasy and love,
the way you would most like to live?

Do you have a kind and accepting authority
within you
that reminds you to love and accept yourself
exactly as you are?

Do you hold space for yourself
to be and to grow
into the delightful being that you are,
to let the expression
of this delightful being come out?

Do you allow yourself
to express your love, your doubt,
and your creative force?

✢ ✢ ✢

The Work of the Adult Ego

Ultimately, the work of the adult ego
is to trust the inner being
with its creative pulse of life
and to direct one's conscious awareness
toward that inner being
to learn wholeness.

Heyoan is saying that once you understand how the creative process works, the major function of the adult ego is to use your God-given free will to make healthy holistic life choices based on wholeness, trust, and truth. This includes all the choices you make each minute, each day, each year, each life.

See how important developing a kind, healthy adult ego is? Each choice we make is a choice for how we use our creative life force of love. Each choice is a choice of how we live our lives. With each dualistic choice, we split our creative energies and decrease our creative power. This results in disconnection, separation, distrust, and pain. With each choice based on holistic principles, our creative abilities grow and we create contact, connection, and communion, all of which create more love, joy, and self-respect.

In the next chapter, I will present edited transcripts channeled from Heyoan of some of the unitive concepts and principles that he has taught through the years. These help set a foundation for creating the lives we long for.

Chapter 4 Self-Review: Some Questions to Ask Yourself about Your Entanglements

1. List what your life's preconditions might be.

2. Explore and list your possible creation of blocks in the womb. What were the conditions of your mother's life and relationship to your father when you were in the womb?

3. Explore and list your possible creation of blocks shortly after birth. If you don't know the circumstances of your parents' lives, ask them, if you can.

4. Trace through and list your creation of blocks in early childhood. Check out your childhood pictures. What do you see?

5. Explore your painful memories from early childhood. What types of blocks did you create then?

6. Study the vicious cycle and its structure. How do you cycle through the four basic steps of your vicious cycles? Choose the step you get caught in the most now in your life.

Chapter 5

TOOLS TO RE-CREATE YOUR LIFE

Holistic Concepts

I have channeled lectures from Heyoan since the early 1980s. The lecture material is presented in a nonlinear poetic form. It has become the spiritual foundation for Brennan Healing Science. It provides new broad holistic spiritual concepts that challenge our view of spiritual realities and religious doctrines as well as our physical life. I have published these books each year since 1998 in the book series *Seeds of the Spirit*. Heyoan uses words—prose and poetry—in a different way to help us move out of our stagnated dualistic reality and to re-create our lives by incorporating these holistic ways of thinking and being. Sometimes he challenges us with outrageous or perhaps even taboo ways to be with ourselves and others. Heyoan teaches us to view ourselves and experience our lives from the broader perspective of re-creating our lives.

In this chapter and in Chapter 19, I have included some of Heyoan's relevant teachings in the form they are presented to students at the school. The words come directly from the spiritual world's perspective and speak directly to us personally. When I channel Heyoan's lectures, I see

him with a group of guides who call themselves the Council of Light. Sometimes I see them gather around a table to the right of the stage, shuffling papers as if preparing for the lecture they are about to transmit through me. Sometimes, rather than Heyoan referring to himself as the originator of the lecture, as in "I say this to you," he says,

"We say this to you."

With regard to this material I am about to present, since Heyoan did teach a great deal of the information about the Human Energy Consciousness System (HECS), it is necessary to remember how our creative process moves through our HECS as described in Chapter 2. These next teachings are descriptions of logical outcomes of the personal psychological and spiritual experiences one has while in the creative process. He guides us on how to compassionately work with what blocks our creative flow: our wounds, vicious cycles, emotional reactions, internal voices, and superego. Freed from these blocks, we can then rightfully experience the pleasure and love that result from following our creative pulse that naturally arises from the core of our being.

Life Creation of Wounds and Defenses

When you are very young, you do not have defenses. Adults usually do not understand this. When you are young you have such a vibrant life force, it runs through you and your body follows it. You jump and laugh and shout and disturb the adults. You don't behave how you are supposed to. You are taught with a reprimanding voice to behave, a voice that tells you to be quiet or that you are doing it wrong. The very young child does not know the difference between doing it wrong and being wrong or having something wrong with it. Therefore, when the adult simply tries to teach a child how to walk, how to sit at a table, etc., the child consciousness hears any of the following things: "I am wrong. I am bad. I am not enough. There is not enough for me. I can't do it without you because I'm going to do it wrong. Everything is perfect and I must be perfect." The child then lives on her/his periphery in order to do everything right. But then what happens? Where is the life force? It's still in there. The creative force of life with which you create your life becomes trapped in the child's defensive maneuvers and negative conclusions.

The Vicious Cycle

Many times it may seem as if there is no freedom of choice in life. It appears that all of the traditions in your life, all of the training, all of the education, the religious practices, and your upbringing have created certain ways that you are that are impossible to change. But as you learn the simple steps of what is needed to change, just a simple way of choosing to go into the soft pain rather than defend, your life becomes an understandable spiritual path to practice.

The vicious cycle of defense is simple, but wishes to appear extremely complicated. In your vicious cycle, you can recite over and again your many life stories that tell how terrible things have been, how the patterns of life repeat, how life is doing you wrong. You can repeatedly recite many different ways and incidents to prove it all.

*Your vicious cycles
are simply defense camouflaged as life.
They are just regurgitated, undigested,
unassimilated experiences.*

*Yet
life is always moving into the unknown.
Each moment is new and different than the last.
It is the process of constant co-creation.*

All your defenses are designed to keep you caught in vicious cycles that avoid the true solution: to simply feel your original soft pain that puts you into a healing spiral that releases the creative force within you and changes your life.

Utilize everything you have learned to become clear in the moment. Find the moment in which you automatically switch from wholeness to duality. You can learn to recognize that moment. Name it so that it becomes familiar. That is the moment that you fall into the linear time, and the three-dimensional space of the traumas. When you learn to recognize it, you can learn to choose, with clear intention, not to self-identify with duality. You will learn to shift your identity to wholeness and the ever-enlightening process of co-creation from your divine center, your core.

That, my dear ones, in a nutshell, is the enlightening or awakening process. It is awakening to the point of now, that is here, always, outside of the limitations of the so-called space-time continuum.

*Consider the possibility of an
ever-enlightening future, which is actually
an ever-enlightening walk into the self.
It is a walk into the light and
source of life and creation within you.*

Going through Creative Healing Cycles

It is not that easy to learn to
go through these cycles,
but it is good and it is healing,
so give yourself time—
time to understand this vicious cycle
of longing, and then your self-judgment
that smashes your longing down.

Yet with your intention
and positive choice to go forward
with what you want to create,
you release your core essence,
the very core essence that you need
to create your longing and fulfill your life's purpose.

All of these things are held within
the four dimensions of your being.

All of your pain can be healed
through this process of utilizing
the creative force of love that flows
through your four dimensions
on the creative pulse of life:
expansion, stasis, contraction, stasis;
expansion, stasis, contraction, stasis.

This is the ever-present creative pulse of life.

How You Create Pain for Yourself

Consider the possibility that you actually cause more pain in yourself than that created by any childhood experience, from any lifetime, or all of them together. You actually create more pain in yourself by self-rejection. You put that self-rejection around your original wound. It is your self-rejection and self-judgment that create your hard pain, the pain around your wounds. This hard pain is difficult. It feels poisonous and caustic. It takes courage to go through that into the wound. But once you have surrendered inside to go inside, everything changes.

Yes, it is deep pain. In the beginning, you may feel vulnerable—primarily because you haven't been there for perhaps many centuries.

When you hold the child consciousness that does not understand the pain, then the pain is soft and sweet and comes with a pulse of life. For it releases the co-creative pulse of life through that area of your being that has, perhaps, not been touched for centuries. Yes, in the beginning you must go through the hard pain. That is but a moment. The hard pain is the resistance.

Hard Pain, Soft Pain

Hard pain
is the pain of resisting the coming together
of the two halves of duality.

Going through your resistance and feeling
the soft pain of early wounds
has the great benefit
of bringing the two halves of duality
back together.

It is important to recognize the difference
between the soft pain of early wounds
and the hard pain of resistance
to the belief systems
that all humans were taught so strictly
to believe in and to act in a certain way.
It is not nourishing for your soul.

Rather, it holds the dualistic split in place,
thereby causing more hard pain.
It puts a shell around the wound.

When you have broken through the shell
and done the work
of breaking through that wall within
you will recognize the sweetness and the
vulnerability
of the child consciousness that is there.

You feel very young
when the two halves of the split come together,
because you are young in that energy consciousness
that was left behind the creative force
many lives ago, or perhaps just in this lifetime.

The Source of an Emotional Reaction

An emotional reaction can be ignited
from your inner duality,
or it can be ignited by an external event.
But an emotional reaction is
only ignited by those things.
They are not the source.

The source of all emotional reactions
and all judgments is internal.
It will be found within the isolated
portions of your being,
held within a time capsule
of your unresolved residual experiences,
ideas, images, and beliefs about reality.
All of these things are fragmented.
They are your half creations,
your half ideas still held in pieces.

Therefore they are not powerful
when considering the immense infinite unity,
the immense divine underpinnings
of every portion of your being.
They are simple child's play.

✛ ✛ ✛

Depowering Emotional and Irrational Reactions

It is a good time now in this process, which has been going on for many years, to consider that emotional and irrational reactions are not a big deal. They are simply things that happen around your surface, a defensive mechanism. You can recognize this simplicity in yourself and others. You do not have to take them so seriously nor solemnly think that it must mean something terrible about you. I'll tell you a secret. You can all handle your own and someone else's emotional and irrational reactions. Practice saying, "Oh! It's an emotional/irrational reaction. Ho hum. Boring. Boring. Boring. What a waste of time to give them such credence!"

Don't waste your time
giving credence to emotional or irrational reactions.
Recognize how boring they really are!

The true pain was created a long time ago. The hard pain of the ER/IR and self-judgments that follow in spinning vicious cycles is not really healing pain. As long as you take it so seriously, you may think it will heal you. You may think you have to experience this hard pain and learn to "stand up for yourself, to not to take it anymore." (We are not so sure what you mean by all of these sayings and neither are you, if you really consider it deeply.)

Experiencing hard pain
simply means that in this moment
you are not prepared, or do not feel safe,
to simply sink into and feel the soft pain within you.
It is as simple as that.

Here is another challenge that we would like you to consider:

If someone has an emotional or irrational reaction
and directs aggressive or chaotic energy
toward you,
consider it a challenge
to simply center into your core.

Notice that your defense might come up quickly, especially for certain things that were repeated in your childhood family. As a child, you found defenses against these things, but as an adult, the defenses are really obsolete.

As you center into your core and reestablish a connection to the wholeness of your being, when your self-identification is anchored into the wholeness of your being, episodes of emotional or irrational reactions—whether they are yours or another's—will become boring. They become a diversion you need not take and a challenge to find your own reactions, calm them down, and center. Recognize the light, the truth, the divine will within you. Recognize your power, your choice of free will, and your ability to understand, know, and feel both. Recognize the strength of your presence and your love, and your ability to feel the ancient pains within you that release your being and your pleasure current, your creative current of life.

The process of spiral healing into the core is simple.
It is a moment-to-moment choice.
It is your choice moment to moment.

Growing on the Spiral Path

Growth arises in quantum leaps. The spiral path of healing is not a linear one. You may find yourselves working on something for a very long time, perhaps years, perhaps decades, and wonder if it will ever change. And then you feel it leave you. You know that you are clear in that area of your being. It does happen. We guarantee you that it will happen for you, perhaps in surprising ways, perhaps in ways that you have not thought of or don't yet understand, but still change does occur. Change comes sometimes at the most unusual moments and in ways you may not comprehend: surprising ways, when sometimes you think the worse possible thing is happening to you and it turns out to be the best.

Consider the possibility that your negative self-judgments about the troubles that you have, your lacks—the things that are wrong with you or the things that you do not have within you (or so you believe)—come from your child consciousness. It has not developed into an adult. It is split in half. All of those things that you thought were wrong with you—perhaps for many years, perhaps for an entire lifetime—we see in a completely different way, in a completely different light. Anything, any area of yourself that you judge as negative, that you think is a terrible shame and perhaps hide deeply within you, no matter what it is, is something that has been split. It is energy and consciousness. It is energy consciousness that has been separated, torn in two by some event that perhaps existed many lifetimes ago. Since then you have not been able to perceive, see, hear, know, or

understand yourself in a healthy holistic manner. Since then, perhaps a millennium ago, you have held yourself in negative judgment. You have accused yourself of many malicious acts and at the same time you have denied the hard pain of the negative self-accusations.

Dealing with Negative Internal Voices

In the beginning you will learn to feel the wound and deal with it; you face the shame of your pain. For example, you may ridicule yourself when you are in pain, and say, "Oh, you shouldn't feel this way. What is wrong with you?" and so on.

It is possible to recognize these negative voices in your head. There are many names for them: negative inner authority, superego, internalized parents. They are voices in your head that speak from the perspective of a child. They are simplified because they have arisen from your inner-child consciousness within you. Your pain occurred when you were a child and as a result you made certain conclusions about reality. You took the negative voices of various different authorities as you were growing up (in whatever lifetime it may be) and made them your own from the perspective and understanding of a child. As you were growing up you heard the voices, you heard the language, you used it, you learned it. They are still in your wound. It is the language of the child consciousness that has been torn in two, perhaps into many pieces. At that very edge of separation between the pieces of child consciousness, at that very separation you can feel the hard pain and the insistence of those negative voices. One of the first things that you learn in self-understanding is to hear them and recognize them as not the truth.

Each time you begin a new spiral into a particular wounded or painful experience, it is difficult to make those voices stop. There are many meditation techniques that can help you center your mind. The work is to recognize them and name them. Just simply give them a name. Even though they don't stop, you can still name them. At this stage of personal awakening it is important not to add another judgment about what is wrong with you if you can't stop the negative voices. That is jumping right into a spinning vortex or a vicious cycle. So rather than focus on making them stop, recognize them and name them as a first step. Then just let go. Yes, they might still be complaining, telling you how you did the latest wrong thing and now everyone will be mad at you, or something awful will happen. Just name the voice. That voice is the defense that encapsulates the real pain. The voice creates hard pain; it is very, very hard, difficult pain to judge yourself. So it is good to recognize it. Name it and recognize it as an irrational defense coming from child consciousness that is very young. This is why it is irrational. The strength of that voice will give you an idea of how long the pain has been there and how much it hurt when you were very young.

The Superego's Interference with Your Creative Force

When you go into childhood pain and learn to recognize how you have taken on scolding, reprimanding words, you will know and recognize them as your superego. It is good to learn to recognize the superego and how it interferes with the creative process.

*The creative force of love, your
creative process of the moment,
comes through you
on the wings of your sacred desires,
sparked by your sacred longing.*

*This is the key to creation:
Let the creative force of love upwell
through the directions
of your sacred desire
for self-expression.*

*Creation through
the unique love of the self
is unlike any other.*

✢ ✢ ✢

Creating a Personal Mantra

So what, then, my dear ones, can you do in addition to recognizing the voice? Consider the possibility that there are many different responses you can have once you hear the voice and recognize and name it. Now it is also okay to change the name of that voice as you progress on your path. You will be surprised how it changes and how you may wish to give it another name.

Once you have recognized a negative voice, you can also create a mantra to help heal yourself of it. You may already have mantras that work very well for you. There is another mantra that we have in mind. It is a mantra that recites one of your core qualities so that you can begin to really know, feel, see, hear, and directly experience your core quality.

Find one core quality that you can use as a mantra. Whatever that core quality is, condense it to one word. It can be several syllables, but condense it to one word. Your core quality will help the core light expand throughout your intention, your purpose and your auric field as it moves up through the dimensions, through the physical. By using it as a mantra, that core quality will bring you into a more centered place while you are recognizing and naming your negative internalized voice.

And now, feel, see, hear, smell, touch, know a core quality within you by focusing into the center of your core essence, the center of your core star, which is between the third and the fourth chakras. Find your core light. Spiral into it. Let it radiate out spherically.

Now focus into the center of every chakra, the very center where the tips come together, and find the core essence. Having done that, find how the core essence upwells within every chakra center. Now find the core essence in every cell of your body, in every cell of your being.

Give yourself plenty of time and accept however much of this meditation is possible for you. Let go of any self-judgments that you may have.

By using your core quality mantra, you will find this core light upwelling into every cell of your body. It may very well happen at the same time that you hear the negative self-judgment. You will notice that the more you move into core essence, your label or name for your negative inner voice will transform.

Now, in this state of meditation, find one of your most habitual negative inner voices. Give it a name while still holding the core essence. Good. Find your core mantra. If you can't, just experience both the negative voice and the core essence at the same time. Focus on both.

There are certain experiences throughout your personal history that you have not been able to describe or understand. Many of them come from the juxtaposition of seeing and hearing both the core essence and the negative voice at the same time. That is something that is very difficult for a young person. When you were a child, you could not understand this, and you tore yourself in half. Not on purpose—you simply didn't know how to utilize these experiences to bring yourself into wholeness.

The Spiral Path into Your Core

The essential path of healing is led
by the core energies that upwell into the heart
and bring you into the sacred now.

The spiral path of healing takes you into your
wounds to heal the blocks and release the love you
could give to yourself and others.

We spiral into the wound to release the core.
We acknowledge the core.
We recognize the core qualities
in ourselves and others.

Support and spiritual guidance
are always at your service.

We are with you wherever you are
to help remind you of your core qualities,
which can bring you comfort, peace, and love
while you enter into the dark tunnel of the soul—
the darkness and pain within—to heal it.

Core Essence

When you very carefully delineate
the dualities within you,
you will begin to explore the relationship
between your dualistic interpretation
of experience and your core essence.

Your dualistic interpretation of experience
is based on your dualistic underlying belief.
When you dissolve that dualistic interpretation,
you will then be left with pure core experience.
What follows is the process of learning to recognize
your core energies as the major creative force
in all your experiences.

Personal Healing Requires Core Identification

Personal change involves more than an isolated personality change. It requires a deep connection and identification with the Core.

By creating an internal neutral observer that witnesses your movement through your habitual vicious cycles, you can practice recognizing the steps of your vicious cycles and learn to self-identify with Core. It takes time and practice to learn the steps in the vicious cycle, and to find its breaking point. That is a point where you can gather enough power to make a choice different from the habitual one. It is the choice to give up your defense and feel your soft pain. First you learn to experience the original soft pain of the young child who was so hurt. Then you can feel the true soft pain of separating yourself from the divinity that you are.

Moving with the Ground of Your Being

It is only you that stops yourself, and so the first work, the first step is self-nurturing. The first step is to be with yourself, to ask yourself each moment, "What do I long to do right now?" "What is it that I wish for?" Oh, how sweet the longing, how sweet the yearning, and even sweeter the fulfillment of those yearnings.

You are a creative being. Release the chains, the chains with which you hold yourself prisoner to these self-judgments, with which you unknowingly limit yourself. Truly, when you reach in and center into the core, you know that these are words of truth. *Yes, in the physical world you must deal with frustrations, for fulfillment isn't immediate as it is in the spiritual world.*

Yet, the spiral path of fulfillment into the self is very rewarding, for through it, you become who you are, in the sense that you allow yourself to fulfill that which you have incarnated to accomplish. You already made a promise to yourself before birth that you would fulfill these needs and longings. You have physical, psychological, mental, and spiritual longings. To fulfill them has been your promise to yourself since the day of your conception.

It is your truth.
Such great pain is caused
by denying your basic truth
in the ground of your being.

You deny the very ground of your being
by denying yourself your true needs.

So, my dear ones, become more consciously aware of what your needs are and what your longings are. Set about giving yourself permission to fulfill each one, to take care of yourself in all areas of your being.

Finally, we must not forget love and pleasure! Heyoan reminds us that the creative force is based on the principles of love and pleasure.

The Pleasure of Creation

One of the highest pleasures human beings have is this experience of creation.

Creation is ever-evolving.
It never ends.
Creation is not just form,
light, and color.
Creation is not just manifestation
in the space/time continuum,
and other spiritual worlds.
In the creative process
you also create wonder and pleasure.

As you experience "eureka," as you become awakened, energies rush through your body, your life energy fields, your psyche, and your being with great pleasure. A supernova explosion of awareness is created!

Release Your Joy of Creation

My dear sweet friends,
what are your longings?
What are your desires?
What do you wish to create in your life?
With whom do you wish to create it?
How do you wish to create it?
Take away the reprimands of the superego.
Let your joys and desires come forth, especially now.

Most human beings are quite shy to show
the exuberance and the excitement
of the true creative forces that flow
through the channel of sacred desires.

Your sacred desires
are connected to your heart, where love emerges
as it upwells from your core essence.

In the very center of your core star
is undifferentiated life and life force.
It radiates out from the very center of your being
infinitely in all directions
as it comes up through the levels.

✝ ✝ ✝

Core Creation

Align once again with your purpose,
with the purpose of your life,
the purpose of this particular incarnation.
Settle into your beautiful bodies,
recognizing the light within every cell therein.
Notice the core star in every cell of your body,
in every organ.
Experience the light there.
Feel this light as it moves through your being,
upwelling from the ineffable deep
inside the core star.

What is it that you wish to create in your life?
Set your purpose well.
Let go the grief, the sorrow, the hopelessness,
the feelings of being trapped, the self-denigration,
the resistance to change,
the fear that change might bring you harm.

Instead, align with a greater purpose of your life.
Both your life experiences
and the conditions into which you were born
are your teaching tools.
They are the tools that teach you to face
that which you have decided to face,
change, and integrate
into your wholeness in this particular lifetime.

Release the burden of guilt, doubt,
and self-judgments
within which you lock your cells
and your creative energies.
Consider the possibility that self-judgments
are merely another way to resist your creativity,
to resist change.

For I tell you this, and it is true: not one
of those self-judgments contains any truth at all.

And so we ask you,
how would you would like to spend
the rest of your life?
What wonderful experiences would you
like to generate in your life?

Whatever you wish and long for,
whatever you would like to come about in your life,
is indeed already in the creative
process coming down

through the higher levels of your
field into manifestation.
It is up to you to choose to focus
on that manifestation,
the sacred longing you carry in your high heart.
Clarify what that is for you right now.

The next moment it may feel, see,
and look different,
but what is it right now that you long for?

Consider the possibility that all of
this can come true.
It simply depends upon you
and how much you block the creative energies
coming through you,
how much you choose to either block
or allow and surrender to your
individual creative process.

You were not the creator of the conditions
into which you were born in this life.
You as an individual have not created
your entire life as it is.
You are indeed a creator,
yet all individuals, all beings, are creating
and thus together create a world in the physical.

Because of your individuality,
each of you experiences this world differently
according to your preconceived ideas,
your belief systems, and your emotional
or irrational outlooks.

In addition to that, you,
from deep within your heart,
deep within the core of your being,
create an upwelling of unconditional love.
That is why we call it the sacred human heart.

This is your tool, this beautiful heart,
the well of love within you
that arises from deep within,
from the ineffable, the divine,
and upwells into your pure heart,
which you create.

You do this collectively
into the pure heart of humanity.
Human love is the gift that humanity
brings to this planet.

Honor your heart and honor your love.
Honor the uniqueness of your love,
which is individual, unique to each person.

Remember your unique love
and its many facets as it upwells
from deep within the heart
and moves throughout every cell of your body
in a unique fashion with your unique core qualities,
which you have already developed in other life
experiences.

Chapter 5 Self-Review: Heyoan's Tools to Re-create Your Life

1. Meditate on each concept or principle you are drawn to.

2. Journal if you wish.[2]

PART II

HEALING OUR CREATIVITY THROUGH THE FOURTH LEVEL OF OUR FIELD: RELATIONSHIPS

*"We start our process with our essential core essence,
and seeing our life task and all life from the perspective
of developing and uncovering more core essence.
Time capsules are simply seen as either shading our internal radiance,
or as road maps of the parts of ourselves that we do not recognize as love."*

— BARBARA BRENNAN

Chapter 6

PRACTICAL HIGH SENSE PERCEPTION

There is not nor ever has there been
a separation between
the spiritual and material worlds.

— HEYOAN

The Nature of High Sense Perception (HSP)

High sense perception is perception that extends beyond the range of what is considered to be normal. Normal perception works through the physical body's perceptual organs and nervous system. HSP works through the human energy field's perceptual organs, which are part of the chakras.

When I was beginning to observe the human energy field (HEF) and the Human Energy Consciousness System (HECS), being a physicist by training, I also observed *how* I was observing them with high sense perception and *how* HSP functions through the HEF. This gave me vital information on how to teach others to open and use their HSP. With these observations, I put together a logical, understandable, and functional system of how HSP works through the HEF and the HECS. I will describe it next.

Basic HSP

With HSP, we have more senses than the normal five senses we are used to. **Each chakra of the human energy field has a particular HSP sense. While chakras take in bioplasma for energy to charge our four dimensions from the surrounding natural fields of bioplasma, they also take in the information the bioplasma contains.** Bioplasma is full of information. Most people in the "modern world" are not aware of the existence of natural bioplasma fields all around us. Yet they do unconsciously respond or react to them as the bioplasma moves through them. One can also refer to the bioplasma as energy consciousness.

The energy consciousness that we sense and of which our four dimensions are composed is not just bioenergy and information, it is a signature of who we are. Actually, it is more than a signature, *it is us.*

While perhaps you do not yet experience it *as you*, you can learn to experience your bioplasma as consciousness with energy, or, in short, energy consciousness. The energy consciousness that is taken in by the chakras of the HEF carries an enormous amount of information. Unfortunately, at this time, most human beings are not consciously aware of the information coming to them through the chakras. Yet most human beings do unconsciously react to it in some way.

Chakras Are the Sensing Organs for Specific Types of HSP

The chakras are sensing organs. The chakras sense the information in the bioplasma as it moves into them. We respond or react to this incoming energy consciousness. We may or may not be consciously aware of our response or reaction to it. Re-creating your life requires becoming aware of your responses or reactions to this life process that is constantly moving through you. I will clarify the difference between responding to and reacting to incoming energy consciousness later in this chapter.

The following list of the chakras of the HEF describes how each one receives information through a particular HSP sense:

The first chakra senses touch, body movement (the kinesthetic), and body position and stance (the proprioceptive sense).

The second chakra senses emotional feelings.

The third chakra gives us a vague sense of knowing (intuition).

The fourth senses love and loving kindness.

The fifth chakra senses hearing and taste.

The sixth chakra gives us the ability to see the HEF, the hara, and the core star, as well as the spiritual worlds within which they exist.

When using the sixth chakra to perceive, we are no longer looking at reflected light. We are looking at the light that is self-generated by the HEF, the hara, and the core essence. Since this light is generated by what we are looking at, it gives much more information about what we are looking at than what is given by reflected light.

The seventh chakra gives us the ability to know the high spiritual worlds and can be used at the same time as all the other chakra senses to integrate the physical and spiritual worlds, thus propelling us to another realm.

The seventh chakra is very useful for receiving detailed information that integrates the physical, mental, and emotional realities with the spiritual world. The information can be about anything. Its nature is spiritual rather than religious. It can be directed toward or pertain to an individual or group. It can be personal or pertain to everyone. It can be used with the HSP senses to integrate the information into a higher state of clarity and understanding that is practical in both the physical and the spiritual worlds. I do this regularly when channeling lectures from Heyoan. It is delivered with the power of loving kindness that completely accepts things as they are with no judgment. Sometimes this information needs to be studied and/or meditated on to understand it.

Important Differences between Information from Reflected Light and Information from Radiated, or Self-Generated, Light

How we see with our HSP does not work the same as seeing with our physical eyes. Our HSP sees light that is *radiated* from the person, thing, or situation we are observing. Our physical eyes see sunlight that is *reflected* from what we are observing. This fact has a lot to do with why we get so much more information with HSP than we get from physical sight. This is basic physics.

The mechanism of HSP works very differently than the mechanism of our physical eyes. Our physical eyes move and focus on the object we want to see. The lenses in our eyes direct the sunlight *reflected* from the object onto the light sensors on the retina. Our eyes control the amount of light coming into them with a variable aperture—our pupils expand and contract to control the amount of light the retina receives. The light sensors on the retina are sensitive to light in the wavelength range of 4,000 to 8,000 angstroms (reflected solar light which we call "visible light").

This makes sense since we, being daytime creatures, naturally evolved eyes to see in the same spectral range as daylight coming from the sun. So when we use our physical eyes to look at something, we are actually looking at the solar light that is *reflected* from the things we look at. We do not see visible light that is *generated* by the objects, because it is far, far, far too weak to see. We look at the sun's light that is *reflected* from the objects we look at with our eyes. This reflected solar light can give a great deal of information about the sun's light, but much less information about the object from which it is reflected. This reflected information only gives information about the qualities of reflectance of the object and what can be inferred from it.

Self-generated **light provides a lot more information about the object or person that is generating it than reflected light does.**

HSP gives us the ability to perceive the self-generated light originating from the human energy field, the hara, and the core star. This light energy is beyond the visible light range of 4,000 to 8,000 angstroms. As *generated light*, it contains a lot more information about what is creating it than reflected light can. Another interesting observation is that this self-generated energy consciousness light, which radiates from living creatures, has more levels and different characteristics from what is generated from inanimate objects.

Thus, HSP gives a lot more information than what we see with our physical eyes, since most of that is sunlight reflected off the surface of whatever we are observing.

All the HEF, hara, and core star information that is perceived with HSP is *generated* energy rather than reflected energy. HSP also gives us information from various types of HEF energy consciousness that are also *generated within* rather than *reflected from* the human energy field, such as

sound, touch, and vibration. This is also true on the hara level and in the core essence.

Developing HSP

Developing HSP takes years of grounding and personal process work of clarifying and strengthening ourselves in all four dimensions of our being. The healer must be well grounded and able to be present and clear in all four dimensions of being at once: the physical, human energy field, hara, and core essence dimensions.

If the healer is not grounded, the information received will be confusing to understand and impractical. The information will be fractured, incoherent, and difficult to apply to life. This usually results in many kinds of so-called mysterious esoteric meanings to fantasize about, accompanied by a false sense of self-importance. However, such a person is not to be judged but held compassionately, because it is simply an emotional defense against the difficult and sometimes painful reality of that person's life situation.

Unless an individual has studied and practiced a great deal so that their energy system can handle extremely strong, coherent, brilliant, high-frequency light and power without their HEF splitting, it is not healthy for that individual to attempt to utilize the seventh chakra for channeling information. Nor is it useful, for if a person's field is not strong enough to handle such extreme power running through it, the field will split and the information will not be coherent or clear. One will not be able to interpret it in a relevant, useful way that pertains to life in the physical and its relationship to the worlds beyond the physical.

Each level of the HEF and the chakras in each level exist in a different and specific frequency range. This then gives us a model to use to sense the state, or health, of each level of the HEF. Using HSP focused on specific levels of the HEF gives us an enormous amount of information about the HEF, for understanding the psychological dynamics of a client as well as the state of health of each level of a client's HEF. Using HSP to perceive the state of the HEF shows us what exactly is needed to heal each level. By clearing, charging, and restructuring each level of the field according to its needs, health is regained. This type of work will automatically include the client's experiences related to the trauma that caused the HEF injury.

We have used this model in BBSH for years to train students for healing and to sense the HEF. It works very well. This model is based on my years of observing the HEF.

HSP Mechanics of Opening the Seals of Perception in the Chakras

Figure 6–1 shows a diagram of a chakra and the path that the incoming energy consciousness or the HECS bioplasma must take through the chakra in order to be sensed. HECS bioplasma is entrained into the chakra by virtue of the chakra's "spin" and charge. The structure of the chakra causes the bioplasma to spiral down deep into the chakra (provided it is spinning clockwise as viewed from outside the body). Thus, in order to have your HSP working through any particular sense, the chakra that provides that sense must be functioning in a healthy manner, i.e., it must be spinning clockwise as viewed from outside the body, both on the front and the back of the body. This means that the bioplasma that is spiraling down into the chakra into both the front and the back of the body is spiraling toward each other in opposite spirals. Just before it reaches the center of the chakra, the incoming bioplasma encounters what is known as a seal. In order for you to sense the incoming bioplasma, it must enter and pass through the seal.

Once the energy consciousness has been able to go through the seal in the chakra, it goes into the "sensor," which is deeper in the Human Energy Consciousness System, and you then get the information.

You can learn how to regulate your HEF (including your chakras) in order to control the frequency and power of energy consciousness going into your seals of perception. In the esoteric literature, the ancient methods were referred to as "opening the seals." This was done through deep meditation methods that were handed down from teacher to student through practice. Now we can use analogies to simple physics to understand a focused way of doing this from the perspective of our 21st-century worldview.

The seals are very small from the physical perspective, and are within the vertical power current (VPC) as is shown in Figure 6–2(a). Figure 6–2(b) shows the seven seals magnified. The vertical power current is deep inside the physical body located approximately inside the spinal cord. Ideally, the VPC is not curved like the spine, but is in a straight vertical line. Seals look a little like lenses; however, they act more like electronic gates in that only a particular frequency range and power level range can go through. This requires a lot of personal regulation of one's HEF to direct the energy consciousness through a particular seal at a particular level. This takes practice, but it is well worth it if you want to receive clear information through your HSP. There are seals in both the front and back aspects of each chakra. In addition to this, there are seals for each level of the field.

This may at first seem complicated, but it is actually quite simple and easy to work with. First you choose your sense. Choosing your sense determines which chakra you will use to sense the HEF. Seeing, feeling, or hearing are usually the most popular ones to use. Since each HEF level is different, to stay clear about the information you will receive, you also need to choose the level of the field that you wish to observe. For example, you want to *see* your client's *fourth* level:

1. If you want to *see* a particular level of a client's field, you must first charge and open your *own* vision chakra (sixth chakra) on the level of *your* field that corresponds to the level of the client's field that you want to see.

   If you want to *see* a client's fourth level, then you must tune your HSP of your sixth chakra to the fourth level of your field, and correspondingly open the seals in your sixth chakra on the fourth level of your field. This then, if charged enough, will allow the energy consciousness of your client's field through the seal in your *seeing* chakra (your sixth chakra, commonly called the third eye). So you must focus your attention on your client's field in the area you wish to see it. If your chakra is balanced, your focus steady, and your field strong enough to allow energy through your seals, then you will be able to see your client's fourth level wherever you focus your attention.

2. Your curiosity is a great tool. Follow it by focusing your attention on what you are curious about or what your intuition shows you to check out. HSP focus is very much like focusing your physical eyes on what you want to see. You must allow enough energy consciousness from the client's field to come in through the seals of your vision chakra (sixth chakra) in the frequency range (or HEF level) of your client's field you wish to see.

    For physical vision, you must have enough ambient visible light to see anything. For HSP it is a little different. If the HEF you want to see is very strong and radiating brilliant auric light, then it will be easy to see, or even in rare cases too bright for you to be able to look at. But usually, especially if you are a healer dealing with people who have an illness, their field will not be very bright (and you have no such thing as lights to turn on, like in the physical world). You must provide the extra energy by charging your own field. The weaker the client's field, the stronger the charge you must create in your own field to perceive the client's field. This means charging your field, not theirs, to increase your HSP. Charging their field must be done precisely in the way they need it.

Thus the techniques to learn HSP are different from the techniques to learn to give healings.

Remember that with our physical eyes we see reflected light from most of the things that we look at, except, of course, light from the sun, stars, fires, light bulbs, etc. If it is too dark to see in the evening or night, we turn on the lights to look at the reflection from all the things around us. **With HSP, we perceive light that is emitted, meaning it is radiated from the HEF and UEF, not reflected from them.** This and a few other things make HSP different from physical sight. I will explain these in a moment.

3. If you have accomplished numbers 1 and 2 above, and you still do not see the field, then you have not charged yourself to the power level you need in order to open your seals so that they can transmit bioplasma through them. Remember, it is important to first ground into the earth and charge your lower chakras to build up a charged foundation in your field before focusing on the center of your particular chakra that has the sense you want to use.

4. Unfortunately, most human beings have several chakras that are not functioning properly. This is one of the things that make HSP so difficult at first. It is necessary to become familiar with the habitual imbalances in your field and learn how to right them. There is a good, simple way to do this. To charge the chakra you wish to use for sensing, start by charging your whole field, first by

grounding down into the earth and breathing deeply into each chakra, beginning with the first chakra. Charge each chakra and make it spin clockwise when looking from the outside of your body. A great way to ground is to stand with your feet a little wider than your shoulders. Bend your knees and keep them bent. Do not bounce up and down as this just scatters the energy. If you need to rest, come out of that stance and shake your legs. Then try again. Breathe deeply. Use your hands to charge each chakra as you make your way up your chakras with your focus and your touch.

5. Since I have chosen sight and the sixth chakra for this description, use the rasp breath as I first described in *Hands of Light* (page 163) to charge the sixth chakra. Simply take long, deep breaths that rasp across the soft palate in the upper back of your mouth. Then direct the energy into your sixth chakra by focusing on the place where the tips of the front and back aspects of the sixth chakra come together *in the middle of your head in the third ventricle area, where the seals are located.*

    (Do not focus on your forehead as many people try to do. You can also use the yoga technique of the breath of fire, rather than the rasp breath, as it also works. However, if you are not used to it, you can become dizzy and disoriented because it could overcharge your field beyond your ability to regulate it.)

6. This method works for opening the seals in any of the chakras. The rasp breath can be used to charge the whole field first, provided that you stay grounded. Then focus on the chakra you wish to charge to open

the seals there. In fact, it is a good idea to first charge your entire field before trying to use HSP. Start with the first chakra, then move up all the chakras, deep breathing with the rasp or breath of fire to open and charge each of them. Do not try to perceive anything with HSP until you have charged all seven chakras. Then go back to your chakra that corresponds to the sense you wish to use and focus on the rest of the exercise to initiate HSP.

Common Problems Encountered When Learning to Open HSP

1. If, in charging your sixth chakra, you get color and no form, you have succeeded in opening the front of the sixth chakra, meaning that it is functioning and its tip is centered in the VPC. However, the back chakra is not functioning correctly. If you get form and no color, you have succeeded in opening the back aspect of the sixth chakra, and it is functioning correctly with the tip seated into the VPC, but the front of the sixth chakra is not functioning properly.

2. If all the alignment is okay and you can regulate your energy consciousness flow but you still do not see with HSP, then your field is not strong enough to run enough energy consciousness into the seals to get through them. You will need to energize your field before trying to open your HSP. Most likely you need to get more exercise, check your diet and eating habits, work your psychological process, and also practice grounding. Or, for the moment, you could just dance! Dancing works great. Put on your

favorite music and go for it. If that doesn't work, resort to the other tools like the diet and process work. It may not be as much fun, but sooner or later you will have to do it!

3. The main problems we encounter in opening HSP are usually the ones posed by our psychological issues. In order to learn to regulate your field, you must practice. The practice must be one of first learning about your field and your personal energy psychology. (I discuss this in *Hands of Light* and at length in *Light Emerging*.) As you learn how your psychodynamics affect the functioning of your field, you will know how important it is to understand yourself and your childhood pain, as well as your need to develop a healthy functioning adult ego to deal with your defenses that prevent you from feeling your early childhood pain. I have described how your psychology defense systems distort your HEF in *Light Emerging*. Here I will simply say that when you defend against feeling your early pain, you block the energy flow through some of your chakras to do so. Since the chakras are the means to access your HSP, blocking them makes it impossible for you to perceive with the HSP that comes through those particular chakras. Thus in order to open and develop your HSP, you must deal with your psychological issues and learn to regulate your habitual field distortions that result from your defenses. To be able to regulate your field distortions you must develop a healthy, functioning, and compassionate adult ego.

How to Tune to the Level of the Field You Want to Observe

This leaves us with the question of how to know which level of the field you are charging. I found a simple method to do this because each chakra sets a base note for each corresponding level of the field. To find a particular level of a field:

1. Make your hands feel the same as the chakra that corresponds to the level where you want to bring your conscious awareness. This sets the frequency of your hands to the same frequency of the chakra.

2. To do this, hold your hands open-palm on your body at the chakra location, and deep breathe to charge your field.

3. Bring your conscious awareness to the feeling in your hands. If you can't feel it at first, don't worry. You can learn to do it by practicing. This does take some practice and confirmation from someone who has learned to do it. But once you have experienced and practiced it, it becomes easy.

4. Once you have "found" the level, bring your attention to that level all over your body by making it feel the same as your hands, which you have already synchronized with the chakra.

Changing the Way You Use Your Mind to Process Information

5. When first witnessing or trying to use HSP, most people make the assumption that it is like physical perception. To some extent this is true, but most of it is not—some of the senses are the same, others are not. HSP requires that you run energy consciousness through your brain in a different way than you

are accustomed. All of us have been programmed by our upbringing, culture, and schooling to run energy through our brains in a certain way. Anyone who went to school will have received teaching that molded the way they use their brain. This molding includes how the energy consciousness flows within the brain as well as the frequency ranges in which the brain is run. In the United States and Europe and many other countries of the world, emphasis has been placed on learning through memorization and deductive reasoning. This charges the frontal and temporal lobes and increases the frequencies to beta waves. Eastern countries such as India and Tibet have, in the past, focused on a tradition of contemplative learning meditation, which creates a very different frequency range and flow of energy consciousness through the brain. This results in the center of the brain being charged more and at very low frequency ranges—alpha, theta, and even sometimes delta waves. One's experience of reality makes a huge shift as one moves from the beta wave reality into the slower alpha and theta waves of meditation. Both methods of gathering knowledge are perfectly legitimate and useful. The Yoga Sutras of Patanjali is one of the most ancient texts on earth. It delineates **five states of mind**:

The Five States of Mind from the Yoga Sutras of Patanjali:

1. Restless, wandering, can't focus

2. Stupefied, dull

3. Distracted

4. Pointed, a constant flow of awareness toward one thing for any length of time; this can penetrate to the essence of anything

5. Still = complete clarity, completely focused, can connect with the real self, intuitive wisdom arises

I am sure it is easy to recognize the first three states of mind that Patanjali points out. The fourth is a state that can be reached fairly easily in meditation by focusing on an object or mantra and continuing to return your focus to that object or mantra each time it wanders. The fourth state of mind is also used by natives who live in the jungle of the upper Amazon. They use it in group meditation led by a shaman. With the fourth state of mind, they observe the life habits of animals to make it easier to catch them. The fourth state of mind is focused on in meditation as practice to eventually move into the fifth state, which takes years of practice. If you want to know how close you are to the fifth state, just count to ten without thinking another thought, or just think of a number such as one or ten without thinking another thought!

Dancing between the Active and Receptive States of Mind for HSP

HSP can be seen as a dance between the active and receptive states of mind. More specifically, HSP uses Patanjali's fourth state of mind in a dance with the rational mind in the receptive state as well as the active states. Here are the steps to use HSP for level one of the HEF:

1. Using your rational mind, clarify and decide what you want to know.

2. Align your intention to find it, then focus your mind on it using Patanjali's fourth state of mind, a concentrated flow of awareness.

3. Make the kinesthetic connection. Send a pseudopod of energy consciousness to that person and

the area of the body you want to read. (You may have already done this automatically when doing the previous step.)

4. Once you make a strong open kinesthetic connection, move into a receptive witness state of mind and allow the information to unfold. Notice that I did not say, "allow the information to *come in.*" I said, "*unfold.*" I will explain this right after these numbered steps. We use the term *witness* as in when you observe or witness something without changing or judging it; you simply allow yourself to know the information. Do not assume that you must bring the information into your field to know it. This is a big mistake that most bodyworkers make. You do not have to do this. I will explain more about this in the next section.

5. Stay in the witness state of mind and let yourself know the information.

6. Continue with Step 5. Do not try to interpret the information. If you do, you have jumped out of the witness mind into the active mind and have stopped your HSP. You are now trying to figure out what the information means. This is not HSP. You have stopped the reading. You will need to go back to Step 1 and start all over!

7. Once you allow the information to unfold, you have succeeded in maintaining your HSP and the reading. As the information unfolds, its meaning will become clear or it will not.

8. If not, go to Step 1 and ask another question. Let your curiosity guide you.

9. The information that you will receive will answer your question, provided you have asked a simple question. Once it is answered, your curiosity will be sparked again to find more information to add to what you already now know to make it more complete. You can continue with anything else that sparks your curiosity.

10. To do HSP successfully, you must learn to move rapidly between the witness state of mind and the active state of mind of focused intent, traveling through the body on purpose by following your curiosity and actively going for what you want clarified.

11. The more you practice the better you will get. Ultimately the big question is, are you projecting or perceiving? This knowledge will come with feedback. The more your HSP is verified, the clearer you will become about how it feels, how you see (what it looks like when you see with HSP), and how you hear (how it sounds when you hear with HSP).

Expansion and Contraction in HSP

In Chapter 2 I described the expanding and contracting phases of the HEF and HECS pulse of life. One can also use HSP in those same phases. The healer can pull information into his or her own body in order to perceive information about the client; i.e., the healer can feel, see, and hear the information about the client inside the healer's body/HECS. I have observed that most people who are bodyworkers automatically pull the information into their bodies/HECS to get it. Unfortunately, this is not the best choice; for example, to sense what is happening in the client's injured leg, the healer must pull the pain into the healer. This means that the healer spends the day pulling the pain or disease disfigurations into their own physical and HECS bodies. This makes for a rather uncomfortable day, as well as requiring a great deal of self-healing afterward. See Figures 6–3(a) and 6–3(b) for clarification.

Bodyworkers' propensity to pull the information into themselves comes from a basic misconception stemming from how our senses in the physical world work. We assume that we must pull the information into our bodies to get it. In HSP this is not the case, because our energy bodies are much more flexible and fluid than our physical bodies.

On the other hand, the healer can learn to expand to perceive information in the client's physical body and/or any part of the HECS: the healer feels information in the client's body/HECS, sees information in the client's body, and/or hears information in the client's body/HECS. This is done very simply, by sending out an amoeba-like pseudopod of energy consciousness from the fourth level of the HEF to connect to the client. The problem is that most people then assume that they must draw the information back into themselves, and thus create a tube inside the pseudopod and pull the information into themselves. This is not healthy for either person involved. All one really has to do is to bring one's HSP into the pseudopod and get the information at the site. It is similar to long-distance viewing. It is just not necessarily a *long* distance!

Exercise to Learn How to Make the Kinesthetic Connection for HSP

1. Sit down and simply close your eyes. Be sure not to look at the ceiling before you do this. Keep your eyes closed until you get to the part of the exercise when it is time to open them.

2. Reach up with your arm and see what you can feel on the ceiling with your hand. Keep trying until you can feel something.

3. After doing this for a while, just note (don't look) what you are doing with your hand. How are you using it? Are you using your fingers and/

or your palm? Is your palm facing up or down?

4. Are you feeling the ceiling up on the ceiling or down in your hand? Keep checking this out until you can tell.

5. If you are feeling the ceiling down in your hand, purposefully try to feel the ceiling up on the ceiling, rather than pulling the information down into your hand. Keep it up on the ceiling. You can do it this way. It is the best way as described above.

6. Make your perceptions simple in the beginning. Here are some questions to ask yourself:

    a. Is it rougher or smoother than the area around it?

    b. Is it warmer or colder than the area around it?

    c. Does it protrude down from the ceiling or is it recessed up into the ceiling?

    d. Is it metallic or organic?

    e. Do you like to feel it?

    f. Is it associated with air, water, heat, electricity, or light?

    g. Guess what it is.

    h. Point at it with your finger and look at what you are pointing at to verify your perceptions.

    i. How many questions did you answer correctly?

7. Now repeat the same process in the following way:

    a. Reach up and feel the ceiling.

    b. Once you are connected with the ceiling, slowly move your arm down until your hands are both placed palm down on your lap, while you still maintain your connection with the ceiling.

    c. Now repeat the ceiling exploration steps you did the first time, while keeping both hands in your lap.

d. Then, after answering all the questions about what you found, and still keeping eyes closed, once again point at what you have found and open your eyes to verify what you perceived.

e. Practice this until you succeed. When you do, you will have succeeded in not pulling the information into you, as well as creating a pseudopod from your HEF without having to use your hand to make the kinesthetic connection. Thus you are freer to move your hands in any way you like to do long-distance healing through your kinesthetic connection!

8. Now repeat the same process without ever lifting either hand off your lap.

9. Next do the same thing long distance. If possible, first get permission from a friend with whom you would like to do this.

a. Make the kinesthetic connection to a friend and observe them.

b. Ask yourself simple, direct questions about them.

c. Note the time of your observations.

d. When you get a chance, call them to verify your perceptions.

Dancing between the Active and Receptive Mind

1. Decide what you want to know. Actively search for information you want by imagining to reach out with your mind or hand and spatially scan where to find it. You will eventually *feel* something. When you locate it, make the kinesthetic connection with it *to feel it* better. Once you make the kinesthetic connection, continue to *feel it and notice what you feel*. Move into a receptive witness state of mind and allow the information to unfold. Gather your feeling information about it, i.e., make a list in your mind of what it feels like. Do this in a receptive witness state of mind and allow the information to unfold.

2. Do not try to interpret what the information is.

3. As information unfolds, its meaning will become obvious or it will not. If not, go to Step 1 and ask another question.

4. If the information becomes obvious, write it down if you wish.

5. You may want to keep a journal of your HSP observations for later reference and verification.

The Nature of HSP Information

There are two basic types of HSP information, literal and symbolic. Just as their names imply, literal information is transmitted through physical as well as HEF perception, and symbolic information uses symbols to transmit information.

Literal Information: If you look at someone with an injured leg and see a broken bone with literal HSP, it will look like the broken bone looks in the physical. If you look with literal HSP into the first level of the HEF at and around the place the bone is broken, you will see the broken lines of energy consciousness in the first level of the field. The particles of light no longer flow through the lines of the first level, because the energy consciousness current of the first level stops when the lines are broken. This is just like the electric current in a wire that stops if the wire is broken and does not make a complete circuit.

If you then look at the second level, you will see the congestion of the energy consciousness of the second level building up where the first level lines are broken. This happens because the first level current is no longer guiding the unstructured energy consciousness of the second through that area. Instead it stops flowing *through* the area and accumulates *in* that area, usually causing a pileup of red energy consciousness on the second level of the HEF.

Injury to the HEF on both of these levels stops the physical from healing as fast as it could. When a healer repairs the injured HEF levels, healing of the physical is much more rapid. In acute injuries, if healing work is done on the injury right away, the recovery can take days or hours rather than weeks.

Symbolic Information: Symbolic information helps get around the healer's fear of information that is not good news for the client. This helps the client figure out what it means at the pace at which they are psychologically ready for it.

There are three types of symbolic information:

1. The client's symbols. In this case the reader will not know what the symbols mean. This method creates the least fear for the reader.

2. The healer's symbols.

3. Universal symbols such as the circle, the spiral, or the equidistant cross.

Some healers use all of them, some only some of them. I do not use symbolic information much at all. I prefer the literal.

HSP and Levels of the HEF that Correspond to the Physical World, the Fourth-Level World, and the Spiritual Worlds

The first three levels of the HEF are related to functioning in the physical world. Opening your HSP gives insights into the HEF levels that primarily deal with life in the physical world. The fourth level of the HEF relates to the astral world. Once you open your HSP on the fourth level of the HEF, you not only perceive the fourth level of your own and other people's HEF, you also perceive the astral world and astral beings who exist and live without physical bodies in that level. This brings about astral world experiences that most likely do not fit into one's reality base unless you have had prior training, which many people do not have. When you open your HSP beyond the fourth level, you perceive the higher levels of the HEF as well as the spiritual worlds that correspond to them.

Power Levels in Your HEF for Different HSP and Healing Skills

As you develop your HSP, you will find yourself being able to do more things at once.

It is very important to increase the capacity of your HEF to handle larger amounts of energy consciousness flowing through it. The more energy consciousness power you can handle running through your field *while still being able to regulate your field*, the more skills you can use at the same time. Each skill you wish to use takes effort and energy. For example, if you wish to give a healing and use your HSP at the same time, it will take more power in your field. The key is that you must be able to handle and regulate this power without your field breaking or becoming chaotic from the increased energy consciousness.

The following is a list of typical skills a healer can learn as the regulated power levels in your HEF increase:

- The first level of power, P1, is what it would take to bring your conscious awareness to a particular level of your HEF, say, in your hands. This means that you can experience that HEF level in your hands.

- When you are able to reach P2 and still regulate your HEF, then you will be able to experience a particular level of your HEF all over your body, i.e., you will bring your conscious awareness to that level all over your body.

- At P3 you not only can do the skills of P2 but also are able to use HSP to experience the client's HEF at that same chosen level in the place you put your hand.

- At P4 you will be able to make a change for healing in the client's HEF at the chosen level.

- At P5, you will be able to make the change for healing and also use your HSP to observe what you are doing when you are doing it. This is a very important combination of skills!

- At P6, you will be able to add the skill of observing the effect of your healing on other levels of the client's HEF.

- At P7, you will be able to add communicating with your guide to all the other skills you are doing.

- At P8 you will be able to add the skill of communicating with the client's guide and listening to the intraguide communications. Please note that there is a big difference between communicating with a guide and channeling.

Creating Coherency in the HEF

One of the most powerful, healthy, and rare configurations of the HEF is a coherent field. Coherency means that the levels of the field will be in sync, allowing for the most efficient transfer of energy throughout each level, as well as between the levels in either direction (up or down through the levels). To make one's field coherent, it is necessary to make all your chakras on each level of the field the same size as all the other chakras on that level. As previously explained, the chakras exist on each level of the field—on the structured levels, they are composed on lines of light; on the unstructured levels, they are composed of unstructured energy consciousness of

that bandwidth. Creating coherency in one's field is not an easy task, and is the result of working on the self as you walk the spiral path of healing into the Core. Figure 6–4 is an image of a coherent field. As coherency is increased in the field, the possibility of clearer and more useful HSP also develops. Yet I have never seen a coherent field. I think that we are in a long-term evolutionary process of creating coherent fields. An increase of coherency in the field creates the possibility of a large increase in energy in the field.

HSP Is Different from Physical Perception

In the process of opening my HSP, I discovered that I had made a lot of assumptions about how perception works. I assumed that it would be like our normal senses in the physical world, but HSP does not function like our normal five senses. I had some rather difficult and confusing experiences when I was in the early stages of opening my HSP. Here are a few of them:

Trying to Communicate on Two Levels at Once: Here is a simple example just to show some of the challenges of HSP. I was driving my little daughter to school one morning. Heyoan was speaking to me about something. I could see his form all over the windshield of the car. At the same time, my daughter chatted away about school things.

Suddenly she shouted, "Mom! You're not listening to anything I am saying!"

I didn't know what to tell her, since at that stage of my development, I was not able to listen to both her and Heyoan at the same time. I didn't want to try to explain what was going on. I was still much too shy to speak to anyone about these things.

Shortly after that incident, I realized I just had to learn to rapidly shift the frequency bands I was tuned to. I could tune in to my daughter, then quickly tune in to Heyoan and go back and forth. After several years of practice, I learned to use several types of HSP (such as sight, sound, and feeling) all at the same time. Eventually, I could do that and also observe two people at the same time.

Yet, given the importance of what is happening in any particular healing, it is important to focus on and scan through different levels of the HEF to be clear about how the healing is progressing. It is important to rapidly shift the frequency into which one is tuned to be clear about how the client is handling it in different parts of their HEF, as well as their emotions and their physical body.

Issues Caused by the Difference between HSP and Physical Senses: HSP is much faster than the physical senses. For example, it is easy to receive the answers to questions before they are asked. People do not understand that as soon as they frame a question in their minds, it can be answered before it is asked by physical voice. This is sometimes very disturbing to people who do not understand HSP. I spend a lot of time impatiently waiting for the person to stop asking their question in the physical world, because the information is coming in so fast that I fear I will miss some of it if they don't stop talking.

As I said, I can communicate on several levels at once, but I have to slow down the information stream to communicate on the physical level, because the physical is so very slow compared to the higher HSP levels. It's like the speed of sound compared to the speed of light! For example, this morning a friend of mine called (on the phone) and asked, "Can I ask you a question?" By the time she finished those six words, I had already heard the HSP words *she has a polyp*," I had seen a picture of it in my mind, seen its size and location in the colon, that it was hanging from a very thin thread, and that it was benign. She then continued to finish her sentence by saying, "Would you check out my colon?" Sometimes I fear that I will forget the information before the person stops questioning.

"Reading" Physicians' Patients before the Physician Mentions the Name or States the Question about the Patient: A physician who came to the physicians' support group that met on one evening during each resident training week at BBSH asked, "Can I ask a question about a patient of mine?"

I immediately "read" the patient's field for him and told him about his patient's physical state and psychological issues that were related to a recent death in her family. He replied, "You read her before even I told you about her condition? Don't you want me to tell you what the problem is?"

"No, it's not necessary," I answered.

Several years later, I saw him again and asked him if the information was useful. "You were correct," he replied.

This did not make sense to the physicians who study at BBSH until I explained how it works. As soon as a physician thinks about the patient, he/she connects through the HEF to that client. I can see the HEF form make the connection. Once connected, the physician becomes a corridor or gateway through which the information can flow that he or she wants. As the physician learns how to open his or her HSP, I will not need to read it. The physician will do it automatically. Many of the physicians who have graduated from BBSH are great at HSP, and are able to use their vast knowledge to solve difficult diagnoses. They usually, for obvious reasons, do not tell their patients what they are doing.

HSP—Seeing a Student's Determination to Get Something from Me: As a teacher of many students, I first noticed this in the classroom. But actually, it happens in all of life's settings. It is like having the feeling that someone is staring at your back—you look around and there they are!

This HEF phenomenon happens when a person—usually a student—who is in the same room or in the same vicinity with me decides that they *will* have contact with me *no matter what*. (There are a lot of people who want to ask me things, and it is just impossible for me to answer all these questions on a personal level.)

Here is what happens. As soon as a person makes this decision, they send a very narrow (one-and-a-half- to two-inch diameter) flow of demanding energy consciousness to me and stick it into my HEF. Sometimes it even has a hook. As you might well imagine, this is very uncomfortable. My system automatically goes on alert and I quickly follow the mucous cord to its origin. In the beginning, I used to always move so that someone else was in the pathway between the student who was creating the pseudopod and myself. This simple movement would break the student's concentration so that the student would stop doing it. At that time, I was still too shy to talk about these things, and didn't want to hurt the feelings of the student who was doing it, since they had no idea that they were doing it. Later I just taught the whole class about what the student wanted to know, without pointing the student out. I also added the issue of gooey string demands to the lecture to help them understand how this is done and its effects on us.

HSP—Confirming a Workshop Participant's "Seeing": The first time this happened to me was many years ago. I was working with a workshop participant who was trying to perceive inside the body of another participant who had just been his partner in an exercise. He wanted to know if what he saw was correct.

So, in order to verify him, I decided to watch him looking. I said, "Look at your partner again. Tell me what you see."

My plan was to simply check out what he was looking at by following the pseudopod of energy into his partner, view it myself, and then verify the description he would tell me on the physical level. However, that is not what happened. To my surprise, with HSP, I saw a picture inside his head of what he was looking at. I was so excited that I began jumping up and down on the stage in front of everyone with my hand clasped over my mouth!

Protocol for Using and Giving HSP Information in the Helping and Healing Professions

As you can see, as your HSP develops, you will be privy to an enormous amount of information that is received on purpose, accidentally, or incidentally. I have seen this type of information misused in many ways. This can become a big problem for both the seer and the one being seen. I have had a number of experiences that have taught me to set a strict protocol for handling this information. Below is a list of my recommended protocol:

Protocol for HSP Information:

1. Never take or give information in an inappropriate setting, such as outside your office or your appointment time. You can, of course, make special appointments, including phone appointments (make sure the person is not alone and not outside of their home). Never give any information outside on the street, in a car, train, hallway, at a conference, concert, party, or other social gathering. (I have been asked in all these types of inappropriate and unprotected settings. The person probably has no idea of the possible powerful effect of such information on him.) At times, it may be appropriate in a workshop on HSP as a demonstration, but only if it is benign information that can be taught to all students present. If not, don't give it at all.

2. Verify your information with at least three senses, and reread it at least three times. I use four: visual, auditory, kinesthetic, and channeling from Heyoan. I go for the information several times.

3. Gather information until you have enough to make a clear explanation to someone without HSP. Learn to translate the information into plain English or whatever language you/ they speak.

4. Get very clear on what information is appropriate to tell them. Many times all the information is not appropriate.

5. Always tell anyone with a serious or life-threatening health issue to see their physician of choice. Make it clear that it is very important that they go. Tell them that you do not diagnose illness, unless, of course, you are an M.D. and licensed to do so.

6. Never tell anyone that they have a serious or life-threatening health issue unless you know exactly what they can do about it to help.

7. Never give regular healing sessions to anyone with a serious illness, unless they are seeing a physician of their choice who is in charge of their case.

8. If they refuse to go to a physician, send them to a licensed therapist who will handle the issue. Or give them a *short* deadline by which they must go to a physician, and prove to you that they did. You may have to stop giving healings in such a painful situation. You cannot ever replace the need for the physician. Many people who come to healers are terrified of getting a diagnosis, and go into denial. Some people stop going to their physician (or any physician) when they get a diagnosis.

9. As a healer, ask permission from the client to speak with their physician to find out if the physician is interested in discussing their case with you. Get the physician's contact information if they are interested. Some physicians are interested; some are not. Some do not like healers at all.

10. At one time, when I had a practice in the Washington, D.C., area, one physician came to the healing of his patient and took notes as I read the field and explained what I was doing and why.

Some Other Important Points:

1. If the physician is interested in the information you can give, find ways to communicate with him or her. Misuse of and vague information undermines the healer-physician relationship that is very important for the future of health care.

2. Working together with a physician can be very helpful to a client if done properly.

Chapter 6 Self-Review: Your Personal Journey of Opening Your HSP

1. List the primary senses of HSP that you use.

2. Which is your favorite sense?

3. How are the senses you have developed related to your childhood experiences?

4. How are the senses you did not develop related to your childhood experiences?

5. List any uncomfortable experiences you have had because of HSP.

6. Did you keep them secret because that was appropriate, or because you were uncomfortable about your HSP?

7. Is there a better way to handle HSP information?

8. Practice following the protocol for appropriate use of HSP. What is hardest for you to follow? Do you have boundary issues about this?

Chapter 7

ENTERING FOURTH-LEVEL REALITIES

Nothing is created outside of co-creation.
There is no individual creation
unless you consider your relationship
to the entire universe manifest and un-manifest.

— HEYOAN

What is the fourth-level reality about? **The fourth-level reality is the world of relationship. It is the energy consciousness aspect of our relationships with our families, our friends, and all others. As an energy consciousness world, the fourth level contains objects and thought forms as well as beings, ranging from angels to devils.**

Join me on this fascinating journey into the exploration of fourth-level realities.

Flat Land

There is an interesting little book called *Flatland*, written by a mathematician named Edwin A. Abbott. In the flat, two-dimensional world of Flatland, only the X and Y coordinates exist, as on a flat piece of paper (the right to left coordinate is X, and the up and down coordinate is Y). Therefore only two-dimensional beings can live there, since it is like a flat piece of paper. The creatures in Flatland do not have a vertical Z coordinate, or third dimension.

In the *Flatland* story, the two-dimensional creatures go about their normal daily lives and everything is fine, until one day a three-dimensional being reaches down from the third dimension (the vertical Z coordinate) and tickles the poor confused two-dimensional creature inside his belly. At first the two-dimensional creature ignores it. But the tickling continues. So he, being a Flatland mathematician, works out the problem and discovers that the only way he can be tickled inside his belly is by a three-dimensional being. He gets very excited about his discovery and tells his friends about the existence of three-dimensional beings. Then he *claims* that a three-dimensional being is tickling him inside his belly! Of course, no one will believe him. Eventually, they all say he is crazy. The more he speaks of the strange three-dimensional creatures, the more the others say he is crazy. He realizes it is just better to not speak of it.

We have a similar problem when speaking to others about the fourth-level realities. I find that the *Flatland* story is a helpful jumping-off point to start to consider the possibility of such realities, to begin to understand them, and then eventually accept the possibility of fourth-level realities, or fourth-level worlds. We healers that deal with fourth-level realities have a similar problem, to make sense of something that is seemingly beyond our life experience. But is it really?

The Many-Worlds Theory in Healing

Training for healership includes the experience of other dimensions of life, or "other worlds." Information about other worlds has been with humanity from time immemorial. With the development of science and experimentation, such ideas were not acceptable as there was no proof of their *existence*, i.e., their *aliveness*. The idea of our existence in other dimensions is now being brought back into our consciousness to be reconsidered as a source of information to broaden our understanding of ourselves and our lives, and to enhance our ability to make our lives healthier and happier rather than to simply dismiss them as ancient superstitions. The question before us is, *How can our modern-day understanding of the natural world help us look at the so-called "other worlds" that have been in our psyches for thousands of years?* Most of us go no further due to the fear that our present-day traditions have taught us to have about these other worlds. Let's deal with our fears and take a look at the distant past and other possibilities to see if there is valuable information there.

Native American Shamans

The Native American shamans in both South and North America refer to such experiences as being in the "dream time" or "dream worlds." They used group and individual ritual and meditation to go there to retrieve information, such as to discover the living habits of the wildlife that lived in their territories to make hunting easier. They did it for religious purposes, as well as to maintain their balance with the natural world, all of which was/is sacred. These traditions continue today.

The Ancient Goddess Religions

The goddess religions reigned the earth for thousands of years before the coming of the present-day masculine-oriented religions. Women were honored as vessels between the ineffable and the physical world, into which man planted his seed to continue life on earth. Many ancient statues of priestesses had snakes wrapped around the shoulders, arms, or neck. The snake is the ancient symbol of the kundalini, the force of light energy that travels up the spine to clarify the body and mind for enlightenment. Many meditation practices are taught to achieve enlightenment through the raising of the kundalini.

Later, Christianity, in its sweeping movement northward, met the British Isles and encountered the ancient goddess religion, the religion of the native peoples who lived close to the earth. They lived within the natural cycles of life, as did all creatures. They lived their lives through ritual and honored each season with ceremony. Everything was considered to be alive, i.e., it contained life energy. In Avalon (now called Glastonbury), the priestesses had developed healing methods using life energy as well as herbs. They went to the top of their sacred hill, called the Tor, to penetrate the veil between the worlds. It was a natural thing to do.

Lacking any understanding of what the priestesses of the ancient goddess religion in Avalon were doing, the invaders accused them of witchcraft and slaughtered them. The witch hunts and slaughtering continued in America in Salem, Massachusetts. These are known as "the burning times." The witch hunters did not know that the word *witch* means "woman who heals with herbs."

Yet through all that, those Christians did believe in other worlds that they called heaven and hell. But because of the vast differences in the two religions, the Christians saw the women of the goddess religion as heathens and condemned their members to hell. How painful for the "witches" as well as for the Christians who did it. What a shame that people of different belief systems judge and condemn those who do not hold the same beliefs!

Modern-Day Cultural Views of Other Worlds

In the American culture of European descendants, while we still hold to our ancient religious traditions, we also have begun to label our experiences of other worlds as going into altered states of consciousness—especially since our hippie days in the '60s! There has been some very good research mapping brain waves and correlating them to types of altered-state experiences. So let's look at a modern-day work of exploring other worlds or altered states of consciousness. In the explorations of Robert Monroe, at the Monroe Institute in Virginia, near Charlottesville, no prejudice is found.

Robert Monroe's Work

Robert Monroe has done extensive research into what he has labeled the *belief system territories* that he and his colleagues experienced by entering different states, or levels, of consciousness. He was able to relate these states to certain frequency patterns that had been measured in the centers of the brains of practitioners of long-time meditation, such as Tibetan monks. Monroe developed Hemi-Sync, a simple way of re-creating these meditation frequencies in the minds of anyone. Using headsets to direct a slightly different frequency into each ear, Monroe could control the input frequency into the center of the brain. Thus he was able to duplicate the various frequencies that corresponded to different states or depths of meditation that Tibetan monks were practicing.

Tibetan monks have several reasons for regular meditation: to calm the mind, to experience serenity, to experience other worlds, and also to prepare for death. Poha is the study of meditation to be able to traverse these other worlds/states of consciousness by practicing holding conscious awareness focused on the clear light of higher states of consciousness. According to Buddhist tradition, upon dying, one goes through other worlds, called bardos. These worlds are also seen as states of consciousness through which the soul travels and is tempted. Yet the temptations are actually projections from the unclear parts of the deceased's psyche.

Basically, every culture on earth has their own way of dealing with the idea of worlds beyond the physical. On my path to become a healer, and during the time since then, I have had many otherworld experiences. These experiences have gently—and a few times not so gently—taken me step by step into an understanding of the worlds beyond the physical.

The HEF and the Worlds of Energy Consciousness

The worlds beyond the physical correspond to the higher levels of the human energy field (HEF), while the first three levels of the field are associated with the building of a physical body and physical life. The higher levels (four through seven, and beyond) are a very important part of one's self associated with life beyond the physical, but also have an impact on one's physical life as well.

When one learns to perceive the fourth level of the human energy field, one can also perceive the world of the fourth level. It exists beyond the physical three-dimensional world, yet also, in a sense, surrounds the physical. The fourth-level world has a frequency band above, through, and below that of the physical.

Once you learn to observe and enter the fourth-level world, it takes some getting used to. The fourth-level world is not like the physical world. It does not function like the physical world. Upon entering it the first few times, we naturally expect the fourth-level world to function according to the physical laws of the physical world. It does not. At first this is very confusing, and many times quite frightening. Yet with close observation, one can discover certain basic laws by which the fourth-level world functions. While still challenging, entering the fourth-level world with this understanding is a great relief.

Opening Your HSP, Your Personal Journey

As I described in Chapter 6, to enter the fourth-level world, you must first open your high sense perception (HSP) on the fourth level of your HEF. To do this, it is important to open your HSP on levels one through three of your HEF first. This helps a great deal with self-orientation once you enter the fourth level.

The first experiences of high sense perception are usually pretty simple. You may have a dream that has a particular meaning about something that might happen to you. You may see a vision. You may hear words in your head. If, on the other hand, you are in a very difficult or life-threatening situation, then any HSP experiences will probably be much stronger.

In the beginning, the HSP sense that opens first will determine the type of experience you have. If your auditory senses open first, then you will hear sounds, music, or information. If your vision opens first, then you will see things beyond the normal sense ranges. As you open more senses, your experiences will include information from those senses. You will begin verifying your information by combining the different senses, as we all do in the physical world. For example, you may hear a loud rumbling noise, feel the ground shake a little, and then look up to see a truck approaching. You had already expected to see this from the information you received from the first two senses and, of course, your past experience with loud, heavy trucks.

If you allow your experiences to unfold and do not try to interpret them right away, your HSP will then develop. Take some time to gather information and don't go for the simple, pat answers right away. Just let it build into a workable system for you.

Experiencing the Fourth-Level World through HSP

As your HSP develops and you are able to regulate it to the fourth level of your HEF, you will eventually perceive fourth-level beings. At first, it might be in a dream. That is easier to integrate into your reality system.

Dreams are probably the most commonly accepted of fourth-level experiences. For example, people have dreams of angels, or simple precognitive dreams of things that may happen, such as car accidents. Precognition and dreams come in any of the HSP senses that are listed in Chapter 6. But since you are asleep, you tell yourself that it is okay, you are not going mad, and it is just a dream. You probably even hope for another dream. Angels are allowed to come to us in dreams in our society. Dreams are okay. Everyone has them. However, that may just be the beginning.

When I first started to see angels, I kept it quiet and criticized myself, saying, "Who do you think you are? Only special people see angels." Later, having seen more angels, I just told myself I was seeing visions. A vision is almost as safe as a dream. All religions talk about people having visions. In a way, calling it a vision is a way to get out of dealing with whether or not it is *real*, i.e., as real as the physical reality. A vision is still iffy, sort of real and sort of not real.

If you continue to have visions, you will eventually reach a threshold that challenges your interpretation of reality. Here is how it works. Say you first have a vision of a spiritual being, perhaps an angel or a guide. Then you hear it speak to you. Hearing an angel or guide speak is common for visions. Your interpretation of reality as a vision is still intact.

Then you ask the vision a question and the angel/guide/being in the vision answers your question! You have taken your first step away from using a vision as a satisfactory explanation. Well, perhaps visions answer questions, although that may be getting a little iffy for some folks.

The next step may be that you feel the presence of the angel/guide/being. This is getting further away from a vision now. You see the being and he/she speaks to you. You ask a question and get an answer. You feel his/her presence, then he/she touches you and you can feel that too. You are beyond the concept of a vision. It no longer works for you. *The interaction is now relational.* You even sense the quality of feelings toward you and the intent of the angel/guide/being. Perhaps you even experience the being's environment around you. Now you have clearly crossed over and are experiencing the fourth-level world.

Let's go back and look at this experience to see what is happening in the HEF that corresponds to it. First you *see* a vision. This is information coming from your sixth chakra opening on a higher frequency of the fourth level of the HEF. Remember, the fourth level corresponds to the fourth-level world, which is a broadband world and expands both below and above the earth's physical-world vibration systems. The fourth-level world is full of beings that range from very highly evolved, and therefore very light, bright, and angelic, to beings that are not yet as evolved as the normal human being.

After seeing the angel/guide/being, you hear it *speak* to you. You have just opened your fifth chakra on the fourth level, on the same frequency range. When you ask your question, you are also using your fifth chakra. When you experience the feeling toward you, such as love and caring, you have opened your fourth chakra to the fourth level of your HEF. When you feel the being's presence and its touch, you have opened the first chakra on the fourth level of your HEF. If you understand the interaction and communication, you have opened your third chakra on the fourth level of your HEF. If you have feelings about yourself with respect to this interaction, you have opened your second chakra on the fourth level of your HEF. So essentially all six chakras are open and functioning on the fourth level of your HEF, which corresponds to the fourth-level realm. Thus you are also experiencing your own fourth-level body. If you continue surrendering to this experience, you will open your crown chakra on your fourth level of your HEF. You experience yourself being in and a part of the fourth-level world, where the angel/guide/being is, rather than experiencing the fourth-level world outside of yourself, as if you were in an interactive movie.

How Childhood Experiences Influence High Sense Perception

My first entries into the worlds beyond the physical went unrecognized for many years. I didn't realize I was entering spaces of life experience that were beyond the three dimensions we are all used to. But after studying the seemingly unexplainable phenomena for many years, I began to realize that all my experiences could be understood much better from the perspective of fourth-level realities. This reality is very different from our normal, three-dimensional physical world.

All of us have experienced the worlds beyond the physical as children. Some childhood experiences are fantasy; some are fourth-level reality experiences, such as invisible playmates that most adults can't see but children can. Here are some of my childhood fourth-level reality experiences. Did you have similar ones?

How Childhood Experiences Influence Our View of the Fourth-Level-Reality World

My dad took me fishing at five in the morning. He taught me to row the boat silently, so that the oars did not make a sound when they entered or exited the water. I was good at it. I loved the silence, permeated now and then with the sound of a fish popping the surface of the still lake when it struck for an insect. I could literally feel the surface tension of the lake water breaking. Each morning there were wafts of mist here and there over the lake. I could hear the gentle breezes rippling across the water now and then, creating tiny rivulets here and there. By the time we left to go about the day, the sun was bright in the sky.

All this was training in high sense perception. I spent hours upon hours sitting silently in the boat, not moving, all senses alert to the natural world around me. I never saw this as a type of meditation; it was just being quiet. I am grateful to him for that.

Mom's influence on me was different. There is a long-running tradition of the "sixth sense" in my mother's heritage; apparently my grandmother used it all the time, as did my mom. In my father's family, the men going back in time were all members of the secret society of Freemasons, which helped form and build the United States.

The "other worlds" never seemed to be anything "special." They were just a natural part of life. Mom had an unshakable faith in God, *the faith of a grain of mustard seed*. It never wavered. When she had a quadruple bypass operation several years ago, she watched the angels around the operating table during the operation. She always knew when something was going to happen. She always knew when the phone was going to ring, and if it was going to be good or bad news. Just a feeling, she said. Sometimes she would get a feeling that someone was about to die. She didn't know who it was, but it would happen. Some of her sisters, my aunts, went to healers regularly.

The Effect of Negative Childhood Experiences on High Sense Perception

When I was "bad," my mother punished me. She put me over her lap and spanked me. It hurt a lot. But my Dad was scarier. When he came home from work and my mom told him how bad my brother and I had been, he would break into a rage and hit us.

When I got older, I realized that my brother would tease me all day long, telling me that I *was not born, but my parents found me under a rock*. I would get very upset and freak out at my brother about this. From these experiences, I learned to use my high sense perception to determine *where the next blow would come from*. So the development of my HSP was twofold: that of the peaceful, meditative, natural world I perceived both in the boat on the lake and at play in the fields and woods, and also that which I used to avoid any negative encounter with my parents. I think that these negative encounters were one of the reasons I sat in the woods so much when I was a little older.

This is a general problem that must be dealt with for all those who have high sense perception, *because the majority of people who have developed it did so out of defense*. Such people tend to look for danger and what is wrong *rather than what is there*. For example, when one of my clients was a young child, her mother repeatedly locked her in a closet. It was dark and scary in there, except for the crack of light under the door. She told me she learned to (mentally and emotionally) go out through the crack of light under the door and spent her days "floating" to places she wanted to go. *She had a great deal of fear, and used her HSP to be alert to the next scary thing that might happen to her.*

We are careful in BBSH when teaching HSP to our students that they know the difference between looking for what is wrong and simply looking for what is there. Looking for what is wrong will easily distort HSP toward the negative, and the student will miss the whole person. We have developed special methods of teaching so that the student can find their internal splits that affect not only their HSP but also their ability to develop professional healership.

My First Experiences of the Interface between the Worlds

There was another strong negative influence to the youthful development of my HSP: witnessing the deaths of the many animals, which were either farm animals or wild game my father caught to feed us. I very carefully watched the process of death as the animal transitioned from one world to another. I watched the life energies be drawn inward and upward as they struggled in the transition. It was both fascinating and educational to watch, and, of course, very terrifying, since I knew it would happen to me someday. As a result of these experiences, I became curious about the interface between the physical and spiritual worlds. I wondered what it would be like to leave this life for one in the spirit world. I even tried to imagine what it would be like to be dead, to not exist at all. Sometimes I would lie awake most of the night trying to make the transition. I couldn't do it on purpose.

Sometimes at night when the moon was full, and it was very cold in my bedroom, I would project myself out the window and go to the moon. Was it a dream? Who knows? I had lots of "dreams" of floating around my bedroom.

My biggest problem at night was when I would get up to go to the bathroom, which was downstairs. Sometimes I would wake up in the morning having wet the bed. This was very upsetting since I clearly remembered going down to the bathroom. Finally Mom took me to a doctor about my bed-wetting. He told her to just spank me every morning I woke up with a wet bed. She did. I think that motivated me to find a way to stop it. I tried really hard. I decided that I must have been dreaming when I went to the bathroom. Then I found a clue to stop the bed-wetting. I noticed that in the "dream" I would go down the stairs like I was skiing straight down a slope. So, each time at night when I would "ski" down the stairs to the bathroom, I knew I had to somehow force myself to go back to the bedroom and get my body. It took some practice, but finally I was able to stop, turn myself around, and get my body to walk down the stairs the normal way. This stopped the bed-wetting.

I also had another interesting experience that occurred during my seventh or eighth grade of school. I remember sitting in a swing in the backyard of the house, and crying profusely for long periods of time, because the love of my life had not been born yet. Just a few years ago, I remembered this experience and realized that it was actually true. My husband, the love of my life, had not yet been born!

Putting all these experiences together and trying to make sense of them as I was growing up just made me more curious.

A Few of My First Fourth-Level Spontaneous Experiences as an Adult

First I want to make it very clear that none of the experiences described in this book were related to drugs or alcohol. I do not drink alcohol, do not take recreational drugs, and never did. I have never smoked cigarettes. All these things are terrible for the physical body as well as the HECS. They disturb the natural health of the field and also decrease its frequency and coherency. Here are my beginning fourth-level experiences, and I will share more fourth-level experiences in Chapter 10.

The Tunnel Test: During my transition from bioenergetics therapist to healer, I had some unusual experiences that went on in the middle of the night. For two nights in a row, I felt someone trying to pull me out of my body while I was sleeping. I resisted. The third night, I woke up to see a being in the corner of the room. I thought it was an angel.

I said, *"Hi, angel!"* then fell back asleep and had a profound experience that started as a dream:

I had gotten up to go to the bathroom in the middle of the night, and was sitting on the toilet looking at my face reflected in the brass plate around the door-knob. As I gazed at my reflection, my hair turned from blonde to a black Afro haircut. Then the face turned into a dark-skinned man.

Suddenly, I was in bed again and was no longer dreaming, but two beings were pulling me out of my body. On one side was the man with the Afro wearing red-orange robes, and on the other side was the angel. No matter how hard I resisted, the power was too great for me to stay in my body. It felt and sounded like a strong wind blowing through my center. It created a great force of internal suction that was sucking me out of my body. My eardrums vibrated as if an internal wind were blowing across them.

As they pulled me out, they said, *"We're going to test you to see if you can follow God's will, so that you can become a healer. Do you agree?"*

"Okay!"

"Let's see if you can let go enough to go through this two-foot-thick concrete wall."

"Okay!" I said, remembering that there is great space between molecules. I let go and surrendered. We went right through. Then back into my body.

"Good. Now, this one is a little harder. Ready?"

"Yes," I said, nodding my energy-field head.

They took me down deep into a dark tunnel. Everything went black. The pressure was enormous. I felt like I was being squeezed to death. Finally, I could see a light at the end of the tunnel. We did not go all the way into the light, but returned just before going into it. Later, I realized that it was the tunnel between life and death. (See Chapter 15 for the HEF description of death.)

At the time, I was receiving healings with a teacher in New York City, as I was training to become a healer myself. The next week, as I walked into my healing, my teacher asked, "Well, how are you?"

"Ah, well, during my intensive something kept trying to pull me out of my body, but I resisted. Then I saw an angel in the corner of the room."

"That was me. You kept calling me an angel. I was trying to pull you out of your body, but you kept resisting me."

"Oh, wow! That was you?"

"Yes. Since you resisted so strongly, I asked Sai Baba to help."

"Oh, so that is who the guy with the Afro was! You two took me through the tunnel of life and death to see if I could surrender enough to God's will to be a healer. Right?"

"Yes."

"Did I pass?"

"Yes, you did pretty well."

Within three months from the time I passed the tunnel test, my massage and Bio/Core Energetics practices became overwhelmed with requests from new people who wanted healings. I had done no advertising. People would come, get better, and tell their friends. I couldn't handle all the calls or the bookkeeping, so I hired a secretary and a bookkeeper. I referred all my regular Bio/Core Energetics therapy clients to other therapists. My healing practice thrived.

Angels and Guides! Oh, So Many of Them

I have seen many angels and guides for many years. They come in all sizes. The angels that I have seen all have wings. Guides generally do not. Guides appear in different shapes and forms, according to the culture and belief systems of the people with whom they wish to communicate. Heyoan told me that guides take whatever form we need to accept and recognize them. Their main purpose in communicating with us is to teach us and help us on our path toward wholeness. According to Heyoan, guides are beings that have incarnated many times, and so have a different relationship with physical earth life than angels do.

Angels live in the realms of higher vibration of the fourth-level world, as well as the higher spiritual worlds above the fourth level. I don't always understand what they are doing. Several archangels came to the healing sessions I was giving at the Pathwork "City Center" in New York City. Again, I couldn't understand what they were doing. I was too shy to mention these types of things. I never spoke about it unless the client mentioned it.

For example, the strong, virile Archangel Michael marched into a healing and repeatedly swung his sword in different geometrical designs over my client!

"What are you doing? Be careful!" I exclaimed telepathically. He just kept on with it. There was nothing I could do to stop him.

The very next day, when I jumped into the car to go back home up in the Catskill Mountains, the driver asked, "Here, want a bookmark?" He then handed me a bookmark with Archangel Michael's picture on it. The picture looked just like the angel that had come to the healing session the day before. Archangel Michael kept coming to the client's healing sessions each week, and kept swinging that big sword over the client. I finally gave up trying to stop him and realized it was his work. The client got better. In fact, she was one of the few who had no side effects from her chemotherapy. She put a sign on each chemo bottle that read *Pure Love.* Later she told me that she prayed to Archangel Michael every day. That must have been why he kept coming.

Archangel Gabriel also came to a healing session. It was a different client. He blew his horn all during the healing. At first I thought it was great, but after a while I wished he would stop. It was so loud I started to lose my concentration. I still don't know why he did it. Without mentioning what I was seeing and hearing, I asked the client if she knew about archangels. She immediately talked about how connected she felt with the Archangel Gabriel.

I found both Archangel Rafael and Archangel Ariel much less invasive. Archangel Rafael came in with soft, sweet love and lots of color. Archangel Ariel was so ephemeral, the atmosphere of the room would light up like crystalline air that softly blew right through both the client and myself.

I'd expected that the archangels would be much bigger, more brilliant, powerful, and awesome. But Heyoan reminded me that spiritual beings appear any way they wish to, and do so according to how it is best needed for the healing client.

According to the Pathwork Guide, angels have never incarnated. Therefore, they do not have the same type of individualization as a being who has incarnated. The Pathwork Guide also said that to have free will, one must incarnate. Without incarnation, there is not even the idea of individual free will or individual self-will. Thus, it is just natural for angels to follow God's will without any hesitation or thinking about what they might choose to do instead.

There is a common belief that the bigger the being of light, guide, or angel, the more highly evolved it is. This is not always true. I have seen many that are quite small yet very effective in helping the people they guide. However, I did see one really *big* angel once. It reminded me of the huge Buddha in Nara, Japan. It came to the Bridgehampton (New York) Community House, where one of the BBSH class weeks was meeting. It was during a time when the administrative work was very hard to keep up with; the school was rapidly growing too big for its space. I was under a lot of work pressure, and was also having difficulty with someone who was apprenticing in one of the classes. Sometimes, when I am under a lot of pressure, I rebel against the spiritual guides who are

in charge of BBSH. This time I threatened to quit (psychically, to the guides) if things didn't lighten up a little. I demanded that the guides and angels help out to get things resolved, or at least give me some kind of confirmation that I was on the right track.

With HSP, I demanded, *"Either I get a sign that I should continue and I am doing my life task, or I quit!"* (I probably wouldn't have quit, but that was the only way I knew how to ask for help in those early days of the school.)

The next class week at school, during the opening meditation, a huge angel appeared over the entire hall. I mean really huge. The ceiling of the hall was at least twenty-five feet high with a balcony all around the perimeter. The angel's skirt fell over the entire hall. The hemline of the skirt was as high as the ceiling of the hall. *Just the hemline of the skirt was about twenty-five feet tall!* There was so much light it was blinding.

"Okay, okay! I get it!" I exclaimed with HSP to the guides and to the huge angel.

Trying to Project My Conscious Awareness into a Book

Several years later, in East Hampton, New York, I was reading a book about Edgar Cayce and how he projected his consciousness into books so that he could learn its material while sleeping or meditating. So one afternoon, just as I was lying down for a rest, I put the Cayce book under my head and projected my consciousness into it. Suddenly, I found myself floating outside my body way above the house. This was disconcerting, since I thought I was going to get out of reading the book, and get the information without reading.

While I was taking a nap the next day, I decided to use the same technique to get out of my body to go to New York City where my husband was working, just to find out if I could see him. We were still living in a small rented house in East Hampton toward the east end of Long Island. New York City was ninety miles to the west. I got out of my body, but as soon as I tried to go to New York City, I went the other direction. I tried this several times, and each time I would fly out over Block Island to the east. I just couldn't do it. Since my head was lying on the bed in the direction facing south, I would go out of my body and turn to the left, where I thought I would be heading west. But it was never the right direction. I never succeeded in getting to New York City that way. I kept getting mixed up between east and west. This is because travel in the fourth-level world works very differently from the physical. The challenge of astral travel is focusing your mind, i.e., how long can you keep your mind focused on one thing. Whatever your mind is focused on is where you go. As soon as you change your mind's focus, you change what we would call "direction" on Earth. You go somewhere else. So, perhaps I couldn't keep my mind to stay focused. How the fourth-level world functions is discussed in the next chapter.

Confusion in the Fourth-Level World

Once you have crossed over with your HSP and are experiencing your fourth-level body and the fourth-level world, the confusion starts. You most likely have brought with you the assumption that the fourth-level world and your fourth-level body function like the physical world and your physical body. That is simply not true. In addition to that, as I explained in Chapter 6, HSP does not function like your normal five senses.

Get ready for a roller-coaster ride that may take you into some weird experiences that are not logical and at first are difficult to understand! In the next chapter, I will help you orient yourself as you travel the fourth-level world by offering you some frameworks that have worked for me, which come from the information I have gathered during my experiences.

Chapter 7 Self-Review: Exploring the Basic Foundations of Your Relationship to HSP and the Unknown

Do a brief review of your childhood experiences to highlight the basic attitude toward the unknown carried down in your family lineages on both sides. Here are some good questions to ask yourself:

1. What were the unusual experiences you had at an early age that could not be understood or explained through "normal" reasoning? How did you handle them? What made you curious? What makes you curious now?

2. What were the unspoken attitudes in each of your family lineages about the following?
    a. Realities or the worlds beyond the physical
    b. Personal spirituality in relationship to organized religion
    c. The nature of evil and its relationship to nonphysical worlds and to HSP

3. How has your attitude to the above and to HSP developed as a result of these experiences?

4. What are your fears about having an experience of the fourth-level world?

Chapter 8

FOURTH-LEVEL-REALITY WORLDS, OBJECTS, AND BEINGS

All worlds,
physical and otherwise,
all the levels of heavens and hells
are always in co-creation with each other.

— H E Y O A N

In this chapter, I will describe the fourth-level-reality world and discuss various types of fourth-level-reality objects and beings that inhabit these worlds.

Trekking through the Fourth-Level Reality

Upon entering the fourth-level-reality world, you may not, at first, think it is very different from the physical world. In fact, you may assume you are still in the physical, because the scenery is very much the same. Yet after just a few moments, you will notice the difference, because the fourth-level-reality world does not stay the same for very long. There is a good reason why the fourth-level reality looks so much like the physical. **It is because we are co-creators of the fourth-level reality.** I will describe how this works later. First I will describe the various objects and beings that make up the world of the fourth-level reality.

There are **fourth-level-reality objects**. These objects can include everything you have ever seen or dreamed up, and unrecognizable things that you may have never seen or thought of before— things that are created by humans or other living beings who are also the co-creators of the worlds of the fourth-level realities.

There are also **fourth-level-reality beings**, which take on all kinds of shapes, sizes, and appearances. They can look like normal animals, birds, reptiles, amphibians, fish, and human beings. They can be characters from myths and fables, heavens and hells. They can be anything, even things that human beings have never imagined. They can also be anything the human mind has ever imagined. They can be ancient creatures or young ones; they can be unrecognizable and beyond our comprehension.

In addition to the objects and beings in the fourth-level reality, there are also thought-forms. **Thought-forms are actually a combination of** emotions and thoughts, which I prefer to call **psychonoetic forms, or PNFs for short.** PNFs are usually not very large or well formed, as they are made mostly from negative emotions and irrational thoughts that are neither well formed nor well organized. They can have a lot of negative dualistic energy in them and negative dualistic intention behind them. PNFs are created by humans and other living creative beings. We all create PNFs.

All of the above fourth-level-reality objects, beings, and PNFs can also be found stuck in the fourth level of the HEF. They are usually associated with blocks or wounds in the HEF that contain unresolved experiences from this and other lifetimes. These objects, wounds, and PNFs are taken care of on the fourth level of the HEF with fourth-level healing techniques that will be described in Chapter 14.

Objects in the Fourth-Level Realities

The fourth level of people's HEFs tend to have many types of weapons from ancient battles, such as swords and spears, as well as shields, arrows, and bullets. There are also various knives from being stabbed in the back—both literally and figuratively—and other types of wounds from various causes, including animal attacks, poisons, and objects used for torture. Humans have done such dreadful things to one another over the centuries, it is almost unbelievable! In Chapter 11, I describe some of the objects I have removed from people's fields.

Until these experiences are resolved, no matter how far back they go, they are still in the HEF in some form. Usually, the further back they go, the more compressed they are in the HEF. Sometimes so small, they are not easily seen until they begin to expand and unfold when they are activated. This can happen when one's energy system is challenged by a strong external energy or from internal causes, such as an illness.

In addition to these typical wounds, one finds curses, or hexes, placed in the HEF in the present or past lives, or placed on an ancestor and

carried forward to future generations. These can come in any form and require additional healing techniques because they involve particular types of ritual or ceremony that utilize the focused intention of the individual or individuals placing the curses/hexes. Those individuals used secret knowledge and techniques, sometimes handed down through generations.

These ancient techniques are not limited by the passage of time. Such things as ancient curses and hexes can occasionally be found in the HEFs of some ill or disturbed people. Although rare, it is possible for the ancient knowledge and techniques to still be actively present in the fourth-level-reality world, and can still be used for the old purposes to build up power to use "over" others.

While such things may not be acceptable to the modern educated mind, it is still necessary to understand how the fourth-level world works to heal such cases. It works with *negative intention to harm* by inducing fear in the person upon whom the so-called curse is placed. I will discuss this in more detail in Chapter 12.

List of Objects of the Fourth-Level-Reality World:

- Unresolved experiences from present lives.

- Unresolved experiences from other lives.

- Curses, hexes, or ceremonial objects, such as shields or symbols, placed in the HEF during present or past lives, or placed in the HEF of ancestors and carried down through future generations.

- PNFs, either self-created or created by others.

Beings of the Fourth-Level Reality

Fourth-level-reality beings are beings that live in the fourth-level reality. The nature of the beings varies, all the way from angels and guides, through discarnate beings between physical lives, such as humans and animals, down to monsters and devils. The fourth-level-reality world covers a broad frequency band of life. In the higher-frequency ranges you will find light, coherency, synchronicity, and friendly, kind beings. The higher the frequency, the stronger the light, the more evolved the beings. These are the realms or belief system territories that humans label as heavens. The lower the frequency, the darker and nastier the realm. These are the levels of purgatory and hells we have heard so much about when not behaving ourselves! No one really wants to go to these belief system territories. There are many belief system territories to choose from when you leave this physical world, provided you know how to do it and can do it by regulating the light and clarity of your HEF! But more about that later. Back to the beings; here is a list of the types of nonphysical beings I have encountered:

List of Beings of the Fourth-Level-Reality World:

1. Archangels: The archangels are above the fourth-level reality on the higher spiritual levels of the HEF, i.e., level seven and above. However, they can go anywhere they like.

2. Angels: Angels can also travel pretty much anywhere they want, as can highly developed human beings who have reached the level of the bodhisattvas. Many of them exist at the spiritual levels of the HEF at levels five, six, and seven, and continue above to the much higher levels of the HEF that I have not yet written about. Angels are beings who have never incarnated. They most naturally follow God's will. It would never occur to an angel not to do so. Since they have never incarnated, they have never had free will. All the angels I have seen have wings. The guardian angels that I see have

wings, although that may be just the way *I recognize them as angels.* If there is such a thing as an angel without wings, I would probably put it into a different category, since I was raised a Christian. That is the way they are *supposed* to look according to Christianity. Other religions and cultures probably do not necessarily agree. That's okay with me. . . . We are, after all, just humans now.

3. Guides: The guides are beings that have gone through many incarnations and have reached a level of wholeness that qualifies them to become teachers and guide us along our path of incarnation. The guides I have seen do not have wings. They come in any size, shape, and form, and communicate with us through thought/feeling forms. With HSP, we can see, feel, hear, and touch them. We have several guides: one main guide, then others that come to teach us various things at various times of our incarnated lives.

4. Devas: Devas are much like angels, but are in charge of certain aspects of the physical realm, such as attending to the needs of those living in specific spiritual places. There was a deva at the Center for the Living Force; this "deva of the sanctuary" hovered over the center when I lived there. Others are in charge of specific species.

5. Nature spirits: Nature spirits are connected with the various aspects of nature, such as plants, trees, and flowers.

6. Other beings that have never incarnated and are difficult to recognize; others that have not incarnated on Earth but perhaps in other physical systems in the universe.

7. Discarnate human beings: People between lives. They go to various places in the fourth-level-reality world for in-between physical life learning. Some get lost and wander around after death. There are groups, like the Buddhists, especially the Tibetan Buddhists, that meditate to help these lost souls. The Monroe group does this also. More on that in Chapter 16.

8. Subpersonalities unintegrated into self: These are portions of beings that became disconnected from the whole and are wandering looking for self.

9. Discarnate (meaning without physical bodies) animals, birds, fish, etc.: This includes beings just between lives, sometimes lost and wandering.

10. Fourth-level-reality beings in profound separation: Usually on the lower fourth-level reality. They usually look pretty grotesque and try to scare you, most often as a means of self-protection due to their fear. Since they are in profound separation, they do have some strong negative beliefs and value systems; thus they also could have a negative intent to harm you because they will get pleasure by doing it. They have a strong dualistic belief in separation and are afraid of contact. Hurting you may be the only type of contact they can handle. Sometimes they take the form of little or medium-sized devils. Their "devil" appearance depends on what appearance they believe devils to have according to the culture they lived in their last incarnation.

Psychonoetic Forms

Psychonoetic forms are created by us and by other creative beings. They can take any form or partial form, as they usually aren't always that well thought out. The more we focus on and visualize them, the clearer and more well formed they are. Or from the negative perspective, the more we have stewed on or become obsessed with our negative thoughts and emotions, the more clearly defined and powerful the negative forms will be. Their clarity, frequency, and intention depend on what ours were when we created them. Thus they are scattered throughout the various frequency levels of the fourth-level reality. These forms play a negative role in the fourth-level-reality world.

Fourth-Level-Reality Worlds and Their Inhabitants

Fourth-level-reality worlds can be experienced as spaces whose nature is determined by the belief systems of the fourth-level-reality beings that inhabit them. These spaces—or belief system territories, or bardos—range all the way from heavens to hells and everything in between. There is a big difference between the western view of belief system territories and the eastern tradition of bardos. The western view deals with these spaces as if they existed outside of us; the eastern view is that they only exist in our psyches rather than being an actual place we can go to! Thus in eastern thought, they only exist in ourselves due to our lack of clarity and ability to regulate our state of consciousness. They are states of consciousness we must learn to clear and dissolve through meditation.

The Belief System Territories: The belief system territories are divided into subworlds that may or may not be related to one another. They may be better understood by set theory. It may be possible to use the mathematics of set theory to determine how the belief system territories function. In set theory, one defines the nature of a given set that is limited and determined by certain parameters. The parameters combine to make up the nature of the space. Then, given the parameters, equations are developed to determine how things work within the set. First, the mathematician sets the parameters and then proceeds to derive and solve equations that describe the way things interact within the set. Those interactions then determine the nature of the space. Thus one can find out how things will work within that type of space.

Belief system territories do not necessarily exist in spatial dimensions, because they are created and held in existence by the beliefs of the beings that inhabit them. A belief system territory does not exist until beings of like intent and belief systems are drawn together by their similar beliefs and intents. Thus, in order for a belief system territory to become a spatial territory, its inhabitants must believe that it is a spatial territory. Territorial space—of the dimension that those beings believe in—is created by their belief! The territorial space comes into existence by virtue of the belief in a territorial space by the being that creates it. This is one of the basic laws of the makeup of the fourth-level-reality world.

These worlds are created and held in existence by the belief systems of the beings that live in them. These beings continue to hold their territories in existence while they live in them.

Since we are so identified with our physical bodies, which we believe exist in three-dimensional space, it is difficult for us to imagine something existing without three-dimensional space. We certainly think of angels as being three-dimensional! Are they? Who really knows? Meditation may help us give up this limitation.

Yet if we succeed in giving up our idea of three-dimensional angelic beings, we are left with the problem of communication. Most of our communication is full of three-dimensional, as well as linear arrow of time, references. Remove them and we immediately have communication difficulties. In some ways, the use of the words *belief system territories* is misleading because the word *territory* implies space as we define it in our three-dimensional world. So let's try a new term for now:

Belief system worlds

This makes it clear that belief plays a large role in their existence. *Intention* also plays a large role in creating these worlds, since intention largely arises out of beliefs.

From my observations, it appears that the belief system worlds exist in the fourth-level energy consciousness range of the human energy field.

The Law of "Like Attracts Like"

The Law of "Like Attracts Like" in the Astral World: The fourth-level-reality worlds and subworlds attract beings of like beliefs and intentions. These beings are drawn there, whether or not they are consciously aware of their beliefs. This is probably the most confusing aspect of the astral worlds, because the beliefs and intentions that create them can be unconscious!

The nature of a belief system world is determined by the beliefs and intentions of the beings who create that territory or are drawn into it by the law of "like attracts like."

The Law of "Like Attracts Like" in the Physical World: Many people simplify the law of "like attracts like" in the physical world and thereby confuse it, especially in the case of duality. Duality makes the law of "like attracts like" more complicated, for if one is in the duality of a negative belief system, another aspect of this law will come into play.

First, the belief systems will be drawn together in the physical world via "like attracts like." For example, two different people believing in violence will most likely be drawn together. However, since belief in violence is dualistic, it will also contain a belief in opposites. In duality, opposites attract each other, since they are each one-half of the whole. Thus each person in the violence game will play one-half the role in violence, i.e., the victim or the victimizer. They will probably even switch roles at times. The particular characteristics of each role will depend on each individual's belief system, which contains other fears as well as demands. This leads to a vicious cycle between the people involved. A typical vicious cycle goes like this: withdrawing, withholding, then demanding, followed by unsuccessfully responding to demands. This leads to more with-drawal and withholding, which leads to louder demands, leading to more withholding, finally ending in abuse, which then leads to more separation and withholding. This vicious cycle can start at any point. The bottom line is that no demand can ever be fulfilled, because its own nature is dualistic in that it demands to have fulfillment come from the other. Yet:

Fulfillment can only come from
inside the one who is demanding it
from another person!

So if you find yourself
demanding something from another,
go get it yourself,
for yourself!

This is why self-knowledge, especially under-standing your personal psychodynamics, is so important in dealing with the fourth level of the HEF and the fourth-level-reality, or astral, world in healing.

The Law of "Like Attracts Like" and How the Astral Influences the Physical World: Since the fourth level of our field exists and lives in the astral world, we are, in turn, directly influenced by the astral world through our personal fourth level. That influence cascades down from the fourth level into the physical and has a strong effect on our lives. **Any belief systems we hold will be supported and enhanced by the astral worlds described above and the law of "like attracts like."** This law draws both negative and positive influences from the astral world to us.

Thus if our beliefs are dualistic and unhealthy, our beliefs will be supported and enhanced by beings in the astral world that hold those same unhealthy dualistic beliefs. Thus when we go into an emotional reaction (ER), the astral beings that hold the same split belief will be drawn to us, to verify our duality upon which our ER is connected! In such a circumstance these beings will verify and enhance our negative judgments of self and others. This only makes things worse for all involved.

As I described in Chapter 7, once you open your HSP to the fourth level, you also perceive the world of the fourth-level realities and will have to deal with it, whether or not you are aware of your intention and the belief system with which you are functioning, as well as the belief system of the fourth-level beings with whom you are interacting. If you are not aware of your negative belief system or negative intent, you will believe that whenever something negative happens, it is because someone else is doing it to you! That may be, but because you unconsciously believe in it, you, by "like attracts like," draw it to yourself both from the physical world and the astral world. The lesson to be learned is similar to the steps you followed in Chapter 4 to overcome the vicious cycle.

The physical and astral worlds continue to interface even after death. For example, if you believe you are bad and will go to hell, and you imagine it as fire and brimstone with devils, that is where you will go by virtue of your beliefs and intent. At least you will go there for a while, until you get a better idea/belief/intent. If you have other beliefs about after-death experiences, you will probably experience those. You will go to these places, which are in various levels of the astral world, because of your belief and intent. These various levels of the astral world are created by the beings—human and otherwise—that believe in them. Watch out for what you believe in!

Whichever is your strongest belief/intent, whether or not it is conscious, will prevail.

Since these are your beliefs,
you can choose to change them
if you are conscious of them
and don't like their outcome.

If you are unaware of your beliefs
and just think that is the way the world is,
then you have less of a chance
to change your outcome.

Thus clarifying your intention,
digging out and understanding
your unconscious beliefs
and their effect on your life,
doing your process work to

find how they came about,
and then doing the personal change work
to replace the ones you do not prefer
with ones that work for you
is extremely important!

The Law of "Like Attracts Like" and How Our Physical and Astral Levels Create Global Effects: Each time we have an ER or IR, we create negative dualistic life-forms in the fourth-level reality, which then go to whomever they are directed at. These forms usually stay stuck if the field is porous to them. PNFs generated by our ER/IR actions set up and maintain a negative connection with the person to whom we have directed them. In other words, if you are still angry with someone from your past, you are keeping yourself negatively connected to them through your anger. Give it up and you can dissolve the negative connection.

The negative thought-forms we create also stay in the fourth level of our HEF, even though we send them to others. In addition to that, like the beings mentioned above, the forms we create have the ability to live on their own in the world of the fourth-level reality. They gather together according to their belief systems in the energy consciousness level they are, usually a lower vibration of the fourth-level realities.

This type of process even includes your negative thoughts/emotions that are not expressed out loud! Each time we repeat an ER/IR it charges these dualistic life-forms, and they grow and become stronger. They create a life of their own according to the negative energy consciousness with which we imbued them. They join together to form creative groups of like intent. They are attracted to us each time we have an ER/IR. They come in support of it, and join in the negative creation.

They are simply doing the creative process like all other creative beings, but from the negative dualistic perspective because that is what they know. This is just how the creative universe works. It works the same with you. You will attract negative thought/emotion forms to you of the kind that you tend to create. The negative builds itself according to the laws of creation of the

universe. It is the same process as the holistic one. The dualistic life-forms are just creating according to their beliefs, as are the beings that have reached wholeness.

The Noise-Band Shell around the Earth

Now that you understand this process, consider the effect that this has on humanity. **All these dualistic, energy consciousness life-forms in the lower fourth-level realities create a shell around the earth. It has been known as the "noise band around the earth," but it is really a noise-band shell of dualistic energy consciousness life-forms around the earth.** When approaching Earth from far out in space, the noise of agony, pain, pleading, rage, sorrow, fear, and terror is enormous. Many of us who are now in incarnation were drawn to come here by the pleading. Our desire to help and to heal attracted us to this place of pain and sorrow. We took the pain and sorrow into our being and bodies when we incarnated as a way to heal them. We were, of course, also drawn here by our own need to heal our personal dualities. The noise shell around the earth can also be seen as the negative dualistic collective unconscious of humanity.

Misusing the Noise-Band Shell for Propaganda

Unfortunately, there is another, very disturbing aspect to the noise-band shell. That is the negative use that much of humanity makes of it for propaganda. Advertisers are well aware of the effects of utilizing our emotional and irrational reactions to get us to buy what they want. Political propaganda is another.

Did you notice that
when any particular political group
wants to do something questionable,
it justifies its plans by first charging up
fears in the fourth-level realities
of the population
it wants to convince?

Frankly, this is dangerous.
This is how wars are justified and started.
When the energy consciousness in the fourth-
level reality
reaches critical mass,
it then has enough power
to precipitate into the physical world
as a materialized event!

As I am sure you notice, there is a lot of emotional and irrational rhetoric on either side of any national or international political debate, disagreement, or fight. The worldwide communications web of all forms is full of it. This web gives humanity the ability to precipitate the negative or the positive down into the physical at a greater rate because of the many people who can be drawn into the creative process. Each speech, each exaggeration, each accusation adds more dualistic energy into the dualistic aspect of the fourth-level reality. The problem is that once the energy consciousness in the fourth-level reality reaches critical mass, it will precipitate into the physical world in like kind. This is the purpose of the negative dualistic rhetoric, to build up enough energy consciousness to precipitate what each side wants into physical manifestation. As each side revs up fear and anger as much as possible by blaming the other, it increases the probability of precipitation into the physical. Each time someone repeats it, it grows in strength and determination, each time strengthening the dualistic energy consciousness in the fourth-level reality. The rhetoric is repeated over and over, especially in the big-time network evening news programs in the U.S., just to sell the news! I wonder, do they have any idea what they are doing? I doubt it. Each individual who repeats the negative events adds to the growing cauldron of the split. It becomes physical attack, it becomes terrorism, it becomes war—or will it become peace? It will eventually become what the collective "we" wants it to be.

Our Individual Responsibility in Worldwide Creations

Whichever way we hold any dualistic energy consciousness in our fourth level, we automatically connect to the noise-band shell around the earth and help hold it in place. Consider how you personally contribute to the noise-band shell around the earth and help hold it in place. What are your dualistic beliefs that help hold that part of the noise-band shell around the earth, and thus help threaten world peace? What healing do you need to dissolve your negative beliefs in order to disconnect from the portion of negative beliefs that you help hold in the dualistic collective unconscious belief system of humanity? You can find them by doing the entire process that is described in this book.

Human-Created Fourth-Level-Reality Worlds and Beings

During the years of channeling Heyoan while in an expanded state, I have had many "eureka" experiences over words and concepts that were coming out of my own mouth. During one channeling, Heyoan was challenging humanity's fear of the fourth-level realities. He proceeded to give us a lecture called *Treks through the Fourth-Level Reality—Friends, Foes, or Your Children*. In this lecture, he explained that we humans are co-creators of the fourth-level-reality worlds and that we have no excuse to be afraid of our own creations: Heyoan said that many of the beings in the fourth-level-reality world are, in fact, our children, meaning that we created them. This comment, to say the least, surprised and disturbed me. Heyoan alluded to it a long time ago, as described in *Hands of Light*. But first, let me remind you that each of us was a part of creating, and continues to create, as well as helps hold the fourth-level-reality worlds in place.

The Future of the Fourth-Level-Reality Worlds

The future of the fourth-level-reality worlds depends on how well we are able to learn to regulate and then resolve our erroneous images and belief systems about reality. It also depends on our emotional and irrational reactions, since they play a large role in our negative creations that we contribute to the lower negative aspects of the fourth-level-reality worlds. Hopefully, as humankind learns these techniques and uses them for psychological and spiritual growth, the less negative energy consciousness we will put into the fourth-level reality and those that precipitate into the physical worlds.

Chapter 8 Self-Review: Clarify Your Understanding of the Fourth-Level Realities

Do you think you have had any fourth-level experiences of objects, beings, or psychonoetic forms? How did you handle it? Did you enjoy it? Were you afraid?

1. What did you learn from the experience?

2. What region of the fourth-level world did you perceive: higher, middle, or lower?

3. What was your state of consciousness that brought you to that level?

4. Why did you perceive those regions?

5. Have you developed a possible plan to handle it if it happens again?

6. How have negative belief systems helped hold the fourth-level-reality world in place?

THE PHYSICS OF FOURTH-LEVEL REALITY

The astral world is the world beyond the physical.

The astral world's boundaries
are not the same as in the physical world.
The physics of the astral world
are also different.

As you enter the astral world,
you begin to perceive and to interact with nonphysical worlds.
This process becomes clearer
as you learn new ways of being in fourth-level reality.

— H E Y O A N

After many years of observing and exploring fourth-level reality, as well as channeling information about it from Heyoan, I have put together what I consider to be important information about how the fourth-level reality of the HEF functions. This information can be a handy guide to clarify your experiences and help you function more efficiently in the fourth-level world.

Unfortunately, the term *astral* has become associated with negative experiences. This is caused by the lack of understanding of the basic structure of the astral world and how it functions. It is the basic structure of the astral world that causes it to function very differently from the physical world. Most people who enter the astral world expect it to function like the physical world, but it does not. This is surprising and usually frightening, until one learns how to be in the astral world according

to how it functions. So to continue our adventure, it is best and very necessary to understand how the astral world functions.

The Basic Structure of the Astral World

When we try to observe or enter the astral world, we automatically expect to see things in space and time coordinates, as well as the three states of matter: solid, liquid, and gas. However, the fourth-level reality does not function like the mundane physical world of space and time, and the three states of matter. We may even try to interpret it from what we know of the atomic or subatomic world, but none of these methods work. The basic structure is neither rigid in form nor like fluid. It does not behave as a gas, a molecule, or an atomic particle. Its behavior is not understandable from any of those perspectives. In fact:

The basic structure of the astral world
is not form at all!
Objects and beings are not solid!
They do not necessarily maintain the same appearance,
such as the same size, shape, or color!
Now that IS different!

This takes some getting used to when learning to work with the astral world.

The Physics of the Fourth-Level-Reality, or Astral, World

Now let's explore how the fourth-level-reality world functions and clarify how it is different from the physical world. The following is a list of the physics of the fourth-level-reality world. By applying it to your fourth-level-reality experiences, you will find it easier to orient yourself in the fourth-level-reality world and make sense of your experiences. It is important to know and thoroughly understand how the astral world works. If you end up there, you will need to know how to handle yourself. Remember, running doesn't help as there isn't solid ground to run on!

What follows are twenty-seven major aspects of the astral world to describe what it is like:

1. The basic structure of the astral world is made up of psychonoetic events that have either occurred in the physical world or are imagined.

2. A psychonoetic event includes time, location, background scenery, objects, and beings.

3. We all co-create on the fourth level to precipitate things into the physical world, both individually and collectively. Anything created in the physical must first go through the fourth level; that is the creative process.

4. Imagined events are possible future events that are in the process of creation. Once enough humans get focused—especially emotionally—about something, the probability of physical precipitation is increased. If, in the physical world, we rev up a lot of emotional energy and put a lot of power behind it, we are doing the visualization process that will work to create the imagined event into the physical world. See the noise-band shell in Chapter 8. Many of these imagined events are unresolved and await clearing—they will either be transformed through personal or group process, or gain enough mass to precipitate into the material world.

5. The visualization process for imagined events is specific and purposefully used to create enough critical mass to precipitate it into the physical world. Imagined events can have either positive or negative intentionality.

6. To materialize an event, it must reach critical mass in the collective unconscious of all beings that are in the act of creating a fourth-level-reality world, or astral subworld.

7. The nature of space in the fourth-level reality is determined by the energy consciousness and intent of the event that makes up the space and location where the event occurred, or was imagined to occur.

8. According to the principle of "like attracts like," events coagulate around archetypes of belief systems and intent. This is what gives the fourth-level-reality world its structure. Each archetype could be considered to be a subworld in itself.

9. The physics of any given fourth-level-reality subworld is defined

by the beliefs held by the energy consciousness of that world and the beings that live in that world. For example, in one astral world, there might be what we call "gravity," where everyone is standing in the same way and is pulled down. In another astral world, where there is no gravity at all, everyone is floating around. In every astral world or subworld, the light and colors can be different.

10. Astral time is very different from the physical. In our mundane physical world, especially in scientific study, we have what physicists call the *arrow of time*. It relentlessly moves into the future, always into the future. We also have our personal experience of the moment(s) of time. Sometimes we experience time going by very fast (when we are having fun), and sometimes it seems to move slowly (say, when we are bored). Time even seems to stand still, especially when we experience a sudden shock, like a loud noise, or an unexpected fearful event. Remember those slow-motion events, as when you slam on the brakes to avoid hitting the car in front of you that suddenly stopped when you took your eyes off it for a moment. Astral time is not necessarily linear, or always moving into the future. Time in any particular astral world depends on the beliefs held by the beings that have created and maintain that particular astral world. For example, time can move forward or backward, or even stand still. If the beings in any particular astral world don't know anything about time, or have never thought about it, they won't create it!

11. Astral time is intimately connected to space because the astral world is made up of psychonoetic events. In the physical world, the way we live our space is encapsulated in time. Time continues to move forward in the physical world. In the astral world, time is determined and encapsulated in the space. For example, my best friend and I were in Athens. We were looking over a wall of the Acropolis and we both just automatically broke into tears because we saw the hordes of soldiers that were about to destroy the Acropolis. It is horribly painful when you go to those places because the unresolved event is there still encapsulated in the space.

12. Past physical events encapsulated in astral space can be cleared through personal or group process. When this occurs, the energy consciousness in that event is integrated into the great oneness, which can be experienced as a great colorful loving sea of life. It then ends through the creative process in core essence and the creation of more core essence.

13. The location you find yourself in the astral world is where you are automatically drawn by your intention, mind's focus, and emotions—all of which may be unconscious. When there is a strong level of unconsciousness or a lack of strong mental and emotional clarity, you will be inexorably drawn to a space that you match. If you go out of your body and want to travel, you are going to go to the astral territory that you match. This is what happens when someone suffers a drug overdose and goes into the astral world. The state of mind at the time of the overdose is where that person will go to in the astral world upon death.

14. Movement and travel are governed by the mind's focus and intensity or power of emotions or feelings. If you wish to travel in the fourth-level-reality world, you must align your intention, focus your mind, and allow your feelings about the place to flow toward it. If you want to go somewhere, pretend you are a rocket ship. Your feelings are your fuel and your mind is your guidance system. If you don't have strong feelings about going, then it will be harder to get there. Your mind's focus determines where you are headed. This is the challenge of astral travel: to keep your mind focused on one thing. As soon as you change your mind's focus, you change directions. The more you can clear your field and regulate your feelings and your mind, the better it will be for you in the astral world because there isn't the physical world to slow things down. Things happen instantly, so cause and effect are slower.

15. Your intention can shift your feelings instantly. Willing yourself to go somewhere will not necessarily work, since what most of us call "willing" is really a dualistic forcing current. This may take you to a belief system territory of willful, forceful beings that want to control you and force you to do what they want you to do.

16. Boundaries are flexible in the astral world. Our boundaries are not determined in a structured way as they are in the physical world. Boundaries in the astral world aren't the same as they are in the physical world—unless you *believe* they are, then they will be the same.

17. Shape and appearance are determined by immediate self-view moment to moment, and can change moment to moment. When I first began my healership, I would see a lot of different astral beings in people. I would go into a person's HEF and try to grab these astral attachments out of the field, and they would change form and slip away. It is odd to deal with these astral beings because we are used to seeing people have the same form all the time in the physical.

18. Energy consciousness can be expanded infinitely or squeezed into a tiny space. This sometimes gives the mistaken appearance that more than one energy consciousness can occupy the same space at the same time. Humans have a fixed shape here in the physical world. In the astral world, a being can be really big or little because it is not made of physical substance.

19. Perception depends on clarity and frequency of the energy consciousness of the observer. An astral being will take a certain form in order to connect with you or what it believes itself to be.

20. Once connected, you are always connected. This has a lot of repercussions, especially if the connection is with someone you don't get along with!

21. In the astral world, light is radiated from the object or being—unlike in the physical world, where the light is reflected from the sun. This self-generated light is much more informative about the true nature of the object or being itself than reflected light. This is especially relevant in the lower hell realms, as these realms are really dark because the beings there are not creating any light.

22. Energy consciousness of the fourth level can be infused into physical objects, which serve as a container.

23. *Up* and *down* can be defined spatially, by rate of vibration, and by degree of brightness. The higher the vibration, the brighter the light, and the higher you are.

24. *Good* and *bad* can be defined by vibration, brightness, and intentionality, not size (as in size of being).

25. Power can be defined by frequency, intensity, clarity, coherency, and focus.

26. Fourth-level-reality power is brought about through focus of mind, which determines what the power is about (clarity of mind); buildup of emotional energy about what the mind is focused on, which then fuels the mind's objective; and precision of will. This includes the use of the three aspects of ourselves—reason, will, and emotion—as well as their balance with one another, which reflects and can also help determine one's alignment of intention. The clearer the intention, the more balanced are the reason, will, and feelings; and the clearer, stronger, and more holistic and healthy are the results.

27. Many dreams are fourth-level-reality experiences, such as floating down a stairwell or flying.

Ways to Get Out of the Lower Fourth-Level Reality

There may be times, in dreams or explorations of the fourth-level realities, when you could find yourself in a lower fourth-level-reality world. This will most likely happen if you decide to learn how to do fourth-level-reality healing, and thereby begin to deal with the lower fourth-level-reality worlds. Don't try to learn it without an experienced teacher. In such a case, it is good to understand how to get out of the lower fourth-level-reality worlds. Unfortunately, the first few times you experience them, it is usually pretty scary. So practicing the following ways, or the ones you like the most, will be a big help to you to move into a higher level of the fourth-level reality.

1. Meditate to build a bridge between the third and fifth level of your HEF, which is the same as a bridge between the third and fifth spiritual levels. Do this regularly and before you work. First feel, see, and know the third and fifth levels, then practice moving between them. This is probably the most difficult of the items on this list.

2. Follow the light. Go into the light.

3. Use a mantra, the name of a spiritual leader, the name of God that is used in your religion, or whatever religious figure to whom you feel most connected. They all exist in the spiritual worlds of god.

4. Call your guides, or your guru or spiritual leader.

5. Make a white shield around yourself on the seventh level of your HEF. This requires getting over your fear. It is a tough thing to do the first time. It takes practice.

6. Command, "In the name of Christ/ Buddha/Allah/Yahweh, leave." (Use your own religious/spiritual leader to whom you are connected.)

7. Use "Night Prayer" from *Hansel and Gretel.*

Conclusion

In the fourth-level reality, our strong thoughts and beliefs actually take form. One of my favorite movies that shows this process is an old film called *Forbidden Planet*. In it a group of space travelers becomes marooned on a planet. There they meet an older scientist and his beautiful daughter, who are the only survivors of a previous spaceship landing. Everything seems fine until the new arrivals discover that it is indeed a dangerous place, and at night they must close everything down with thick steel walls, or an unknown monster of unimaginable power will attack and kill them.

As the movie progresses, one of the newcomers and the daughter fall in love and things get worse with the monster. Then the newcomers find a huge underground machine/computer. The older scientist proudly demonstrates that the machine/computer runs by direct control from his mind. Everyone is impressed. However, the attacks from the strange invisible monster continue. After much struggle and more attacks, it becomes apparent that the monster is created by the scientist's id, i.e., his deeper unconscious that he is not aware of. "Monsters from the id," they exclaim! As the old scientist dies in the struggle, the monster fades away and the machine breaks up.

Similar things happen in the fourth-level reality, but there are no machines or computers involved. It is just the way the fourth-level reality works, especially from our unconscious, since we are unaware of it. Once we become aware of what is in our unconscious, and how it also functions through the normal creative processes in our HECS with which we create our experience of reality, we can also become aware of how we create our own problems.

Chapter 9 Self-Review: Clarify Your Understanding of the Fourth-Level-Reality World

1. Study the main points listed that describe how the fourth-level-reality world works. Compare them to how you first interpreted your experiences of the fourth-level reality. Now reinterpret your experiences using the information from the "Physics of the Fourth-Level-Reality, or Astral, World" section.

2. What have you learned from each of your experiences?

3. List any uncomfortable or fearful experiences you have had in the fourth-level-reality world.

4. If you need to get out of the fourth-level-reality world, which of the points listed above in "Ways to Get Out of the Lower Fourth-Level Reality" do you think will be the biggest help to you?

Chapter 10

OTHER FOURTH-LEVEL-REALITY PHENOMENA: ATTACHMENTS, IMPLANTS, AND EXTRATERRESTRIALS

*Please note that the challenge
in dissolving astral objects and beings
is to hold unconditional love the whole time,
without dropping or losing contact with it
for a second.*

*This is a difficult task,
because if you go into a state of fear,
the entire configuration goes back to how it was,
and you must start the healing all over again!*

— HEYOAN

Now that you understand how the fourth-level reality functions, in this chapter and the chapters that follow I will discuss the various types of fourth-level reality, or astral, phenomena, that you will most likely find sooner or later in the healing room. Let's start with the simplest. They are astral attachments.

Astral Attachments on or in the Field

In dealing with this subject, it is important to first remember that the astral world is composed of energy consciousness. This is very important to be aware of as you proceed with your exploration of the astral world.

Remember that in the astral world, the law of "like attracts like" is much stronger and works much faster than in the physical world. **You will attract objects or beings that are drawn to you by virtue of your thoughts, emotions, and beliefs. They will attach themselves to your field and seek to enhance the beliefs that you both share. These *attachments*, as they are called, are usually attached into the fourth, or astral, level of your HEF. Sometimes, they can even be found sitting on the outside of your seventh level.**

97

I have not seen them on other levels. However, they do affect the other levels of the field just by being in your fourth level. The fourth level affects the other levels, especially the second.

If you have a difficult relationship in which you fight a lot, as I did at one time, you will attract many of these attachments. They will seek to influence you to fight more, and feed off the negative energy generated by both yourself and your partner. Negative energy is released in fighting. The released negative energy fuels the fighting and increases the probability of more fighting, because there is always a lot of leftover negative energy hanging around to fuel the next fight!

These negative energy attachments are easy to remove from a client's field. It is a matter of holding unconditional love in yourself and your hand, grasping the attachment gently, and lifting it into the light. It will be transformed as it is lifted into the light. Such attachments can be beings or objects, such as various types of weapons left over from past lives.

The Nature of Astral Power

As discussed in Chapter 9, astral power is brought about through attention of mind, which focuses it; the force of will, which maintains its purpose; and the buildup of emotional, or strong feeling, energy, which powers it—in other words, the use of the three aspects of ourselves: reason, will, and emotion. This type of power can be used for positive or negative results, meaning to help or to hurt, or to take power over another. Both positive and negative astral power function under the same laws.

Negative astral power can be directed by or to an individual or group. Objects can be filled with it. Actually, we do it all the time, usually unconsciously, sometimes semiconsciously; sometimes we indulge in doing it on purpose. Have you ever had an argument with someone on the phone, then cut off the call in anger by slamming the handset down onto its base? Guess where your anger went? Not only to the person with whom you were angry, but also into the phone. Guess who gets that—the next person who uses that phone! How's your ear doing? Have you ever, on purpose, maligned someone? Guess where that angry energy consciousness went? You're right—directly to the person you maligned, no matter where they are on (or off) the planet. The more you do it, the stronger it gets. It is like any habit. You build pathways for the energy consciousness to move—not only through your own system, but also to the people you repeatedly malign. To every action, there is an equal and opposite reaction! They will eventually react! It has been postulated that this type of energy consciousness does not get weaker with distance, like electromagnetic fields do.

Astral Power for Duality or Unity Depends on Intention

Astral power originates from emotional power. However, to utilize astral power, one must also focus on a target. This requires clarity of mind to direct the astral power to a target. A target can be any person or thing! Adding the power of intention from hara creates much more power.

When someone believes that they must fight against something, they have split intentions; i.e., they see themselves as having positive intent, while they see the other as having negative intent. Whenever you engage in the idea of good versus bad, you are engaging in duality. Dualistic intention is not as strong as clear, aligned positive intention.

Talisman: For example, a talisman is an object that has been imbued with astral power and intentionality. Any object can be made into a talisman. Once created, that talisman can be used as a source of power from which to draw the particular astral power with which it is filled. It can also be made for protection from something or someone. Talismans are usually created in ceremony. A talisman can be made for yourself or for others, and can be empowered either with clear, aligned positive intention to help or with negative dualistic intention to hurt.

A typical "positive" ceremony would be one in which you fire a crystal at sunrise for a particular positive purpose, such as staying on your path of healing into your core. Your purpose determines if it is positive or negative. This crystal firing is an ancient Native American ceremony. You align yourself with a particular positive purpose or creation, and just as the sun comes up, you pass your crystal through the fire three times while chanting your purpose. I did this a long time ago with someone who directed me. I found it very moving.

Yet at that time, I did not think about the fact that in such a ceremony it was assumed I would have adversaries in my path. These adversaries were seen as outside of myself. I, of course, now know that whatever adversary that appears to be outside of me is really a challenge to bring out my inner adversaries—those parts of myself that I have kept separate from the "me" with whom I identify! This is the deeper truth to making a ceremony work: the adversaries are within us, not outside us! When you have cleaned yourself and integrate with your inside, you can handle what comes to you from the outside.

As long as we remember that our basic healing is of our inner split, the outer dualistic world will simply become, in our eyes, a reflection of our own duality.

My Experience with Astral Objects

Ceremonial Empowerments and Implants from Present and Ancient Times: I was quite surprised when I saw the first implant in a client. Once again, I questioned what I was seeing. It was a shield over her heart. Heyoan told me that it had been placed there during the time of the ancient goddess religions on Earth, when God was seen as female. The purpose of the shield was to help this woman keep her oath of allegiance with the goddess. She was to never fall in love with a man. She had to remain a virgin warrior who guarded the temple.

It was an interesting set of healings. I simply followed Heyoan's instructions as he explained how to remove the shield; clear the mucous that had accumulated around it from various painful experiences; cauterize the wound with silver, then platinum light; rebuild the field on all seven levels where it had been destroyed; then integrate it with the rest of the field on all levels.

Later, sometime after the healing, I remembered that her presenting complaint had been that she had trouble with men. She had been divorced more than once and had not been able to maintain a relationship with a man in a long time, even though she had five grown children from her marriage. I later found out that she was remarried within a year after the healing.

I have removed many other types of implants done in ancient times for specific purposes, such as scarabs that were implanted in religious ceremony during the time of ancient Egypt, and insects that were implanted in less-ancient history in Africa, as well as by Native Americans. The purpose of these was either to give power or to harm. I have seen crystal implants imbued with power to help, to empower, or to do harm that were implanted during the time of a land that is referred to as Atlantis.

I have even seen a form of a ceremonial dagger, which was used in the third eye of students of a certain young guru who said he was from Tibet. He was not intending to leave that astral form in the students' third eye, but did so out of ignorance. I never met him, but he was known for riding around on a motorcycle in Washington, D.C., in the mid-1970s. He was giving shaktipat to a lot of people to open their third eye. He did it with a ceremonial dagger. Unfortunately, in the process, he was tearing their third eyes (their sixth chakras) open, and damaging the seal therein. Since his students could not control their HSP nor their astral levels that he opened, their astral vision became distorted! They were having some very terrible psychic experiences.

Soon they found out about me, and a stream of these poor, frightened souls came to me for help. I simply repaired their sixth chakras and their seals. I then closed their sixth-chakra seals to stop the terrifying visions; I did this because they could not regulate their fields, their chakras, or the energy flowing through their sixth chakras. Now they could not get enough energy through their sixth chakras to reopen their seals. This allowed their vision to become healthy and appropriately focused on the physical plane. The healings automatically stopped their erratic, unregulated astral-vision distortions, because I repaired their chakras and the seals inside them.

In other clients who engaged with the astral world before coming to me for healing, I have seen many kinds of astral objects in various places of the energy field. These objects were more than likely placed for ceremonial purposes in both ancient and even more modern times.

My Experience with Astral Beings

Self-Created Beings Attracted to an Unmet Need: One of the first times I encountered a fourth-level-reality being was during a healing session when I was working to help a woman heal her pancreas. She had chronic pain in that area of her body. As I was clearing the HEF on the fourth level inside her pancreas, I encountered a nest of baby harpies! I was certainly surprised, and turned to my guides for help. They said to gently take hold of each little baby harpy, remove it from the client's HEF, and lift it into the light. As I did this, a harpy bit my fingers! The guides suggested that I hold unconditional love energy in my hands and fingers as I did this. That worked much better. The baby harpies did not want to be removed from their nest. After gently removing the babies, and lifting them into the light, I also removed the nest and dissolved it into the light. As I lifted them into the light, their forms dissolved. Free from this distortion, their forms turned into those of white doves.

I was then instructed by the guides to clean out the pus and other poisons that had accumulated in the wound. Then the guides instructed me how to recharge it with appropriate energy consciousness on the fourth level. I continued to clear the field up through the remaining levels and then finish the healing.

After the client rested, I told her what I had seen. Since she was a healer, it was okay to discuss these unusual things. In the weeks that followed the healing, she had much less craving for sugar and worked in her sessions on her substituting sugar for her need for love from her mother. The fourth-level-reality baby harpies represented this need as well as her frustration and anger about that need not being met in childhood. Remember, fourth-level-reality beings take the form of what they believe themselves to be, and are attracted to others through the laws of attraction, i.e., "like attracts like." Thus they were able to find a home in her pancreas.

As I was telling the client how the harpies had turned into white doves when they were cleared, Heyoan leaned over and said,

They were doves all the time!

Thus the harpies in my client's pancreas were created by her unconscious need and anger about her experience of not enough care from her mother. So we can say that she created them, or we can say that she attracted them. Either or both can be true. Please note that this is not to say whether or not her mother did enough for her. Rather it was the conclusion of her unconscious that was the important point in the case. It is not the therapist/healer's opinion that counts here. It is the recognition that the client believes it to be true, and has to deal with that fact and resolve it within herself with the support of the therapist. The healer also adds the power of healing and the reconstruction of the HEF to help resolve the issues. The result is a more powerful recovery. The client can learn how to take care of herself and drop her own self-judgments about her inability to do so, along with her underlying feelings of unworthiness or "badness."

Astral forms related to psychological issues are not just figments of the imagination. They are actual energy consciousness forms that block the field and help hold negative life patterns in place, as well as interfere with the creative processes with which we create in our lives.

Fantasy: One of the problems with regard to fourth-level-reality world phenomena is to distinguish between truthful helpful guides and fourth-level-reality beings that are not so developed but just want to pretend to be, or that just want to make contact with a human being. One such case was interesting in this way. A woman who was lacking a social life, and not well integrated within herself, attracted some fourth-level-reality beings that claimed to be her spiritual guides. She came to her therapy session very excited that she had finally contacted her guides! When I witnessed the beings during the session, they were of low development. They were dark, not well formed, and with negative intent to deceive. I became very concerned about her inability to have clear contact with reality. I sent the beings into the light, and explained the situation to her. We then proceeded with "normal" therapy sessions, devoid of psychic phenomena. This helped a great deal. She needed to reconstruct her normal life rather than delve into psychic phenomena. By my confronting her to stay in her physical life rather than go off into fantasy, she started reconstructing a normal life in the physical world.

Fourth-Level-Reality Attachments—Black Kali: One of the very last sessions of my fifteen-year healing practice in New York City, just before I switched into full-time teaching, was one in which I saw the Black Kali for the first time. I was working on a client who had multiple sclerosis. Toward the very end of the healing, I saw a huge Black Kali with fingernails clenching and pointed teeth biting into her field at the seventh level. At first, I tried to remove it. That wasn't so easy. I realized I was out of my league. I told her about it, and suggested that she go to someone familiar with Tibetan Buddhism, someone from the Far East who was more qualified than I. I do not know if she ever did. She moved to a different place, and I did not hear from her again.

Joint Sessions between Human Beings and Astral Beings: After I became used to dealing with fourth-level-reality beings, I began to give joint therapy/healing sessions between beings in the fourth-level reality and human beings in the physical world. They were pretty much like sessions between two people in the physical world. Here are a couple of examples of these

types of healings. Usually when a fourth-level-reality being is hanging around a physical person, the being wants something from the person. And usually it is about something the fourth-level-reality being wanted to finish while living in the physical but did not succeed. Sometimes it is just about making contact with a loved one who is still in the physical to let them know that the supposedly "dead" person, now in the fourth-level reality, is in fact not dead but living in the fourth-level reality. Sometimes it is about not being able to let go of a relationship in the physical after leaving it and moving into the fourth-level reality. The following is an interesting example of such a case.

While I was still living at the Pathwork Center (then called the Center for the Living Force), I went to the Netherlands to give intensive Core Energetics sessions to the Pathwork members who lived in Holland. One of the clients was in trouble. Shortly before I arrived, she had almost died twice within a couple of weeks. I shall call her Clara. Clara told me a most interesting story about her grandmother, who had passed away a few weeks before her episodes started. Clara had been raised by her grandmother and was very close to her. When her grandmother died, Clara was in a lot of pain and was missing her. Clara had successfully made contact with her departed grandmother. But now she had a problem. Her grandmother kept calling Clara to come to the other side. Two weeks before I arrived, Clara's grandmother had convinced her to come to the sill of the third-story window to jump out! Clara spent some time on the windowsill, then finally dragged herself back into her room. She was in agony. She missed her grandmother, but also didn't want to die. Then another episode happened the day before I arrived. While taking a hot bath, Clara was almost gassed to death. (I never found out how the gas got turned on, but it did.) Clara also said her grandmother was still calling her to the other side.

Luckily, Clara had scheduled a week's intensive with me. She had sessions every day. All of them were joint sessions with her deceased grandmother on the other side of the veil between the worlds. The sessions started with dialogue between the two people, via my HSP as well as Clara's, each saying things they needed to say to complete their relationship for this lifetime. Slowly, day after day of joint sessions, they came to completion. Finally, on the last day, the grandmother left. They both let go of each other, and the grandmother went up into the light beam that appeared in the corner of the room. After that, Clara had no more problems with her grandmother.

I have given many such sessions since then. They were usually not so drastic as Clara's situation. They were mostly brief contacts, where the supposedly dead person makes it very clear to the one in the physical world that they are okay and still alive, but in a different reality. (Many like it much better there than here in the physical.)

Fourth-Level-Reality Children: One of the most common types of long-term relationships between the fourth-level-reality humans and physical humans that go on for years is between children who die and their parents—apparently, mostly their mothers. These fourth-level-reality children remain members of the family, growing up in it like the other children. Most of the time the mothers are aware of it. They communicate with their fourth-level-reality children, but don't talk about it to other people. They do tell me about them.

Another similar phenomenon is the common case of physical children who have fourth-level-reality playmates. Many children have them. They are usually called imaginary playmates, but anyone with fourth-level-reality vision—like the physical children who play with them—can see these fourth-level-reality children. It is very common with children of healers.

Fourth-Level-Reality Connections to Physical Life: The most curious experience I ever had involving fourth-level-reality people and physical people happened one day when a new client from another country came in for a healing. By this time I was used to guides and other types of beings regularly coming into the sessions along with my clients. But this time was a little different. The woman came into the room and shut the door. A few minutes later, three fourth-level-reality men

formally dressed in black suits sort of stumbled into the room through the closed door, while they were looking seriously in all different directions. They looked very embarrassed, not quite knowing what to do there in the room with a healer. I thought it was strange, since most of the healing attendees I had seen before always came as part of the healing, either to help in some way (as they had been some type of spiritual leader or guru to the client), or as relatives who wanted to make contact. These guys were different. They were strong, powerful, and very serious. They kept checking out the large room I was working in. After a while I ignored them, as they didn't seem to be intent on making contact with the client, but remained very alert. When I finished the healing, they left with her. She didn't seem to know they were there. I didn't mention it.

A few years later, I was speaking with a therapist friend of mine from another country, whom I will call Sally. Sally asked me if the woman she sent to me ever came for a healing. I asked what her name was and it turned out to be the woman in the session with the three guys in black suits. I told Sally about the strange guys who had sort of pushed their way through the closed doors to come into the room, and who were very embarrassed. Sally laughed and said that the woman she sent was the wife of the head of a secret service agency of that country! We had a great laugh over that one! I think that was one of the most outrageous events of my healing career. Apparently the guys in the suits were some sort of bodyguards, or perhaps they just wanted to be! Who knows?

I would like to say that
you can take any of these experiences
that I have described, in any way you like!

— *Barbara Brennan*

Some may make some sense to you, others may not. For me they have been a great learning. They have *taken the braces off my brains* about my rigid ideas of what is and what is not reality. I wanted to share them with you to open up the view if you wish to; that is completely up to you. I have no judgments either way!

So-Called Extraterrestrials, Popularly Known as ETs

The subject of ETs is taboo, but I shall attempt to deal with it anyway. As a research physicist, having worked for NASA at Goddard Space Flight Center, I can't imagine a universe so limited that it would not create intelligent beings at least equal to us, and most likely more advanced than we are. Our solar system is very young, as is our average-sized galaxy. Yet we continue to think we are the best, most evolved species. Oh well, we are probably not the only ones. How sad for us to limit our vision of the future in such a way. The probability is that someday we will find very intelligent life out there somewhere. Or they will find us—maybe they already have!

First we imagined that we were the top species on a planet that was the center of the universe. Galileo really paid for this one—Earth wasn't even the center of the solar system! As our science gets more developed, we simply find bigger and better things all the time.

Can you imagine when we do find extraterrestrials that are more developed than us? How are we going to handle it psychologically? Yet the probability is that we will. After all, we exist on a small planet that revolves around a rather mundane G3-type sun that is neither special nor unique in any way in a universe full of them. Our galaxy isn't even an old galaxy—some galaxies are many light-years older than ours!

It is hard to find other planets like ours in other solar systems because we have not yet developed the tools to do so. But it does not mean that they aren't there. In addition to that, just because our bodies are adapted to our earth's environment, it does not mean that other life systems must be like ours. Indeed, the evidence so far is that life is able to adapt to all types of what we think of as hostile environments. Life creates ecosystems in which it then thrives. A great example of this is the life ecosystem found on the super-hot thermal vents deep in the ocean. Until we found them we did not believe that life could exist in such hot temperatures. But it does!

If the ETs that were so popular with the New Age communities exist or not, I do not know. I have never seen one, at least in the physical world. I have, on the other hand, seen ET-like beings in nonphysical worlds. I have been in their ships in the nonphysical world. My house in Montauk is even near the radar tower where the large ET entity is supposed to have appeared as a result of the Philadelphia Experiment. I have seen shows on Area 51, a U.S. Air Force facility in Nevada rumored to be the place where the U.S. government hides alien technology or visitors. I remember when ETs were all the rage with some of my more "far-out" (as a 1960s person would say) students. *But alas, I have never seen one.* Perhaps I would like to meet a real—meaning physical—ET, provided he/she/it were friendly, tolerably looking, noninvasive, and not interested in having me for lunch; but so far, not one iota of luck in that department!

Speaking of ETs, I once gave a workshop at the Omega Institute at the same time a well-known teacher was giving one of his workshops. He happened to be sharing the other half of a duplex cottage I was assigned to for sleeping. That weekend that cottage was a real buzz, with him on one side and me on the other. A couple of times I thought that the cottage might take off. One of the interesting things I observed about Whitley was that he walked just like Jeff Bridges in the movie *Starman*: on his toes, head lifted up and forward, whole body leaning forward as if lifted and tipped forward by a string that was carrying him just off the ground. I was with a group of my BBSH teachers who were assisting me. When Whitley would walk by at lunch, we would all use our X-ray vision to observe a very interesting object that was apparently, from what we could tell, implanted in his head. It carried a high frequency that was driving his brain at higher frequencies than that of normal humans. Not only that, it was also an observation device that was connected to a "ship" in a different fourth-level reality. Through it, "they" (the fourth-level beings) could observe us as well as our activities. We wanted to ask him how it felt, but were too embarrassed and shy to ask. I never got to see who "they" in the ship were.

Close Encounters with Elisabeth Kübler-Ross

This brings me to some interesting experiences with Elisabeth Kübler-Ross, a wonderful woman who gave her life to heal others, who never held back, who was a great leader of our time, and who opened many a door for many of us.

My story starts with my idea of asking her to endorse my book *Hands of Light*. First I sent it to her and asked her if she would endorse it, and then I called her.

She said, "This is a very unusual book! Can you come visit me in my home in West Virginia?"

I drove there as soon as I could. The long hours of driving were highlighted by one major thing that lasted the entire trip. It seemed that no matter which way the road turned, the cluster of stars known as the Pleiades was in full view in the bright and mysterious night sky. I have always been attracted to the Pleiades and feel as if I have a personal connection to them. Perhaps I even came to Earth from there eons ago. I often feel homesick for the Pleiades. I wake up in the middle of the night and go out on my deck to gaze at them, with an inexplicable yearning to return home to their beauty and advanced society. I realize that the Pleiades are not even a group of stars that are close to each other, but just look that way from Earth. However, that does not stop my yearning.

When I arrived, Elisabeth came out on the porch to greet me. I pointed out the Pleiades in the beautiful night sky, to which she said, "That's where we came from! Now come on in and have something to eat."

Upon entering her kitchen I came upon an amazing sight of every type of fresh, home-baked dessert I had ever seen. Every countertop and table was full. There were pies, cakes, turnovers with fruit inside, cookies, breads with fruit, and other pastries. It was like walking into a European bakery.

"Here, eat up. You must be hungry after such a long drive," she said, while piling as many goodies on a plate as she could. I was too shy to say that I didn't eat sweets. So I enjoyed stuffing myself.

"This is an amazing book. Now tell me everything you know!"

"What do you want to know? Where should I start?"

"Teach me to see auras!" she said, with a cup of coffee in one hand and a cigarette in the other.

I proceeded to try, as she continued with more coffee and cigarettes. She clearly was not going to change her state of consciousness, a prerequisite for HSP. I was trying to think of a polite way to bring the conversation around to her endorsing my book. It would mean a lot, since I was an unknown author at the time. I continued,

"To see auras, you have to calm your consciousness down at the same time you increase the energy flowing through your body. Take a deep breath and center."

"Why is it that I can't see auras but I have seen ETs?" she asked, ignoring my instructions.

"I've never seen an ET," I said, trying to avoid the fruitless HSP lesson. "Or I should say, I've only seen them in the fourth-level reality. The tall ones and the shorter blue ones. What did the ones you've seen look like?"

"I saw those too, but they were real (meaning physical). They levitated a chair right behind me. They took me up into the ship."

"Wow! What did it look like in there? I was up in a fourth-level-reality ship," I said, keeping up with the conversation as best I could.

"It was like an operating room, with tables around the outside of the circle. Everything was light gray or white. They were working on people," she said.

"Yeah, the tables were there," I replied. "Everything was a light gray color. The tables had a lighter cover, almost white. There was a big hole in the center of the ship, like a tall atrium. It seemed to be where they levitate things up into the ship. I didn't see any staircases at all. I want to know how they do that—levitate, I mean. It has something to do with reverse spinning magnetic fields. I think that is how I got up in there, but I don't remember being levitated. The whole thing is like a dream, yet it seems real. Do you know what I mean?"

"It wasn't a dream," she said matter-of-factly.

"It seemed like a hospital or a lab, but no one was there," I continued.

As we continued to talk, things began to get strange. We seemed to melt into and out of the "other world."

Then Elisabeth asked, "Do you channel?"

"Yes."

"Good. Channel for me!"

"Okay," I said, and proceeded to expand my state of consciousness. I expected just a few questions to be asked, but it went on and on. I vaguely remember seeing fourth-level-reality ETs coming into the room at one point at the beginning of the channeling. We both saw them. Then the subjects quickly switched and most of the rest of the night I was channeling about all sorts of things, such as the origin and cure for AIDS, in which I saw an insect in Africa that looked a little like a praying mantis, a book on insects in the Harvard library that listed this particular insect, and even supposedly a cure for AIDS that filtered the patient's blood through some sort of charcoal-like substance that cleaned it, then put it back into the body. The channeling and questions went on and on through the night. When it was finally over, nine hours had passed.

As I took my leave in the approaching dawn, I wondered if it was real. Was the channeling good? Or was it just the mysterious, beautiful night and the stunning experience of meeting someone so famous? Yet it seemed as if we had known each other for decades. But that is probably how Elisabeth always was. I really didn't believe any of the channeling or the ET stuff. But, as always, I said to myself, "Wait and see if anything develops from this. For now, Barbara, enjoy the ecstasy."

We had recorded all of the channeling. I left the tapes with Elisabeth. I don't know what happened to them. I don't remember what else was on them. Nor did I ever try to find the insect in the Harvard library in the entomology encyclopedia. I did leave with one certainty. I had found a life-long friend and colleague whom I truly loved and respected, someone who was not afraid to speak her truth, no matter what anyone thought or the possible consequences of discussing such inappropriate (for an M.D.) things as ETs.

I went to see her another time. I took a student who wanted to meet her. The way there was filled with great expectation. The meeting was similar to the first, but without the ETs and channeling. Elisabeth held back her energy. She didn't seem to care for the person I took to meet her. She told me the next time I saw her that she didn't trust that woman because she did not do her personal work on herself. Yet it was still a wonderful meeting. This time, to top off the visit, for the entire three-hour drive back to the Pathwork Center in Virginia, a rainbow arched across the road just in front of my car. It was glorious!

I saw Elisabeth again just a few times. Each time I would run into her at a conference, she would act very friendly and ask me if I was doing my work in the world. This usually seemed to question if I was sticking my neck out far enough and really being straight about who I am, what I see, and what I am *really* doing. I must admit, I have been afraid to write this book for a long time. But the truth is always best, and I am having fun writing it!

Chapter 10 Self-Review: Exploring Your Experiences with Other Astral Phenomena

1. Have you had any experiences with attachments? List them.

2. How have you dealt with them?

3. What is your belief system about ETs?

4. Have you had any experiences with ETs? List them.

5. How have you reconciled ETs in your reality system?

6. How have you learned to understand astral phenomena better from this chapter?

Figure 1-1

The Black Velvet Void

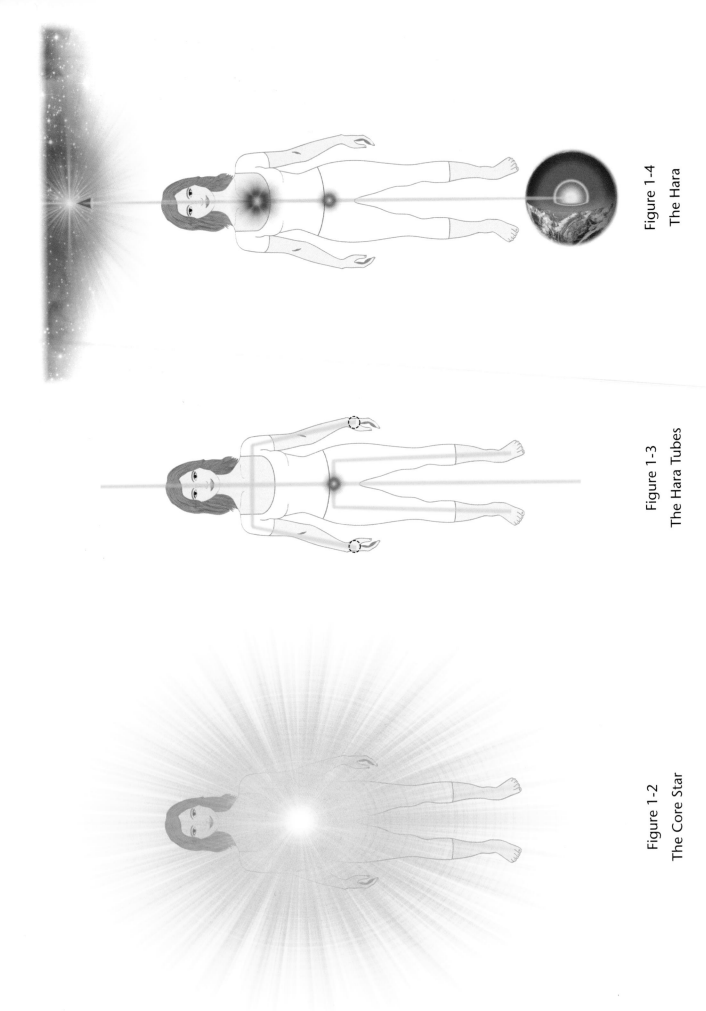

Figure 1-4
The Hara

Figure 1-3
The Hara Tubes

Figure 1-2
The Core Star

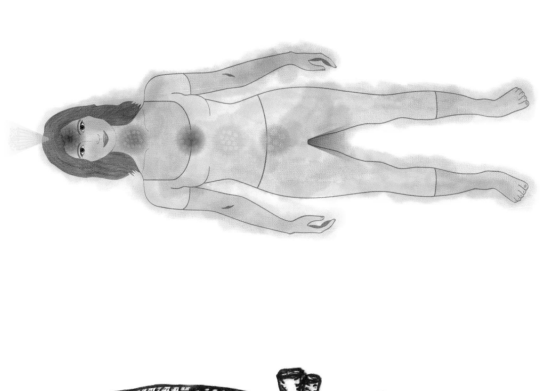

Figure 1-7
Emotional Body Level 2

Figure 1-6
The Kidney as Seen on Level 1

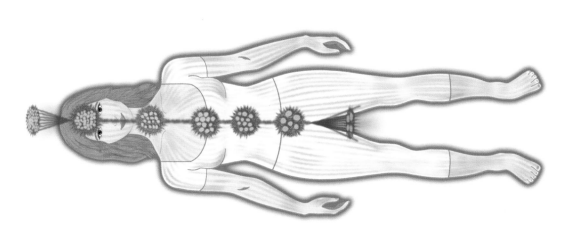

Figure 1-5
Etheric Body Level 1

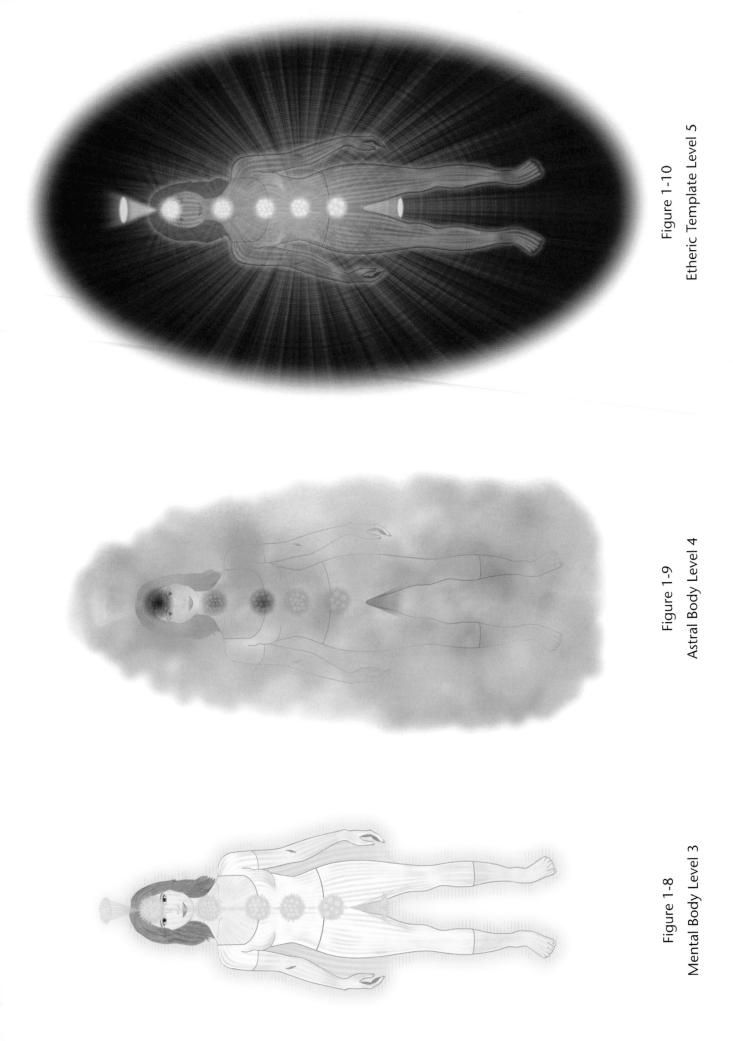

Figure 1-8
Mental Body Level 3

Figure 1-9
Astral Body Level 4

Figure 1-10
Etheric Template Level 5

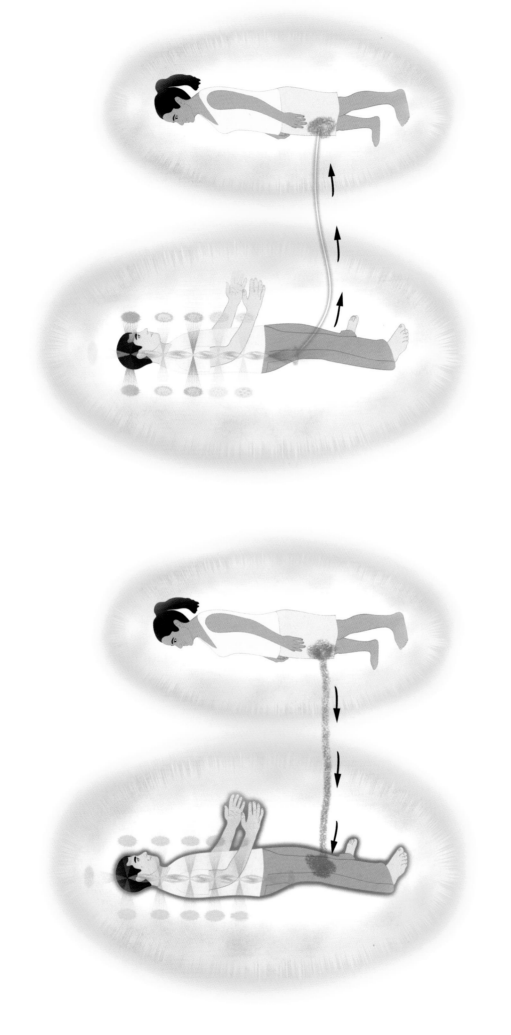

Figure 6-3a

Healer Pulling in Information (Pain) about Client into His Body

Incorrect

Figure 6-3b

Healer Brings HSP into Pseudopod to Connect to Client

Correct

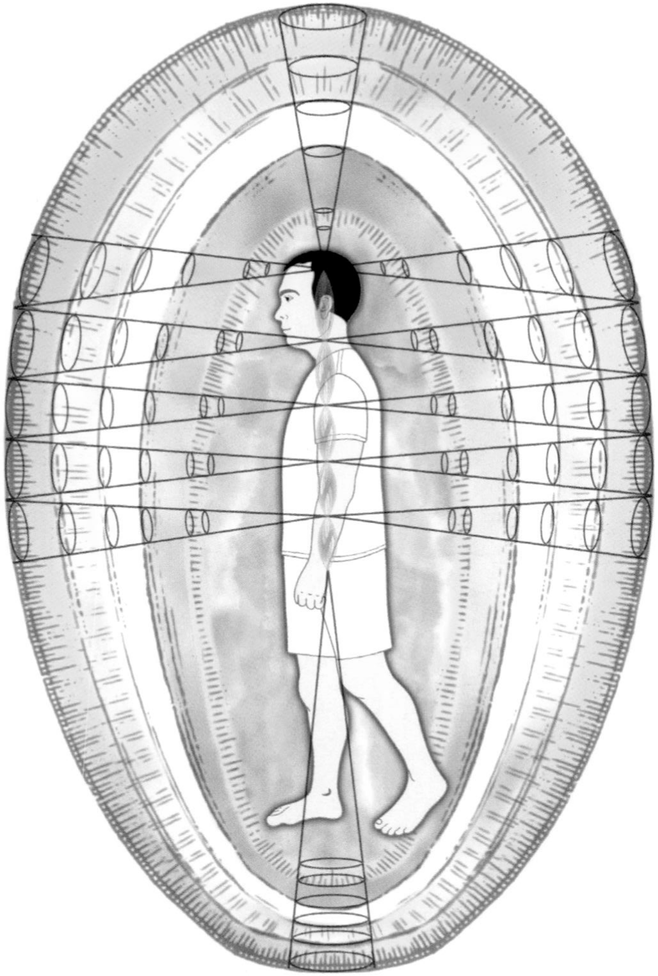

Figure 6-4

Diagram of a Coherent Field

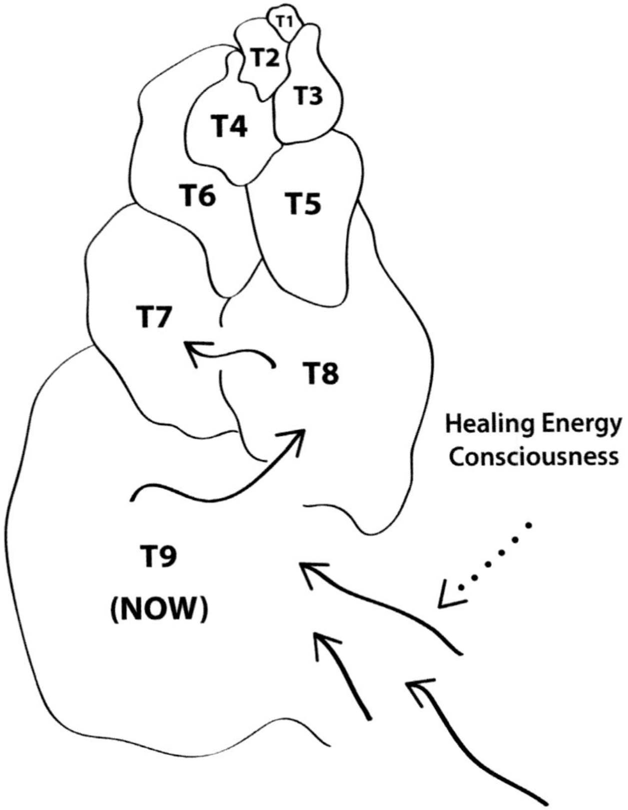
T1
T2
T3
T4
T5
T6
T7
T8
T9
(NOW)
Healing Energy
Consciousness

Figure 14-1

Anatomy of a Time Capsule

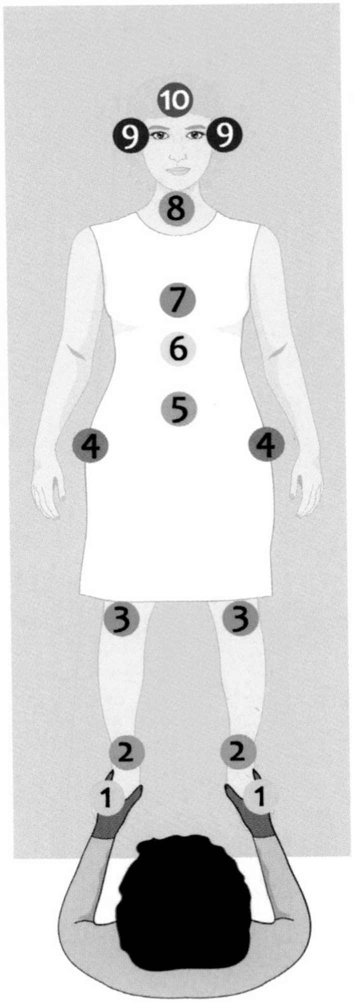
10
9
9
8
7
6
5
4
4
3
3
2
2
1
1

Figure 14-2

Hand Positions for Chelation

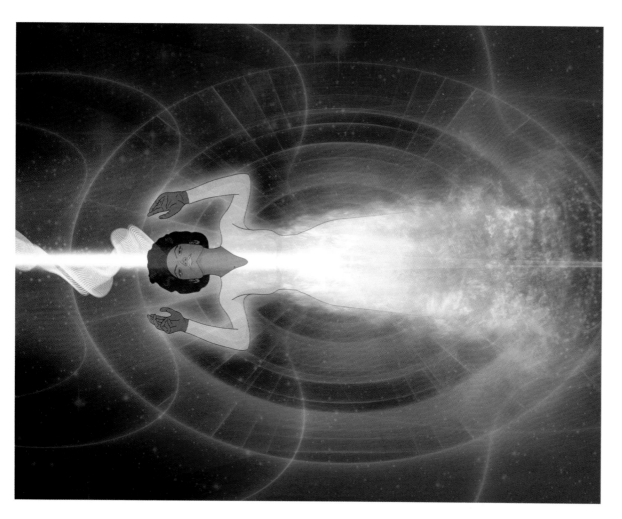

Figure 15-2
The HEF Circulation at Death

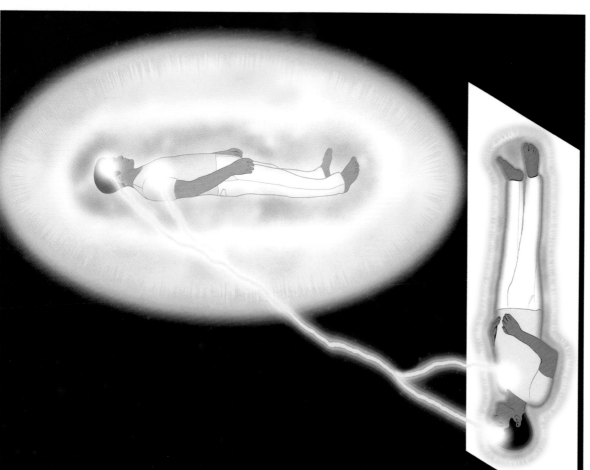

Figure 15-1
Astral Traveling

*The Silver Cord Keeps the Connection between
the Physical Body and the Astral Travel Body*

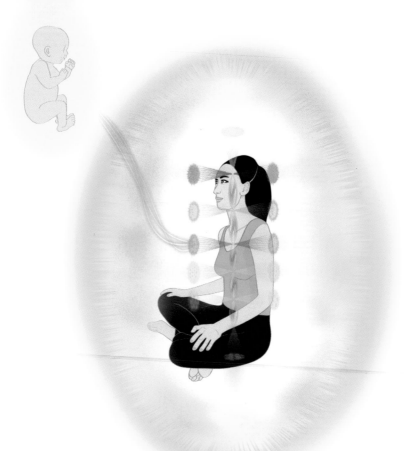

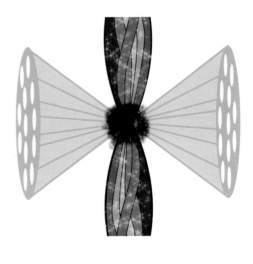

Figure 17-1

Cord Connections between the Person
Wishing to Be Born and the Mother

Figure 17-2

A Dense, Dark Block Deep inside the
Heart Chakra Prevents Conception

Figure 17-3

Relational Cord Connections between Child and Parents

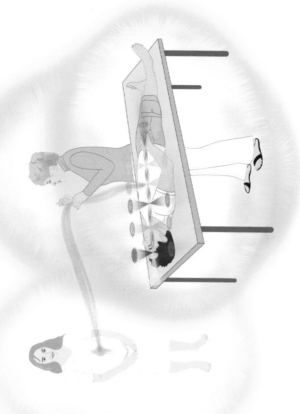

Figure 17-4b

Relief in the Fields of Donald and His Mother after Healing

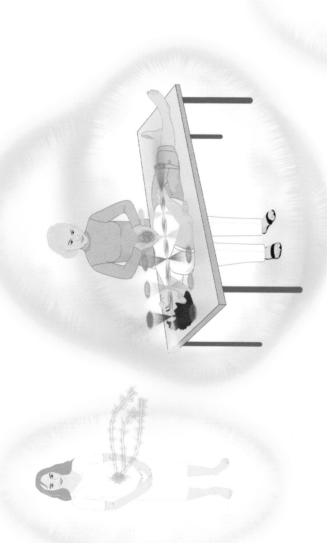

Figure 17-4a

Cord Distortions between Donald and His Mother

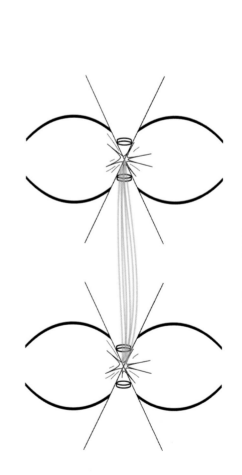

Figure 17-5

The Healthy Anatomy of Cords and Seals

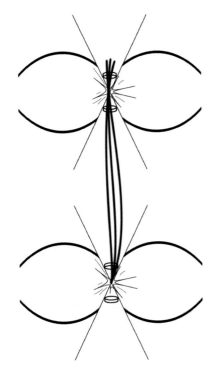

Daughter

Father

Figure 18-1b
TARS Pushing through the Chakra Seals

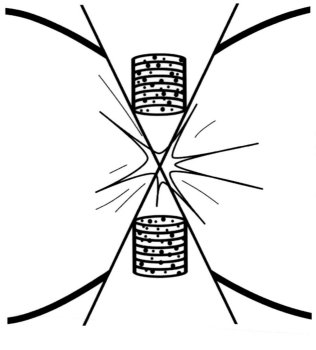

Figure 18-1c
Blind Spots on Seals

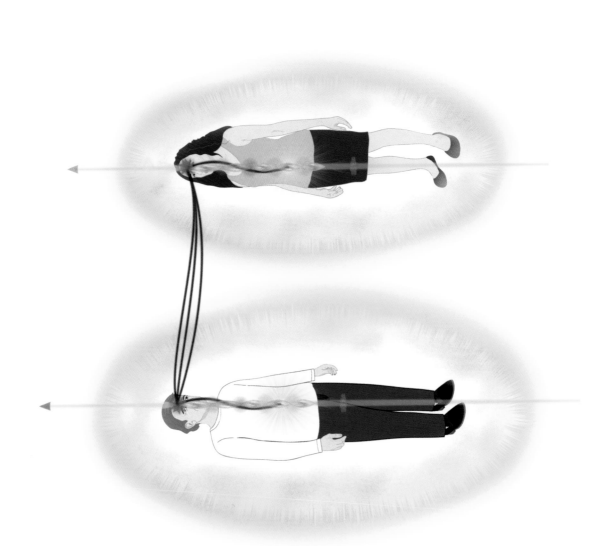

Figure 18-1a
Damage in Sixth Chakra from TARS Blocks a Clear Perception of Reality

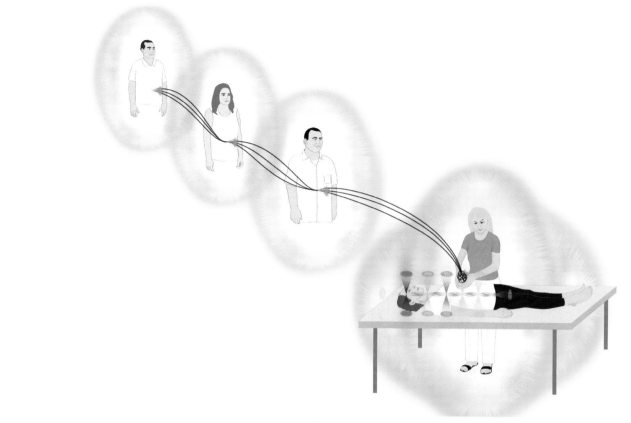

Figure 18-2a

Steps in Healing TARs

Beginning of Healing to Remove TARs

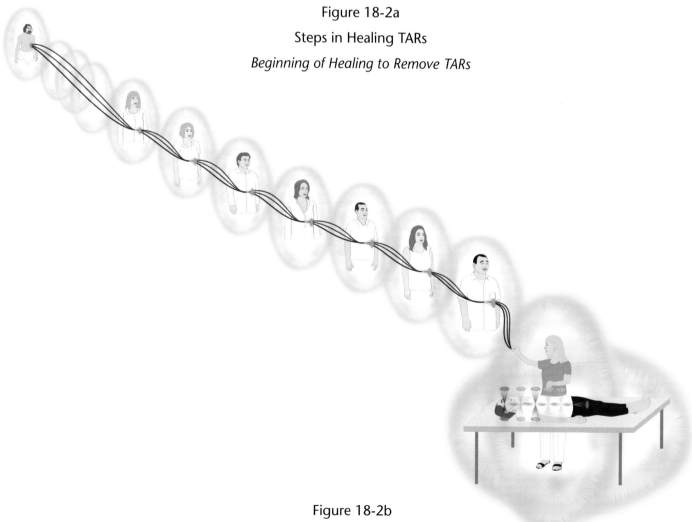

Figure 18-2b

Steps in Healing TARs

Unwinding the TARs

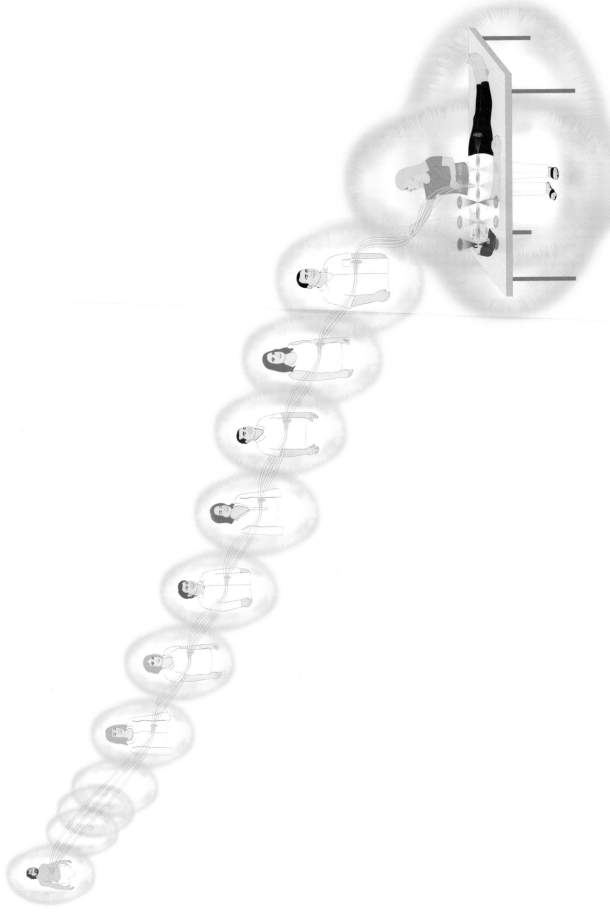

Figure 18-2c
Steps in Healing TARs
All Generations Receive Healing

Chapter 11

EXTREME DUALITY IN THE LOWER ASTRAL WORLDS

That which has been called "hell" or the "nether worlds"
will be cleared and clarified.
For what is hell other than profound forgetting?

The souls that are focused into hell
are in great pain.
They are there simply because
they do not experience their light,
and do not hold self-love.
They do not experience their purity.
They do not experience their life.
This is the great pain of hell or the so-called Hells.

If a being has no self-love,
that being is lost in darkness,
that being is very difficult to reach with love,
because love and light are frightening to such a being.
Therefore, when light comes to that being,
it reacts in defense and attacks.

Consider the possibility
that those beings called "devils"
are in profound forgetting.
Yes, they do mischief and harm,
but they are doing it out of forgetting and separation,
so much so that when the light appears
their defense is very harsh.

You all understand what defense is now.
When you go into defense,
you become frightened and angry.
You might throw energy out
or hold it in for a later explosion.
You might verbally attack someone
or tell them negative things.
That is the same type of defense on a lesser scale.

— HEYOAN

What I am trying to do in this book is to give a more understandable framework of certain worlds that are considered neither to be real nor to exist by the intellectual community. In our culture, via unspoken law, they are considered to be dangerous and dealt with only through "accepted" religious context, or through psychiatric treatment that labels them as hallucinations due to psychosis, imagined and projected onto the world outside the self—i.e., *not real*.

Having experienced these worlds myself, I personally do not agree with many of the religious interpretations of experiences associated with these worlds and the use of the word *evil*. This makes these experiences bad, even dangerous (especially experiences of the lower part of the fourth-level reality). It also labels the person having them as being either possessed by the devil or psychotic. Neither of these labels is very helpful. These attitudes and the actions that are attached to them lead to more pain, both for the individual experiencing the lower fourth-level-reality world and for those who dwell in or are caught in it. After experiencing these worlds, it is easy to see how the words *heaven*, *hell*, and *purgatory* originated. Unfortunately, religious interpretation results in abandonment of the beings caught in the lower fourth-level-reality worlds, while psychiatry discards such experiences as fantasy and tries to eliminate these "hallucinations" with drugs. Neither approach is very kind.

Having worked as a healer with some people who were labeled as "psychotic," I agree that many do need the medications for their own safety. It takes a long time and a lot of healing work, in conjunction with a psychiatrist who is willing to slowly reduce medications, to carefully walk with such a client back into balanced harmony within himself. Never, ever try it without appropriate medical direction. In many such cases, there are not only basic physiological causes in psychiatric issues, but also extreme energy field distortions.

In this chapter, I shall attempt to describe the nature of the more extreme dualistic energy consciousness levels of the HEF fourth-level realities, or lower astral worlds. These are the belief system territories of very negative energy consciousness, extreme darkness, extreme psychological and physical pain, torture, confusion, self-hatred, self-flagellation, and lost-ness. These are the lower astral world belief system territories that religions call *hell* and *purgatory*. Various religions teach that hell is where God sends beings to suffer their punishment for their so-called sins. Other words for such places from around the world are *Annwn, Diyu, Duat, Gehenna, Hades, Jahannam, Naraka, Sheol, Tartarus,* and *Yomi.*

They are worlds of split consciousness. **The beings that inhabit them have profound forgetting of their true selves.** They have extremely negative self-judgments and deep personal pain. Heyoan says,

*In the spiritual worlds of god
there are no negative judgments!*

*There is only
loving kindness and acceptance
of the shortcomings of human beings
who are on a difficult spiral healing
path into their core,
where the so-called light and so-called dark
come together in the transparency of
truth, wisdom, and integrity!*

Many religions teach about the fight between the forces of light and the forces of darkness. Heyoan says that this is simply dualistic thinking, and that our habit of dualistic thinking is what gets us in trouble. Dualistic thinking leads to the necessity of choosing sides. Heyoan says,

*Choosing sides
means supporting duality.*

*Choosing sides
enhances the split and makes it worse.*

New Way to Enter the Darkness of the Lower Astral Reality of the HEF

We need to learn to think holistically, without the tension of opposites, as I have described in previous chapters. The beings that have created and live in the lower astral territories experience profound forgetting of their wholeness. They are disconnected from their innate goodness that exists deep within the ground of their being and are therefore in deep pain.

Recognizing When Negative Intent Is an Effort to Make Contact

So as we take a little trek into the lower astral reality to meet the so-called entities of darkness, keep this in mind to help you maintain your personal connection to your wholeness—your deep inner goodness, the foundation of your being—because upon entering the darker territories, you will be surrounded and influenced by the dualistic negative energy consciousness that is there. That world of negative energy consciousness, and the beings that are caught there in negative pleasure, will also have negative intent (i.e., dualistic intent) to draw you into your dualistic (negative) intent. They will be attracted to that within you that is of the same type of duality as theirs.

They will want to draw it out of you as a way of making contact. This means they will, on purpose, try to bring out the dualistic (i.e., the split) in you and enhance it. They will want to draw you fully into their dualistic world. They will attempt to increase your dualistic split and bring out the negative side of it, which you have been trained—as all human beings have—to keep hidden. You can look at this as extreme negative intent, or you can recognize it in a different way:

It could be the only way they know how to make contact!

I am sure that you have done this yourself, only most likely not on such a scale. Yet the process is a normal one when meeting someone new. When you want to make contact with someone the first time you meet, you look for common ground and common interests, right? So actually another way to look at the astral beings' *seemingly devious maneuvers* is that they simply want contact. Wouldn't you if you were caught in such a negative condition?

Another way to consider this phenomenon *is that beings caught in the lower astral reality enjoy negative pleasure,* so they will try to get you into it by finding, enhancing, and drawing out the parts of you that enjoy the same type of negative pleasures as they do!

This can be seen as just another way of making contact!
Or
perhaps this is the only way they know how to make contact!

Thus by understanding the psychology of the lower astral beings you meet, you will have a good tool to deal with your own fear and negative impulses! After all, you incarnated with them in order to bring them into wholeness!

Thus in your healing career, when entering the lower astral reality, rather than split into the "easy way out" of calling it *hell* and the beings that live there *evil,* you will be challenged to face your own negative pleasure and negative intent in order to heal it. This is a must to qualify to do astral healing work—just as I had to do many years ago when, in the middle of the night, lower astral beings, or so-called dark entities, came to frighten me. Instead, I held on to my faith in the divine worlds, which I had directly experienced, and forced the dark entities to leave with my strong, bright energy consciousness. I, of course, prayed for help. Help came first in the form of the Edgar Cayce meditation group and then the Pathwork Center in the Catskill Mountains of New York State, where I lived and worked for years on my issues. I am forever grateful for that help.

Here is one of my first stories of encountering a so-called evil entity.

The Black "Evil" Entity

My Edgar Cayce study group meditated together once a week. I met some very nice people. Some of them were Quakers. We would study the Cayce readings, discuss them, and then meditate. Cayce's work is marvelous. It can give a clear idea of the spiritual worlds and how to interface with them in a positive and useful way to improve life in the physical. One of my friends in the Cayce group, Iris, studied Tibetan Buddhism. Iris had meditated for many years. I went to her house for a few private meditations with her. In these silent meditations, we both saw the same symbolic visions. I, with my scientific background, would always ask her what she saw, rather than telling her my vision first. This type of confirmation was very helpful and encouraged me to continue in my quest for clarity in HSP and understanding the spiritual worlds.

A few years later, while I was in my last year of bioenergetic training, something happened that taught me that there are many ways to interpret psychic experience, and that it is very important to know how to do so in a positive, useful way. It became clear that a very important prerequisite to learn clear HSP is a strong, grounded knowledge—knowledge of one's psychological processes, knowledge of how one's own energy consciousness system works, and knowledge of how to regulate it. All of this, in fact, requires a lot of training and personal process.

A client of a therapist in the clinic in which I was training, whom I shall call Bud, killed himself by hanging. I do not know why or the circumstances of his life. Bud was cremated and his ashes brought into our group meditation room for a ceremony. I didn't know Bud, but had seen him around when he came for his sessions. I didn't know his therapist either. During Bud's ceremony, my curiosity about death came up really strong. I wanted to know where he was. After the meditation, I put my hands on the container of ashes and projected my consciousness into them.

"Bud, where are you?"

I could feel the sharp, agitated, incoherent, burning energy in the ashes—a kind of consciousness trying to get released. That was all I sensed.

The next day I was home alone when I heard a knock on the door. It was my librarian neighbor and the lady who lived downstairs. They told me that they thought my house was on fire and that I should come outside. I told them I thought it was

the dirty windows! They invited me over for tea. I accepted. As soon as we sat down with the tea, one asked me, "Do you ever go out the door in your forehead?"

"No, but I would like to try!"

So all night long we tried to go out the doors in our foreheads. One of the women couldn't do it. I saw the librarian become a gold point of light and go out the door. I became a gold point of light too. I got to the door and stopped. I stood at the edge of an abyss—an infinite dark nothingness that seemed to be full of undifferentiated life. I was too scared to jump into the abyss, so I stood there and called for Bud. After a couple of hours, the evening became very strange. One woman decided to try automatic handwriting. She was drawing with automatic handwriting when she suddenly stopped, pointed to something she drew on the paper, and exclaimed, *"This is a very evil entity!"*

The dog started barking in the kitchen and the three of us became terrified. We tried to calm down. I stayed a little longer, then I went home. It was then I started seeing the big black entity following me. I didn't know what to do. Luckily I was home alone, so nobody else got involved. I walked around the house trembling and carrying a Bible. I tried putting crosses of water on the walls. It didn't help. I spent the next several nights in terror.

A few days later, I got an appointment with a healer from Europe. He tried to remove the entity, but couldn't. Finally he said, "This evil entity has been chasing you for many lifetimes! You have to gather your power and fight it. You must try to win. But don't worry, if you lose, you will only lose your body!" Well, that certainly didn't make me feel better! It did nothing for my terror except to make it worse.

Finally it was time for my regular session with my bioenergetic therapist. He didn't seem very concerned or worried. He couldn't see the black entity, but he could see my terror. He helped me work on my terror of the unknown, but the black entity would not go away.

He said, "You will need to do more work on this. I can give you more sessions. It's lucky you are not going to a psychiatrist because he would give you drugs and lock you up."

I scheduled more personal bioenergetic sessions in which I was able to deal with my fear and calm myself down to a certain extent. The entity was still there, and I was afraid of it. Since no one I knew could see the entity, I also kept questioning my sanity.

Then I remembered Iris from the Cayce group, so I called her. I didn't tell her about the situation. I simply asked, "Can I come meditate with you again?"

"Okay, come at three P.M."

When I arrived, Iris would not let me go into her house as we usually did. Instead, she took me to the garden. We sat under an apple tree and meditated there in silence. We both went into meditation and came out at the same time without saying a word, just as we had done before.

Iris said, "You are being invaded by a very dark entity. Your aura is black from the chest down. All you have to do is to push him out of your body with white light, overcome your fear, and send him unconditional love to release him into the light. I will help. This 'dark entity' confronted me before you arrived, but I wouldn't let him invade me."

It was the *overcome your fear* part that did not seem so easy. Now, once again, I was more terrified. I calmed myself as much as possible and started to meditate in silence with Iris.

I started pushing "the entity" out of my body with white light that I drew down from my crown chakra and held at his boundary with love. I worked to overcome my fear and feel unconditional love. It was really hard. I concentrated on the light and love and kept pushing him down out of my body with white light. I could see (with my eyes closed) Iris also sending him light and love. He slipped out of my body and walked around behind me and over toward Iris. Then the funniest thought crossed my mind:

If you think you're bad off, think of him. He doesn't even have a body!

I chuckled inside and felt unconditional love for this poor creature who was lost without his physical body. As I filled him with love, he went from dark dirty gray-brown-black color to gray to lighter gray, and eventually he became white light. I saw him go around to Iris, where he became very light. Then, as Iris and I released him with unconditional love, his HEF slowly turned into white light and he was released. When Iris and I came out of our silent meditation, she described exactly what I had seen.

Iris said, "I sent him light and love, but he wouldn't move until you sent the light as well. Then when you finally overcame your fear, you pushed him out of your body with unconditional love. He walked behind you and then came over to me. His colors became lighter. When he came behind me, I threw him up into the light in sparkles. He was released into the light."

I went home in peace. I never saw him again.

A More Useful Interpretation of the Experience with "The Evil Entity": As time passed, I began to see that the experience with Bud was connected to the experience with the so-called dark entity. This put the experience into a much better perspective to deal with it. After some time of working on it in my sessions, and dealing with my fear, it became obvious to me that Bud *was* the dark entity. Since that experience, I have seen several people who have committed suicide who become very dark afterward, when they realize what they have done. Essentially, killing yourself doesn't help. When you leave your body, you find that you are much the same as before, with all the same issues and problems, but no longer have a physical body to stabilize your emotions, fears, and self-judgments. In fact, now you have more self-judgments and usually more fear, and also usually no ability to regulate your experience or your perceptions.

In such a situation as Bud's, once in the astral world one is likely to get lost. The European healer, having been brought into healing through old European tradition, and Iris, having trained in the Tibetan tradition, both called Bud a dark entity because his HEF was so dark. Neither had the information I have since put together from the perspective of a bioenergetic therapist/physicist to reinterpret this observed phenomenon from a more Western-educated perspective. Bud's HEF was dark because he was in such self-despair and guilt for having committed suicide. He was already deeply suffering before he committed suicide. I am not aware of the cause of his state since I was not his therapist, nor did I read it with HSP at the time. Afterward, as with most people who commit suicide, he felt very guilty about it, since after the suicide the problem not only does not leave, but may get much worse. Once he left his body, he no longer had its protection to hold back or regulate the degree of negative feelings about himself and his despair at what he had done.

I remembered that I had first projected myself into Bud's ashes, and then later stood at the abyss between the worlds and called for him. I realized that, looking at it from a new perspective, Bud had come to me for help because I had called for him, and I could see and make contact with him, such as it was. Others, except for the European healer and Iris, could not. Now I realize that he had desperately clung to my legs in an effort not to get lost in the astral. That is common when people commit suicide. There is so much grief and guilt afterward that they sink into an even deeper depression than before. They also tend to get lost, as they are not familiar with how to get around in the astral world.

There are two ways to look at this: it can be looked at from a split dualistic perspective of this black evil entity trying to kill me, or we can see that it was Bud who had hung himself and had gone into a real deep darkness. And who had called him? Me!

As Heyoan said,

Darkness looking through darkness
sees darkness.

But if you are in the light,
light looking through darkness,
you will see what it is.

So I looked and then I saw what that experience was. Bud was down on his knees grabbing on to me to make contact because he was lost. We helped him get released into the light.

The key to this story is: when in fear, you are going to see monsters. Most of the teachings in the world reflect this good versus bad dualism. There are black monsters and there are great wonderful angels. Most of the teachings are like that, rather than "here is a person who sank so low and had such trouble in his life." He felt so bad about himself that he killed himself; I called him and he came for help. It is very different.

This experience had a profound impact on how I interpreted the psychic phenomena of the astral. Much of the teachings in the world are very negative, such as labeling "lower astral beings" as bad or evil and sending them to even lower places, like hell. Frankly, that's a real drag. These people/beings need help. The last thing they need is more negative energy projected or thrown at them. These beings that live in such darkness have such profound forgetting of their true divine nature. They need help like we all do with our own areas of dark psyche. As Carl Jung said, "We do not become enlightened by imagining figures of light, but by making the darkness conscious."

Profound forgetting is a very deep split in the psyche. A split is a division of reality into good and bad. In a deep split, bad is really bad (i.e., evil), and good is angelic. Unfortunately, an individual with such a deep split tends to identify with the negative side of the split most of the time. When the personality switches to the positive side of the split, it is usually an exaggerated, unrealistic positive that does not last long and is not grounded in physical and spiritual reality. The most common expression of this type of split is expressed in an individual with bipolar syndrome. There is, of course, always a physiological aspect of any such split as well as one that shows in the human energy field: the more profound the forgetting, the darker, denser, and more negative the energy. Another way to put it is that a being with a deep split has a very low opinion of itself.

This great lesson is essential for all those
who do astral healing work.
It is so easy to look into dark
astral worlds and see evil.
That is not what the beings there need!

*They are already struggling with
strong negative self-images.
They do not need others projecting fears onto them.
While they may try to frighten you,
they do so because they are frightened of you!
They need lighthearted, loving acceptance
and recognition of who they are!
Beings on the path to enlightenment!*

— *Barbara Brennan*

Step by step, my life began to change into something more wonderful than I had ever dreamed of. After a time of nurturing and study, I was ready to face "hell" again, but in a different way. I was ready to enter into the familiar darkness and despair—but this time, as a healer. I was ready to give healing to those poor beings caught in the darkness and pain in the lower astral. Here is my story.

I Travel to "Hell" for the First Time as a Healer

As I once described in *Hands of Light*, the first time I went to hell I was very surprised, because it was during a healing I was giving in my office in New York City. I was just coming to the end of the healing. I held my hands held over the client's sixth chakra, and sent love and peace to the client to bring him to a higher state of consciousness. The forty-year-old client beneath my hands had come to me because his body had not completed developing through puberty into manhood. I had already given him several healings to enhance the development of his endocrine system, from which he felt somewhat better.

Suddenly I fell into hell! Down I plummeted from the ecstasy of the sixth level of the field into the darkness of the lowest aspect of the fourth level. I was shocked. I couldn't figure out how it happened. I started to judge myself for having done something terrible. I searched through my recent past, but could find nothing. After struggling with my self-doubts for some time, I started looking around me. It was so dark that I couldn't see anything! Finally I remembered several ways

that I had learned to get out of hell some time before, so I began to try them. The first was to look for the light and to go in the direction of the light. There was no light anywhere. There was no "lighter up" nor "darker down"; there wasn't any gradation of the blackness. I didn't know which direction to go, since looking for the light didn't work. I could hear nasty sounds, but I could not see anything at all. It was pitch-black. Then I started praying for help. That didn't seem to help either. So, focusing on my Christian background, and combining it with Hindu chanting rhythm, I started chanting internally (without sound), because I didn't want to disturb the client who was resting quietly.

"Jesus Christ, Jesus Christ!"

From what I could tell, this did not work either, but I kept it up. Then, to my surprise and dismay, I heard several voices in the darkness ask,

"Who is that?"

Now, that really made me scared. According to my upbringing, Christ went down into hell, made contact with everyone, and brought out whoever wanted to come. Everyone there was supposed to know him. BUT THEY DIDN'T!

"Why don't they know Christ?" I exclaimed to myself.

"Shhhh! Quiet, Barbara. Cool it!" I calmed myself, and chanted again.

"Jesus Christ, Jesus Christ!" I continued chanting, over and over.

After some time, I noticed it was getting lighter above my head, and I appeared to be moving up into the light. Soon I found myself in a lighted courtyard of what appeared to be a monastery. Some monks wearing brown robes came to me. They reached for my right hand and said,

"Here, we'll take this."

I looked down to see a piece of my client's soul in my right hand. Then, pointing in another direction, they said,

"You go for counseling."

I turned and floated to the left. I found myself in front of and between the two front legs of the sphinx. A secret door in its chest opened, and then I was in the chamber inside. (All this was going on psychically while, in the physical world, I was still holding my hands over the client's forehead and doing the sixth-level uplift.) Once inside the chamber, I saw Heyoan, who was sitting on a golden throne. I kneeled down in front of him. He gave me an initiation of brilliant golden light. Then he said,

Here is the secret
I told you I would reveal to you
when you were ready.

You and I are one.
I am your oversoul.
We have the same core star.

You, Barbara,
are the incarnation of me in this lifetime.

I did not share this experience with others for years, as it was so deeply personal, and, I thought, possibly egotistical. Now I realize that is true for all people. We all have lifetime guides who are our oversouls. Other guides come to us for specific lengths of time to teach us specific things, such as healing techniques. After we have learned what they have come to teach, they leave. Thus:

The guide who is with you your entire life
is your oversoul.
That guide shares
the same core star as you have!

With regard to that client, it was a turning point for him also. He was reunited with a portion of his soul that was somehow separated from him years, perhaps even lifetimes, earlier. I do not know how he was separated from it. It took a long time and many healings, but the client did, in fact, get much better. His endocrine system woke up and he developed his masculinity.

The Task of This New Millennium

In this new millennium, the duality that humankind has held for many thousands of years is coming out into the open to be healed and made whole. The extremes of so-called light and dark are coming together into wholeness. Organized religions are being confronted by their internal dualities and judgmental control over people.

As Heyoan says,

You don't really believe that
you must be punished
to behave well,
do you?

Chapter 11 Self-Review: Exploring Your Dualistic Experiences

1. List your life experiences that you consider to be on the order of extreme dualism.

2. How did you handle them at the time they happened?

3. How did you later resolve them, for the growth of your inner being?

4. What did you learn about your inner strength and what confidence do you now have about what you can handle?

Chapter 12

NEGATIVE INTENTION AND THE ASTRAL WORLD

*What is called Evil
can be seen as extreme duality,
which is simply profound forgetting.*

— HEYOAN

Now let's look at what happens when negative intention is held to really hurt someone.

Hexes, Curses, and Entities

Hexes and curses can be very dangerous. They are even more dangerous if cultures deny their existence, because they can cause all sorts of illness, physical pain, fear, strange behaviors, and even death without anyone detecting the cause. I have not studied this subject with anyone, so what I have to say is based solely on my HSP observations and experiences as a healer. I also don't know if there is an official difference between the words *curse* and *hex*. Perhaps they are just different words for similar things from different cultures. Curses and hexes simply use the laws that function in the fourth-level reality that I have already described. Each culture has created their own curses and hexes that they use. They also understand and interpret them according to their own systems.

What Is Black Magic and Why Is It So Strong?

Black magic is an organized system using energy consciousness information to harm or to control others by taking advantage of their weaknesses and their lack of understanding of such phenomena. It uses the same principles and laws of how the HEF fourth-level reality works that are used for healing. However, in black magic, those laws are used very specifically, in rituals with objects and symbols, and include the use of creative power sexual energies. These rituals are repeated over centuries by secret societies. As stated in Chapter 10, objects and symbols can be empowered in this way to carry dualistic energies and negative intent. Each time a ritual is repeated, it adds negative energy consciousness, power, and negative intent to the astral forms and negative belief system territories that are focused on. It can be powerful and dangerous. It finds and feeds on terror. It is not something to play with. It is connected to great reservoirs of black negative energy consciousness that have been built up throughout the centuries of human existence.

One of the ways black magic maintains power is that it is kept secret. Most people do not think it is real, or are afraid to find out. Yet they fear it. If they do think it exists, then black magic works on their terror to intimidate them. So bottom line: either stay away from it or learn how it works. A good book to learn more is *The Spear of Destiny* by Trevor Ravenscroft. It is the story of Hitler's search for the spear that pierced Christ's side. It tells the history of that spear after Christ.

My Experience with Black Magic, Hexes, and Curses

A Client with an Unusual Problem—Possession: Shortly after my first trip to hell, a woman called to say that she wanted to see me right away. She seemed so desperate that I found an opening and put her right in. She drove her VW bus to the Center for the Living Force (CLF), where I was living at the time, and parked in my front yard. I went down the outside steps to greet her. She jumped out of her bus and desperately tried to tell me her story, sometimes screaming incoherently. I tried to calm her down and get her up the stairs and into the healing room. Her HEF was a mess, to say the least. I had never seen such a configuration before or actually since that day. She was being invaded and controlled by another individual. He had great power. He was invading and controlling her through her crown chakra, which was spread wide open and torn up, and whose protective screens were gone. There were large, thick, solid black tentacles or roots coming down into her crown chakra. The tentacles went down into and entangled through her vertical power current, all the way down into her third chakra. They seemed to be held there by some power I knew nothing about. That power did not originate locally, but was from some distant culture. No matter what I did, I could not find a way to get them out. They were placed and held extremely strongly by a force unknown to me. I had never met such a strong, immovable force before. I knew I was in over my head. So I stopped

the healing and tried to calm her down to get her to tell me her story, in hopes that I would find a way in to release the roots. Soon I understood why I couldn't do it. Here is the story she told me:

"When I was studying Buddhism, I met a Buddhist monk from Tibet. I fell in love with him and we got married. But it didn't work out. He just wanted to control me. He kept sucking my energy. I couldn't stand it anymore, so I told him I wanted to get a divorce. He refused. Finally I said that I would just get one on my own—after all, this is America. Then the control got worse. Shortly after that I found out that he was not a Buddhist monk! He was a black magician! He has been using black magic on me the whole time to suck my energy. I can't get away, and I can't find anyone to even listen to me. Everyone thinks I am just crazy. Please help me! Please! Please! You have to take it out!

"TAKE IT OUT! I CAN'T STAND IT! I AM GOING CRAZY!" she screamed, jumping up and down!

"I'm sorry, I can't do it. I don't know how to do it, and I don't have enough power. I really tried. You need an exorcism! You have to go to a Tibetan monk—please find one. Try Tibet House. Or go to a priest for an exorcism. I have heard of one in New York City. He might be able to help you. Please go to him."

I wrote his name on a piece of paper, ushered her out of the healing room, and then forcibly walked her to her VW bus. When we got down the stairs to the bus, she started jumping up and down shrieking and yelling as if she was crazy. I attempted to calm her down again. It took a while to get her ready to drive and into her VW. I reassured her again that she needed to see the priest I recommended to get an exorcism. Finally she drove off down the road; actually, I was surprised at how well she could drive. My prayers went with her to heal her unfortunate state. I was just not qualified yet to handle that degree of black magic.

The Ethics of Handling Curses: Early in my career, there was a man, whom I will call Peter, who came to study with me in New York City. I noticed that his third chakra was terribly damaged. The screen was torn off of it, the seals were damaged, and it had a deep, gaping hole in its center. Noticing the extent of the damage, and not mentioning what I was observing, I asked him about his history. He told me that he had studied with a shaman for about three years. He had become an apprentice. His job as apprentice was to assist the shaman in removing curses and entities. It went like this: the person with the curse that was to be removed was taken into the center of a circle formed by people holding hands who held protective energy around the circle. The purpose of the circle of people was to give protection from the curse or entity. The shaman would pull the curse or entity out of the cursed person's aura and throw it into his apprentice's (Peter's) third chakra. When this happened, Peter would fall to the ground, writhing in pain and confusion. Peter was then dragged out of the circle while the shaman attended to the person he was healing. The circle of people kept the curse/entity from reentering the patient's aura. Peter told me that he usually continued to writhe on the ground another three hours till the convulsions stopped. He would then be sick for another two weeks before he recovered. Peter said that the shaman had helped a lot of people this way.

I was concerned for Peter and what would happen to him over the long term with such a damaged chakra. I worked on him almost every class, and also when he studied to be a teacher in my school. When he finally stopped studying with the shaman, his chakra held the healings I was giving him.

Peter also told me that he had studied with several such people. He said that the norm was to remove entities and curses stuck in the field and put them into things like chickens, eggs, or, as in his case, even apprentices! He also said that it was the norm to remove curses and send them back to the person who had sent them. I questioned the ethics of both of these techniques and searched for a more ethical way to do it.

A "Curse" from Transference: It wasn't long before I was challenged again, this time through transference. One of the tough things about being a leader is the transference that students go through while on their sacred healing path into the core. *Transference* is a term used in psychology. *Positive* transference takes place when a client or student transfers his good feelings onto the leader, e.g., a teacher, healer, or doctor. In such a case, at first, the leader is seen as being all good and as going to take care of the student/client in ways they never were, but wanted to be as children. Usually, at first, the teacher is seen through the eyes of positive transference as a wonderful teacher who is going to change their life. Some of this is true, but a great deal of it is positive transference. Then, later, when the student reaches a particular difficult point in his self-transformation process, when the deeper self-transformation work is necessary, *negative* transference arises from within the student. It turns out that the leader is a teacher, not a savior!

At one point during one my students' course of study, she went into a very negative transference with me. Rather than work on negative transference with a therapist, she went to a negatively biased psychic who told her that I had cursed her in a different lifetime, and that the student should "send the curse back"! Of course, I had never cursed anyone. So the bottom line was that the student cursed me for no real reason. Oh well, it didn't have much effect. It was just transference. This is when I discovered just one of the many problems of "sending curses back."

Heyoan taught me how to heal the entire thing, including the woman's troubled past lives. I held unconditional love in my hands, removed the curse from my field, and dissolved it. I followed it back, dissolving it through the entire path it had come. It went to the student, through the psychic who told her to send it to me, and then back to another individual I didn't know. I dissolved the whole thing so no one would get hurt.

The Vacation of Her Dreams—Or Was It: The first time I accidentally witnessed a curse was in the healing room. A woman came to me because she seemed to be slowly dying. I will call her Pat. Her health had been degenerating for two years.

She didn't know why. Pat said that she had gone to several physicians, but they could not diagnose her and whatever they had given her didn't work. As I began charging and clearing Pat's field during the first part of the healing, I saw an astral form attached to her field that was literally sucking the life energy out of her. As I explored Pat's field, I noticed that the form was not just connected to her field but to someone else's who was far away from where we were in New York State.

I followed the connection all the way to the Caribbean. This was very curious to me, as I had never seen anything like this. I continued to read the field on the astral level. It was connected to a native woman there. Then I noticed that it didn't actually originate with the native woman, but simply covered the outside of her field, then continued to a scary-looking man in what I, at the time, would call a "witch doctor's" outfit, complete with mask, feathers, shield, and odd-looking objects hanging around his neck, belt, and in his hand. He was the source of the energy form that was sucking Pat's life energy out of her.

I proceeded to try to remove this thick, sticky, slimy, negative energy consciousness. It wasn't easy. I tried sending it back to the original creator, but that didn't work. So instead, I centered myself, went into a state of unconditional love, and filled my entire field with unconditional love. Next, I focused on my hands, which were working to loosen it from Pat's field, and made sure they were covered and full of unconditional love. Then slowly, little by little, I began dissolving the negative hostile energy into love. It took a long time and a lot of concentration.

Once I had transmuted all of it that was in and around Pat, I proceeded to dissolve the long, thick, gooey mucous string that connected it to the island woman. When I reached her field, I psychically asked permission from her to dissolve it and transmute it into love. She agreed. I transmuted all of it that was on and in her field, and then continued to follow the mucous string to the so-called witch doctor. Upon reaching the outside of his field, I asked permission to dissolve it for him. He refused. So I didn't dissolve it from him. I then resumed and completed Pat's healing, and did a normal closing for her field.

After that, Pat rapidly recovered. I saw her a couple more times. Each healing focused on rebuilding and strengthening the many levels of her field as she rapidly recovered. During one of those healings, I asked her if she had been to the Caribbean. Then she told me her story:

"Two years ago I was in Jamaica on vacation. I met an island man, Jeremy. We fell in love. It was wonderful, we were so right for each other. We were going to get married. He said he'd come back to the States with me. But one morning toward the end of my vacation, a very angry island woman appeared in the backyard of my cottage. She was furiously screaming at me about something. I couldn't understand the dialect. Then I saw the knife. As she lunged at me, suddenly some local guys who had heard her screaming came running and grabbed her and the knife. They kept yelling at her as they dragged her away. Later, the guys came back and told me that she was Jeremy's common-law wife of many years and that they had several children. Terrified and brokenhearted, I left as quickly as I could!"

I sat in silence as Pat released tears of grief. When she finished I told her what I had seen in her field and what had happened in the healing. The island woman had hired an obi-man to kill Pat with negative psychic energy, so that Pat could not get back to Jamaica and take Jeremy away from her and her children.

A few weeks later, as is usual in my life, some new clients came in for healings. One was from the Caribbean. These new clients had written a book on the obi-man of the Caribbean, and brought in a copy for me. They did not know about Pat's healing. That is how I learned the name *obi-man*. The obi-man tradition of the Caribbean came with the African slaves. They are the medicine men of the ancient cultures of Africa. Their purpose is to heal according to their cultural traditions.

The Fire Curse: The next time I heard about a curse was only a month or so later. A woman, whom I will call Jean, came to me for a healing. After a brief introduction, she said, "My boyfriend is trying to kill me with black magic! I'm terrified. I am trying to stop his curses with meditation and prayer, but I'm afraid it is not working."

"What do you mean? What is he doing that you think this? How is he doing this?" I carefully asked, remaining serious.

"I'll show you," she said, as she proceeded to remove the long-sleeved shirt and gloves she was wearing. It was hard to cover my shocked reaction. Jean's hands and arms had been burned so badly that all the skin, and the tissue just beneath it, had been burned away. She had skin grafts that covered her hands and arms halfway up her biceps. The skin grafts were about one-quarter inch thinner than her normal skin, so that there was a sudden thinning and reddening of the skin at the junction between the graft and the normal skin. All the grafted skin looked bluish red. She proceeded to tell me the following story:

"He did this with black magic—I tell you, he is trying to kill me! When I got home from work one day, I called for him, but he didn't answer. Then I realized that he was upstairs doing a ritual. I was terrified. I immediately went into the basement to our meditation room and lit a candle, and started meditating to get protection from what he was doing. I was too scared to meditate, so I started praying as hard as I could. When I opened my eyes, the house upstairs was on fire! It wasn't from my candle. I quickly blew out my candle and ran up to the ground floor for the front door. It was locked. I ran to the back door. It was locked too. I ran to the windows, they were locked. He had set the house on fire and locked me in! But no one will believe me. I covered my face with my arms and hands so I could breathe. Finally I broke a window and climbed out!"

She paused, took a deep breath, and fell into tears. "I was in the hospital for months."

I proceeded to give Jean healings to rebuild all the levels of her field on her arms, as well as the rest of her body. There was a lot of trauma to remove from her field. There were tears in the structured levels, and chaotic dark clouds in the unstructured levels. The fire had not only left a lot of red in the unstructured levels of the field, but it had also shattered and frayed the structured HEF levels on her arms and hands that had been so badly burned.

Using my HSP, it did appear to me that the boyfriend had tried to use ritualistic black magic against her, but just didn't know how, as it is something I have not read much about. Even though it looked more like arson to me, I had no "real" evidence. The most important thing was that the client was protected against any further possibility of psychic attack. This I made sure of by clearing, strengthening, and protecting her field by helping her make her center very strong. Once she regained her strength, she decided to get more needed surgery for her scars to recover their normal texture.

An African Curse, Nine Generations Later: This experience was another surprise for me. By the time I witnessed this curse, BBSH had developed into a four-year program, and I was teaching students how to remove fourth-level-reality objects and beings from their fields in the second year of training. I was surprised how strong and how long a curse can last in the field. Nine generations is a long time.

First a reminder: the big difference between an astral object in the field and an astral being in the field is that beings have free will and do not wish to be removed. They fight you if you try to remove them, like the nest of baby harpies that tried to bite my fingers as I removed them from the client's pancreas. Thus removing beings is a little bit harder than removing objects that are stuck in the field but do not fight being removed. The beings have been put there by someone else, or by the clients themselves, either in this life or a different one. In addition to that, the will of the individuals who put the curse or hex in the field is keeping the curse or hex that must be healed in place, if it still exists.

So back to what I experienced when teaching class. I was teaching astral healing to the second-year students who were doing table healings. They were learning to remove fourth-level-reality objects and beings. As I walked around the room, assisting students, I noticed one student having difficulty. I went over to see the problem. The student "client," who was on the table receiving the healing, was of African heritage. The student "healer" was unable to hold the field steady because she did not have enough energy in her field. She was also not sure what she was trying to remove, also a result of not enough energy needed for the healing. I looked into the student client's field on the fourth level of the field, and saw that her vertical power current was full of small sinister-looking black snakes. Well, that explained why there was not enough energy to complete the healing: the student healer did not have enough power to remove the snakes that had sinister intention (nor was she expected to have that much energy control at her level of study). So I took over the healing, and had the student assist me. I proceeded to remove the snakes—at first, one by one, then many at a time. This took quite a while to do. As I removed the snakes, I took them to the higher levels of the field, where they took their original, nondualistic form as normal snakes (without sinister intent). I also proceeded to trace and dissolve the negative energy of the curse back to its origin. As I went back through time and the generations, I followed the energy consciousness of the curse, dissolving it as I went, all the way back to Africa, where it had originated some nine generations ago! I was amazed. I had no idea that such a thing could be carried down through so many generations!

I have always had a good relationship with snakes; as a child, I used to catch them and play with them. Later in life, I learned that the ancient goddess religion that encompassed most of the globe in ancient times used the snake as a symbol of the kundalini, the survival/healing/transforming force of life. I had seen snakes in people before, but not so many, nor from so long ago! It turned out that the presenting complaint the student client had given to the student healer was that of chronic back pain. It went away after that healing.

A Basic Overview of Beings/Objects and Curses/Hexes in the Fourth Level of the HEF

1. The fourth-level-reality world exists on the same frequency band as the fourth level of the HEF.

2. Objects can be charged with fourth-level-reality energy consciousness to help or to harm. Such objects can transmit this energy consciousness to humans. Some of these objects are called talismans. They are imbued with fourth-level-reality power in ceremonies.

3. Curses/hexes are placed in or on the field by another individual. Such an individual is either trained in or trying to practice some sort of shamanism, witchcraft, or voodoo.

4. Secret societies that use these powers have existed and still do exist all over the planet.

5. If the person placing a curse or hex does not have the power to place it inside the field, it simply sits on the field until the cursed individual has an ER. When this happens, the field weakens enough for the curse to get inside the field.

6. Curses/hexes can last for many generations if put there by a powerful person educated in these things. The power of a curse or hex depends on the ability of the individual placing it to regulate and control their HEF with focus (reason) and force (will), fueled by emotions.

7. A curse or hex should be dissolved, not sent back, as that is like making a curse on the person to whom one sends it back.

8. Fourth-level-reality objects stuck in the field are taken to the fifth level of the field, the divine, the template

(and form) of all things, to regain their original purpose.

9. Once a fourth-level-reality being is created, it continues to exist and evolves as all beings do.

10. Fourth-level-reality beings are taken into the light to regain their normal healthy balanced state.

11. The major tool for fourth-level-reality healing is unconditional love. It arises spherically out of the center of the heart chakra when the HEF is clear and balanced. To reach that state, it is good to go to the core star and then the hara level into a state of clear, effortless intention.

12. The use of will force in astral healing usually leads to duality to hurt or to have power over.

13. Don't try to do this on your own. You need to be taught how to handle your fear of the unknown and what is in your subconscious.

14. Your relationship to the fourth-level-reality world is affected by your ancestral past.

15. Your significant relationships, such as in marriage, include the astral past of the families into which you marry.

16. All negative belief systems are connected to and influenced by fourth-level-reality worlds that hold those beliefs.

17. A complete HEF healing must include astral healing, time capsule healing, and relational healing, as well as other types of advanced healings,

some of which are discussed in this book. A full healing must include at least seven levels of the HEF as well as all aspects of the HECS.[3]

18. The fourth level of the HEF is the level through which all relationships function.

19. The foundation of the fourth level of the field is the heart, the sacred human heart, out of which and through which unconditional love flows.

20. Remember unconditional love is essential for fourth-level-reality healing.[4]

Karma

This is an area of work that should not be taken lightly nor denied, as "modern" humans have. I have seen people close to death and nearly insane from such things. The old traditional ways to fight these things just create more fighting. Heyoan has taught other techniques that do not fight against it. Instead, we use unconditional love to dissolve the negativity of these objects and beings and return them to the light. We must also remove the so-called bad karma from the ones that are acting out their duality and harming others.

Karma can be seen as an opportunity
to resolve any conflict
or to clarify
any misunderstanding about reality
that you have within you.

— Heyoan

Any unresolved life experience from any life will remain in the field until it is resolved. That's

---

3   See *Hands of Light*®.

4   Note to reader: I did not put all fourth-level-reality healing techniques in this book, such as healing attachments and implants in the field, as they require a lot of training, including personal process work, dealing with the healer's fear of the unknown that arises from deep within the psyche, and personal support needed for the student when getting used to the worlds of the fourth-level reality.

a lot of opportunities in the HEFs of most every-one! Incarnation is an opportunity to clear that so-called karma away. We keep re-creating the same type of negative experiences in our present life until we resolve it. These re-creations, although very annoying, do create the opportunity for healing. That is one of the purposes of incarnation.

Chapter 12 Self-Review: Exploring Your Experiences with Negative Intent

1. What fourth-level-reality experiences have you had that involved negative intent or pleasure?

2. Describe what they were like.

3. Were they frightening? If so, how did you handle your fear?

4. What did you learn from them?

Chapter 13

OVERVIEW OF "PAST-LIFE" HEALING

To become individuated, you began the healing spirals,
through the process of what you call incarnation and reincarnation.

You have created these terms—incarnation and reincarnation—
by separating them with your idea of something called time.

You have given yourselves many opportunities and many "lives"
with which to create.
Using a linear time scale, you can go back in time
and remember other life experiences.
All these life experiences are tools for recognizing the self.

— HEYOAN

The great psychotherapist Dr. Stan Grof said,

"Each of us can manifest the properties
of a field of consciousness that
transcends space, time, and linear causality."

Dr. Grof saw the benefits of experiencing our unconscious, unresolved, painful life events that we hold frozen within us. To do so in a therapeutic setting gives us a chance to experience and then dissolve them. Some therapists call it *letting them die to us.* Dr. Grof's work includes processing unresolved experiences from both this lifetime and previous or "past-life" times. Many body psychotherapists do this work now because it is so effective. Such work requires deep personal process with a well-trained, experienced healer/

therapist who has done her/his personal process. Utilizing HSP and knowledge of how the HECS functions enhances and shortens the process of healing. This process makes it more direct, since the energy configuration of the trauma can be directly worked on and removed from the HECS. Once this is done, the physical body heals rapidly.

The subject of "past-life" therapy is a vast one. I will give you a basic overview and foundational information for past-life therapy. Once I have discussed past-life therapy in this chapter, I will move into a new way of looking at the phenomenon called "past lives." I developed these new techniques by observing how the HECS retains unresolved experiences from all life experiences including the present life, as well as so-called past lives.

There are two major things that stand out regarding experiencing past lives:

1. The inescapable feeling that one is trying to resolve a past-life issue, that there is something you still need to learn that keeps escaping you until you do past-life healing. In some cases a whole life can be seen as constantly trying to come to terms with the disappointments of a past life's dying thoughts.

2. Past-life characters can be recognized as other selves or as a part of one's self now that still have problems that need to be resolved.

Using Deep Relaxation to Follow the Body into the Past

I was first trained to do past-life therapy with the use of deep relaxation and regression at the Institute for Psychophysical Synthesis (IPS) in Washington, D.C. In the training, we were taught to be very careful not to lead the client into any specific vision of a past life, or into any particular emotion. Instead, we calmly, through spoken word and an occasional gentle touch, guided the client into deep relaxation in each part of his/her physical body, beginning at the feet. This work was done while the client lay on a sturdy, narrow bed or a massage table. Once each part of the body was relaxed, the guided visualization led the client mentally and physically as the client regressed back in time. Once this was done, the therapist massaged the particular part of the client's physical body associated with the trauma.

This method leads the client's mind and body, step by step, backward in time. This method helps the client to reexperience the old traumas that caused the body block in that particular area of the physical body. This method is repeated each session the client receives. Therapy continues until the client experiences and releases all the recurrences of the trauma, including the first time the trauma occurred. This includes any past

lifetime when the trauma occurred. The HEF is not completely cleared of the blocks caused by the trauma until the first trauma is completely healed. Usually the field releases the most recent trauma of the same nature first. The next healing would most likely release the second-most-recent time a similar trauma happened, and so on, backward through time.

In general, almost all major issues of this present lifetime were caused by unresolved experiences carried forward into this life from past lives. Some of these past lives result in birth traumas in this present life. For example, one client had a chronic neck problem. The umbilical cord was wrapped around her neck at her home birth. She was blue (and silent) for several days after birth. After that she had several injuries to the same area of her neck in her childhood. As a five-year-old child, she climbed up on a statue of a lion in front of the Field Museum in Chicago. Her older brother pushed her off and she fell on her head on the concrete. Later in life, when riding in the front passenger seat in a car that had no seat belts, her head hit the windshield when the driver of the car rear-ended the car in front of them. The result was another whiplash injury that became chronic. Each time she put a little strain on her neck muscles, such as picking up something that was a little too heavy for her weak neck muscles to handle, her neck would click out of alignment and cause chronic pain. Chronic injuries such as these are very difficult to heal. They required constant care and vigilance to protect the injury from re-wounding. Thus,

Chronic injuries offer
a tool for learning self-care
as well as loving acceptance
of one's imperfections.

When dealing with her past life that related to her present condition, she remembered being burned at the stake with the rope tied around her neck. She had strained at the rope to escape, but she was unable to. Asking for help did nothing, as those watching would have been put into her situation had they responded. Each time she tugged at the rope, she strangled herself more! It had been a hopeless situation that resulted in her death.

Now, in this life, she was challenged to find hope. She did so by learning to ask for help again when she needed it! This time she got help.

Following the Client's Lead: It is important to remember that during the time of healing, the healer follows the client's lead. The healer goes wherever the client's psyche and body go internally with respect to the client's presenting complaint. The healing continues until the time capsule is completely dissolved. When this is accomplished, the client's field is clean and he will not have to deal with that particular experience and issue again. He has dissolved the negative belief about himself and his life. The client has participated in his healing process and has become well. He has empowered himself to live his own life through his own choices. This is how the client gains a great deal of self-respect. Yes, the healer helped a lot, but the client is the one who has released his unresolved issues by experiencing, releasing, and healing the pain they caused.

The healer also helps remove the traumatized energy consciousness from the HEF. Once it is cleared, the healer assists in recharging and rebuilding the client's field. The healer also teaches the client the psychological process of how the client has been compensating for the trauma, thus misaligning his field. As healers, we simply assist the client in handling the emotions that the body released. We are there to witness and confirm the client in his process. Clients respond well and make good progress in resolving their life issues that originated in their past lives. Until the healing, the unresolved experiences, left over from their past lives, are still blocking their life energy now, in this life.

My work of practicing the bioenergetic way of dealing with past lives called forth even more the psychic and healing factors from deep within me. Since I could see the field, I was already working with it from the perspective of the natural bioenergetic flows of energy through the body and field. I was enhancing the flows of bioenergy where the body blocked it, removing and cleaning stagnated pools of energy where it had accumulated, and charging the undercharged areas with clean, clear healing energy. Then my vision opened even more: rather than just seeing the energy consciousness of the entire HECS, I began seeing the events that had occurred in the client's life that had caused their problems.

A fairly short time later, I started seeing my clients' past lives. At first it frightened me, so again I did not share what I was sharing with others. I could see how the client's life experiences were related to one another. Experiences left unresolved from previous lives were simply carried forward into this one. They were buried deeper in the field under similar unresolved experiences that occurred in this life! This configuration was a real wake-up call. It showed me that dying does not get you out of an unresolved situation. It only pushes it forward into the next incarnation, and greatly increases your probability to have to deal with the same issue again in similar personal situations on the earth—but at a later time period.

Seeing a Client's Past Life

When I first started seeing the past lives of my clients, I was rather timid about it, and didn't mention what I saw for years. The first time is memorable as it immediately confronted me with the issue of how to handle the psychic information I received.

When my client, whom I will call Sarah, lay on my table for the past-life regression, I immediately started having a vision: I was standing by the Sea of Galilee, near a boat that had Christ's robe thrown over it. In the distance, just over the water, I could see a bright golden light moving toward me. As the light came close, it became larger and brighter. Then I recognized that it was Christ walking on the water toward me! I didn't know what to do with this vision, as the client was Jewish, so I kept it quiet.

All visions that I have had during healings have pertained to the client, not to me. But, having been raised a Christian, perhaps this one was for me. Yet each time Sarah came for a healing, the vision would reappear. I thought it was a past life that she had had during the time Jesus was on the earth and that she had known him. But I never said anything. Perhaps that vision pertained to me, perhaps not. However, it was a good lesson to not share things when one is not completely confident that the information pertains to the client. Later, as I matured in my work, if I was not sure whom it was for, I would simply and quietly ask Heyoan.

How to Handle Seeing a Client's Past Lives

Since that time, I have given many past-life healings. I usually see the past-life experiences before the clients do, but I always wait for the clients to find them. Then I can confirm them. This is a very important way to handle the information you might get with regard to past lives. The problem is if the healer tells what she sees, then it may not be experienced as authentic by the client, and from that moment on there will be doubts. If, on the other hand, the client directly experiences a past life—especially if he feels it in his own body without any direct information from the healer—it will be an authentic experience for the client and therefore very healing. The client will use the experience to resolve life issues that come forward in the past-life experience that provide personal information to the client with regard to solving issues in this present lifetime. That is the power of past-life healing. It brings one into deep resolution that cannot be resolved with the information from only this present life.

A Broader View of "Past Lives"

From years of work with "past lives," and looking at the phenomena as "past lives," I have seen that we have many different types of lifetimes that are related to one another by the unresolved personal issues that we carry into subsequent life experiences. When we finally break the patterns we have repeated throughout many "past lives," our present life very rapidly makes a big shift into a much more fulfilling experience.

Overview of Past-Life Phenomena

There are four major ways to work with past-life phenomena. They are as follows:

1. **Psychic:** Past-life readings or channeling past-life information.

2. **Parapsychological:** Scientific and experimental investigation of past-life claims to prove or disprove that they exist.

3. **Religious:** Reincarnation is or is not an article of faith or doctrine. Most of the world's religions do have the doctrine of reincarnation. It is said that reincarnation was removed from Christianity in the First Council of Nicea in 325 A.D. (There are quite a few books out there that confirm this, but an official Catholic website denies it.)

4. **Psychotherapeutic/Healing:** Therapeutic work to improve life experience and energy healing, which I will focus on in this chapter.

Leaders in the Field of Past-Life Experiences

Dr. Ian Stevenson: In his work as a psychiatrist, Dr. Ian Stevenson noticed that young children commonly made statements referring to *when I lived before* or *when I died before*. At that time, Dr. Stevenson was the chairman of the department of psychiatry at the University of Virginia, and later the director of the division of personality studies at the same university, where he investigated evidence that supported the existence of past lives by searching old records that substantiated recollections of past lives, especially recollections of children. Unfortunately, Dr. Stevenson passed away in 2007, but his work remains as a gift to all. Here is what he did:

Dr. Stevenson devoted fifty years to the scientific documentation of past-life memories of children from all over the world. He studied children who spontaneously (without hypnosis) remembered a past life. His methodology included the following steps:

1. Methodically document the child's statements.

2. Identify the deceased person the child remembers being.

3. Verify the facts of the deceased person's life that match the child's memory.

4. Match birthmarks and birth defects to wounds and scars on the deceased, verified by medical records.

5. Rule out all possible "normal" explanations for the child's memories.

Dr. Stevenson's Results: He ended up with over 3,000 cases of matching results in his files, and wrote a 2,200-page book correlating birthmarks to past-life wounds, entitled *Reincarnation and Biology*.

Dr. Harold Lief, in the *Journal of Nervous and Mental Disease*, made the following statement about Dr. Stevenson: "Either Dr. Stevenson is making a colossal mistake, or he will be known as the Galileo of the 20th century."

Carl Jung's View of Past-Life Phenomena: Rather than focus on whether or not the past lives actually took place, Dr. Jung utilizes the phenomena of archetypes for therapeutic purposes. Dr. Jung explained that archetypes—ancient, universal character formations—are the root structures of our psyches. Our disposition to experience the heroes, villains, lovers, and despots in ourselves derives from the archetypical. In Jungian therapy, these archetypes are brought out into the open for the patient to recognize, understand, and resolve within the personality.

Jung explained, "One does not become enlightened by imagining figures of light, but by making the darkness conscious."

Jung said that past-life therapy offers a blank screen called past life upon which to project the archetypes that lie deep in the psyche. This type

of work grew into many specialties, and became known in general as Shadow Work, since it meant looking at unpleasant and often negative shadowy characteristics inside a person's psyche, rather than repressing them further.

A number of other protocols to deal with patients evolved, which were very important in providing deep explorations into the human psyche. For example, in the psychodynamic process, truth became *that which is real for the client.* Thus the search for truth was transformed into *the search for meaning.* Another important aspect in the search for meaning was the *importance of synchronicity in a patient's life*, synchronicity being coincidence that has a *personal meaning* beyond the immediate facts of the situation.

The Guardians of the Threshold: Other aspects of probing deeper into the darker regions of the psyche was the issue of how deep one should go and when was it appropriate. How could the therapist know, since the deeper psyche is not put together like our mundane daily consciousness? It does not function as orderly as our day-to-day consciousness. Instead, it is symbolic, nonlogical, archetypical, unpredictable, and, at times, it can be very nasty.

A common idea about psychic work is that we each have inner *guardians of the threshold* to prevent us from going too deep, too fast. Such guardians of the threshold look like frightening monsters depicted at the gates of a temple or bordering a sacred Mandala, such as the Black Kali with teeth and fingernails clamped onto the seventh level of the field of the client I mentioned in Chapter 10. They are images of the client's own fear and are there to prevent the client from entering realms of the psyche that he/she is not yet ready to handle.

Past-life therapy, if not handled correctly, nor respected for its powerful effect on the client's life, can be like taking the lid off Pandora's box. It can unleash potent forces over which the client may have little control. Searching into past lives for answers to today's issues should only be undertaken with someone fully trained. Revealing a so-called past life can be shocking. In a "past life," the client may have acted inhumanly toward others, such as being a killer, rapist, or a violent soldier. Such information can become a moral problem that challenges the whole personality. A client may become even more self-judgmental and use the past life as justification for self-denigration, or even harming himself. Past-life information could even lead a client to take advantage of others who supposedly harmed them in a past life. I saw this once in a group I was running. One member of the group claimed to remember another who had done harm to the other in a so-called past life. Therefore, according to her logic, she was free now to harm the person she accused. This was, perhaps, the most shocking thing that I experienced during my career of running therapy groups. I finally had to ask her to leave the group.

Yet past lives are not to be remembered and cast away. They are living energies to be balanced with each other and with the ego, potentially to be integrated into a newer and broader sense of self.

Some people say that once we explore a whole series of past lives, a very prominent feature stands out: there is a constant process of reversal from one kind of personality type to its opposite. I have not found this to be true. In fact, I have seen the opposite. People tend to live lives that repeat similar experiences, in long series, but in different settings. It is as if we repeat the issue till we learn to get it right.

Stumbling Blocks the Healer May Encounter in Working with the Fourth Level

Projection is one of the first stumbling blocks to working in or with the fourth-level-reality world. It is very easy to project your duality onto what you perceive if you do not understand how the fourth-level-reality world works. When looking through a glass darkly, one sees the darkness projected from the self, rather than what is. As I mentioned in Chapter 6 on HSP, one looks for what is, not for what is wrong. Any fears the observer has about the fourth-level-reality world will result in three phenomena:

1. **The seer's projections from fear will manifest right before the seer's eyes.** What is happening in this case is the seer's fear becomes the creative force that then creates the feared event or being, i.e., projection becomes creation.

2. **The seer's fear, which is composed of energy consciousness, draws like energy consciousness to it.** This draws to the seer exactly what the seer feared he would find in the fourth-level-reality world. It is essential to do personal process work to uncover and deal with your fears.

3. **The seer demands to be psychic.** Another stumbling block I have run into often when training healers at BBSH is the student's demand to be psychic NOW! The underlying fear is that the student is completely incapable of learning HSP. Forcing HSP just leads to projection and complicated fantasy that confuses the student and slows down progress. Patience, humility, and focused work in personal process, as well as skills practice, will take the student far in learning HSP.

Misuses of Fourth-Level-Reality Phenomena, and How to Handle Them

There are several major misuses of fourth-level-reality phenomena that I have witnessed.

The most common form of psychic attack that most people actually do, yet do not understand that it is happening, is maligning! Most of us are used to it, but don't like it. I can see the negative streamers and sharp strikes of energy that fly out from those who are maligning to the people being maligned. It does not matter how far away in the physical world their victims are!

How to Handle Psychic Attack: Most people do not know that they are sending negative streamers to people, striking and hurting them. Depending on your relationship with the person who is doing the maligning, you can directly let them know of its effects. You can just tell them that it makes you uncomfortable to talk about others who are not present, or just change the subject. You can also put a protective shield around the person being maligned.

Unconscious negative intent in healers is also a form of psychic attack. It has a big negative effect. I have witnessed many. All of the following examples had energy consciousness streamers and attachments into the clients with whom they were working. They seemed to be completely unaware of what they were doing. I have seen healers:

1. Who clearly did not have enough training make unethical demands on their clients, such as to act in certain ways that had nothing to do with their healing or condition.

2. Who have not had enough training (if any at all) in their own personal psychodynamics, and who have very little self-knowledge about what they are doing and their own underlying motives for some of their actions. I went to such a healer who demanded that I be submissive and not progress in my growth process. She wanted me to stay young and submissive, and insisted on calling me a girl. I mentioned it during a healing. After the healing, as I was leaving, she sarcastically called me a girl. I decided to never go back.

3. Who were undermining, maligning, and proclaiming themselves better than other healers. They seemed not to know that they where creating terrible forms in the field and sending them to the people they were maligning.

4. Who, in a group with only one weekend-type training, proclaimed a person who had a lethal brain tumor

healed, after only a short group healing. They told him not to go to the hospital. He died shortly after.

How to Handle Unconscious Negative Intent: If your client has a serious illness, make sure that he is going to a physician. If he refuses to go to a physician, I suggest that you deal with the client himself, letting him know that he needs to go to a physician of his choice in addition to any healer of his choice. During my practice, several seriously ill people came to me as a way not to see a physician. I always immediately sent them to a physician. I would not give them a healing without knowing who their physician was and getting permission from the client to confer with the physician.

Remember, denial can be a very strong force that covers extreme deep fear.

Stages of Reactions to the Astral That Must Be Dealt with in Personal Process Therapy

There are several stages that students who learn fourth-level-reality healing work go through. Each stage must be dealt with carefully, supportively, and lovingly.

1. **Infatuation** is the first stage. Walking into the fourth-level reality is walking into a whole new world that exists both around and inside you. It is fascinating at first because people are curious. They have heard stories of fourth-level-reality travel, through which you can go out of your body to visit friends close and far, even in other countries, or travel through the solar system and beyond. They are excited to explore new worlds. Most assume that the fourth-level-reality world works like the physical world, except it must be more fun. Let's go, they say. But as we know, the fourth-level reality doesn't act like the physical world! And sometimes, as we have seen, it's not fun at all! On the

other hand, many people have never heard of it and wouldn't believe it if they did hear about it!

2. **Fear** is the second stage. Once people have heard and start to consider that it may possibly exist, their first reaction is fear. Then as we have seen, the fourth-level reality becomes taboo. It is dangerous and against some religions to explore it. So they won't get involved. Probably that is a good thing for them. It takes years, a lot of personal psychological work, and sound grounding in the physical world to attempt it.

3. **Terror** may be one's third stage. Once one has some good fourth-level experiences, like with an angel or spirit guide, they will probably not be afraid to enter the fourth level. Yet sooner or later, when in a bad state of mind or in a bad dream, the terror comes! This is when the individual realizes the extent of the fourth-level world and some of its contents. Heavens are okay. But hells! No! Or they realize that a person could get lost or caught in the fourth-level realities (and sometimes they do), especially some who are diagnosed as schizophrenic. Getting that diagnosis *is* scary!

4. **Creation of an Acceptable Reality System.** The fourth stage of relating with the fourth-level reality comes when the student is able to study and work through his fear psychotherapeutically to create a place in his basic reality system to put fourth-level-reality experiences. By studying the physics of the fourth-level-reality world (Chapter 9), and by directly experiencing that the fourth-level-reality world does function in the way described, it becomes a place that functions in an understandable way. It is different from the physical, but understandable. The student now understands that there is a way to navigate through the fourth-level realities. The student can succeed in fourth-level-reality navigation when the student learns how to regulate his emotional reactions and break the vicious cycle of negative repeated patterns. The student also works on himself to free himself of the underlying fear of the unknown, both outside and inside, by learning how to regulate himself no matter what he is experiencing. Of course, everyone does have a cutting edge. The work of bringing back all pieces of the self that are scattered throughout time and space into center and integrating them into one's whole continues throughout many lifetimes.

Transference and Projection in Personal Process

In personal process, with regard to the fourth-level-reality work, it is very important to understand *transference* and *projection* and their effects on one's experience of reality.

It is also important to learn to have deep contact with the self. *Transference* occurs when a person projects the characteristics of a psychologically significant person (usually an authority from childhood) onto another individual. That authority is said to be "transferred upon."

Projection also refers to the psychological phenomenon in which an individual projects his own inner feelings onto someone else, as if the other person were having them rather than himself. A common example of this is being afraid of someone because you are convinced that that person is angry with you, when actually you are angry with him. You are feeling fear because of your own anger! By understanding these things, and healing the fear that lies beneath them, one becomes much clearer as to what the true reality actually is! I spent many years in therapy as well as in training to become a bioenergetic therapist, which helped me understand these things in my own personal process. I still do personal work on myself with someone.

A lot of personal process work is necessary if one wants to delve into the fourth-level-reality worlds and do healing there. It is much harder to deal with psychological issues related to the unusual experiences one has in the astral world.

When I first started having such experiences, I had no road map as I described in Chapter 7 to help me. As the number of my experiences of the fourth-level reality grew, I drew my own road map. What follows is a description of the various types of fourth-level-reality experiences with various fourth-level-reality beings that helped me to understand what was happening and how to deal with it. First, I will describe a few astral experiences that occurred in my personal life, and then those that occurred in both therapy and healing sessions I was giving.

I had already heard of some of these types of experiences. Some were surprising and taught me that there is probably no limit to the experiences one can have. They helped me get a broader view of how the astral world functions, and the types of beings that exist there. It was through these experiences that I learned how to handle encounters with astral beings, how to communicate with them, and eventually how to help them.

Misuses of Past-Life Work by the Client

I have observed three major ways that a client can misuse past-life work. They are as follows:

Avoidance of Issues in This Life: The client focuses on other lives to avoid issues in this life. The "other" lives are usually seen as having been powerful, rich, and/or famous.

Projection and Blame: Projection and blame put on people in this life for things that you experienced in other lives. It's as if they had treated you badly in that other life and must pay for it now! They may have even lived in that other life, and may have even treated you badly in that other incarnation, but focusing on them won't help you heal a bit. It is your unfinished creation, not theirs!

Unfinished Business Doesn't Give Privileges: Using unfinished business from so-called past lives to take unwarranted privileges in this life. The most extreme example I saw was in a past-life group. A married student, whose wife was also in the group, went around telling the other women in the group that they had been married to each other in a previous lifetime and had had sexual problems. So now they had to have sex to work them out! Several women in the group actually acted as if they believed him, or perhaps they just took it as a great excuse. This class was in the country. Later I found out he had a shack in the woods that he used for this. Unfortunately, I found out after the classes were finished for the year. The commitment made in order to get into that group was to not engage in any sexual activities with any class members, unless, of course, students were married to each other. Such activity changes the group dynamics.

Chapter 13 Self-Review: Exploring Your Past Lives

1. List your past-life experiences along a timeline.

2. How do they influence your life now?

3. What images and beliefs do you still carry that are connected to unresolved experiences in other lives?

4. What have you learned about yourself from your past-life experiences?

5. Have you ever recognized anyone from a past life? How was that for you?

TIME CAPSULE HEALING: RELEASING THE BONDS OF THE PAST

Once you have gone into that early wound and felt the pain,
you find there portions of your creative force
that have been locked inside the wound since it was created.

Thus what you call the past,
locked in a time capsule when that creative force was arrested,
is not actually a past held in time.

Rather, it is your creative light energy,
held by the wound's density that curls light.

Your illusion of a past
is actually your creative energy held in stagnation.

It has not continued to move and flow
in its normal creative pulse.

Granted, you use the concepts of time
in order to understand what you call memory.
Yet consider the possibility that memory
is a frozen idea of an experience
that has actually been contained in the form of a capsule,
which we prefer to call a time capsule.

It is simply a stagnated creative energy
that is no longer moving in the creative pulse of life.

— HEYOAN

We all have internal reality constructs about ourselves, our lives, and other people.

Some of our reality constructs are holistic and are integrated into our healthy adult egos. In the parts of our lives where our holistic reality constructs are functioning, we are healthy and wise—perhaps even wealthy! These healthy reality systems function very well to create the happy, loving, and fulfilling lives we want. We share our integrated clear wisdom with our friends. We enjoy these friendships and even help our friends heal themselves and their lives. Our friends do the same for us.

So why aren't all aspects of our lives perfect? We are unable to create perfect lives because some of our inner reality systems are not healthy. In fact, they are split into separated parts that are in conflict with each other. Usually they are split in half; thus, they are dualistic. We all have unhealthy dualistic reality systems that are based on our inner duality.

Our Internal Dualisms

Our dualistic, unhealthy reality constructs are usually both unclear and unconscious. Our dualistic reality constructs make up our *unhealthy belief systems*, with which we create trouble and pain for ourselves. We even create trouble in the lives of others, especially if they have similar dualistic beliefs. In other words, and to a certain extent, we assist our friends in messing up their lives the same way we mess up our own lives! We don't *consciously* know or intend to help create a negative outcome! We are not aware that the outcome of our advice or actions will be undesirable, both to ourselves and to the others we advise! Thus,

It is important to become aware of our unconscious dualistic beliefs, our unconscious dualistic energy, and our unconscious dualistic intentionality.

To do so, we must search deep within ourselves, through the powerful technique of time capsule healing, to find:

1. Our split or dualistic beliefs and their origin.

2. Our split or dualistic intentions that result from these beliefs.

3. How our split or dualistic intentions fight against each other.

4. What unitive outcome we really do want to create.

Recall from Chapter 3 that blocked energy has split intentions and is dualistic.

Dualistic energy consciousness is composed of two unresolved, incomplete reality constructs that are opposites of each other.

They result in two opposing intentions that simply block any creative act we try to accomplish that is related to them. Dualistic energy consciousness is unsuccessful in creating what we truly want, because it does not have enough clear aligned energy to create.

Each side is backed by a powerful *will force* that demands its way in order to supposedly protect us from our *feared* outcome. This *will force* automatically—and usually unconsciously—kicks in when any type of life situation occurs that is similar to something very painful that we've experienced before.

The reason that it is still painful is that it is still unresolved.

It may have happened in one's youth or even in a past life, or past lives. Such a repeated experience immediately evokes a fear in us that is similar to the one previously experienced, at a time earlier in this life or in a "previous" life. Many times, this fear is unconscious. It has been pushed down into the unconscious in an effort to deal with (or even to survive) a situation over which we had no power to change when it happened the first time, and perhaps many times after the first.

To be successful in one's creative purpose, one's purpose must be unified and aligned. When one's purpose is not clear, it is usually split. What I mean by split, or dualistic, is that one is at "cross-purposes" with oneself. In such a case, there is not enough aligned creative energy to achieve one's creative purpose. As long as any creative energy consciousness is associated with a particular creative endeavor remains dualistic, it will interfere with your ability to complete your creation, *whatever that may be.*

The Purpose of Time Capsule Healing

The purpose of time capsule healing is to gain more creative energy in your life, and to heal lifelong issues that may not make any sense to you when searching your present life to find any causes of these issues. **Time capsule healing releases creative energy consciousness that has been held in a dualistic stagnant, immovable, dualistic state for perhaps hundreds—indeed, even thousands—of years.**

The process of time capsule healing returns our dualistic creative energies to their original holistic state so that they can complete their original purpose. Therefore, with time capsule healing, you can re-create your life the way you want it to be! Why? Because once your holistic creative energy consciousness reenters in your HECS, you have much more creative energy to heal chronic conditions, change what you want to change, live and enjoy your life, and create what you long for.

Description of a Time Capsule

Time capsules are conglomerates of unhealed events from past lives as well as this life that have not been resolved. They include physical wounds that resurface as birthmarks, emotional and irrational behavior problems, and dualistic belief systems that are in conflict with each other, yet at the same time are drawn together by the principle of "like attracts like." All within the same human being! How complicated we are!

Time capsules coagulate around an archetype. Or, put in more personal terms, they accumulate around a wrong idea, belief, or feeling of what life is about and how we are supposed to be in life. This eventually and repeatedly culminates in an injury in the same location in our physical body that the time capsule is located in the energy field. The process for removing a time capsule is similar to the process of removing a block that was described in the healing sequence in Chapter 3.

Seven Major Aspects of Past-Life Wounds: Sometimes we carry our unresolved issues and previous wounds from *previous* lifetimes as birthmarks into the next life. The following are seven major aspects of these past-life wounds:

1. They occur from similar traumas and are in the same location on our bodies.

2. They have similar energy consciousness that draws them together. Thus, in one body location, one can find many past lives of wounds similar to those that have occurred in this life.

3. They are not laid out along a timeline, but rather are enfolded into the HEF in similar energy consciousness and isolated from the rest of the field.

4. The pulsations and flow of energy consciousness of the HEF just go around them.[5]

5. The major difference in these wounds we are focusing on is that they did not originate in this lifetime.

6. Traditionally, they are called past-life traumas. However, in this chapter we will reevaluate that name and move beyond it. As described in Chapter 9, painful experiences in the fourth-level-reality world are not organized in linear time.

---

5   See Chapter 3 for a description of how a block is created.

7. Our painful experiences are held together according to likeness. Painful experiences that are similar to one another accumulate together, and are located in the areas of the physical body where we have physical difficulties or injuries.

We need to remember the nonlinearity of time and its connection to blocks that are now specifically held in the fourth level of the HEF. In the fourth-level-reality world information exists in a four-dimensional field, but, from our three-dimensional physical perspective, it *looks like* a three-dimensional world, because that is how we are used to seeing things!

Yet within a block,
time is no longer an arrow
pointing only into the future,
as it is in the physical world.

Within a block,
time has been frozen
since the moment the block occurred.
Time is encapsulated
within the energy consciousness in the block
in the space that the block occupies
in the fourth level of the HEF!

Let me say that again in another way:

Inside a block that is held in the fourth level of the HEF, time is frozen in the moment that the block occurred. Thus the block is separated from the normal pulsations of energy flow through the HEF. This separation allows the individual who created the block to function in daily life, rather than get caught up in his deep pain from earlier in life.

Instead, we make use of a *new type of time* as a tool for healing. In so doing, we find that

Time, in the fourth level of the HEF,
is encapsulated in the experience,
rather than the experience
being encapsulated in time,
as in the physical world!

The Anatomy of a Time Capsule

A time capsule contains a particular type of wound from many lifetimes, each of which has taken place at a particular time and location in the physical world. They are not laid out on a linear timeline as one might expect. Instead, they are located in particular areas in the HEF, both outside and inside the physical body, where you still tend to repeatedly hurt yourself. They are located where you can't seem to bring that part of your body into complete health and may have chronic pain.

Figure 14–1 is a diagram of a time capsule. I have numbered each "past life" in linear-time order as they happened in the physical. For example, T1, which stands for Time 1, is the first time this particular type of wound happened, many lifetimes ago. For teaching purposes, I show nine lifetime experiences for this particular type of wound. Time 9 (T9) is the last time that this type of injury happened. It could be in a previous life or in this life. Please note that the lifetimes in Figure 14–1 are not necessarily consecutive lifetimes. There may be many lifetimes between these in which the client did not hurt himself in this way. Time capsules coagulate around a particular archetype that has a particular dualistic belief system associated with it. Similar time capsules are usually grouped and compacted together in a specific area of the physical body, with the first experience being the deepest (T1). The next similar experience that happened is Time 2 (T2). (That is what I mean by saying they are not held in a linear timeline.)

Another important point about time capsules, is that the longer they are held in the field, the deeper they are compressed into the field, and the more compacted they become. A few times, I have even seen them set deep into the vertical power current, and compacted to the size of a period at the end of a sentence.

The Major Areas Where Time Capsule Healing Is Effective

1. Any type of chronic or irrational fear, such as fear of drowning, small spaces, heights, insects, snakes, etc.

2. Insecurity

3. Chronic depression and low energy

4. Phobias

5. Sadomasochistic behavior problems

6. Guilt and martyr complexes

7. Material insecurity

8. Eating disorders

9. Accidents

10. Violence and physical brutality

11. Long-term family struggles

12. Sexual difficulties

13. Negative aggressive sexual behaviors

14. Harsh marital difficulties

15. Chronic physical ailments

The Process of Time Capsule Healing

The General Process of Time Capsule Healing: Time capsule healing integrates Brennan Healing Work and energy field phenomena with past-life therapy and regression techniques. Time capsules may affect all levels of the HEF and even the entire Human Energy Consciousness System (HECS). Most of the healer's concentration is to release the time capsule from the fourth level of the field, and then follow the natural responses of the HEF through all its levels as it reorganizes itself. For several weeks—perhaps even months—after a time capsule healing, the entire HECS continues to reorganize itself into a much healthier state. During this period of time, the client is integrating the newly released creative energy, as well as the new freedom he experiences in his life. As his healing continues, his life changes, sometimes in surprising ways, to which he needs to adjust. He experiences more ownership of his life.

After some period of rapid change, the new development levels off and it is appropriate for the client to schedule another time capsule healing. The length of time varies with the individual, and depends on the client's support system and capacity for change in their life.

Sometimes, clients come several times a week for time capsule healings. However, the normal rate is once or twice per week depending on the client's ability to handle adjustment to the changes that result from the healings.

HSP during Time Capsule Healing: Time capsule healing starts by reading the HECS with HSP to find the configurations of so-called past lives held inside the time capsules, and to discern what experiences need healing. The healer does not use HSP information to program the healing or lead the client in any particular direction during the healing. The healer uses HSP information as a way to be more present with the client. The healer does not disclose HSP information to the client until after the healing and after the client talks about the experience (if the client chooses to so do). The healer then shares HSP information in a way that confirms the client's experience, or, in some cases, gives more information than the client obtained to help the client more deeply understand the healing that he took part in by being willing to experience the past in order to heal it.

The Healer's Regulation of Energy Coming Out Her Hands: While there are many techniques that BBSH graduate healers are trained to do for time capsule healing that are beyond the scope of this book, energy-flow regulation out the hands is necessary for any type of healing. We teach it the first day of beginning training in workshops, as well as to all first-year students. We call the simplest of these techniques *Push, Pull, Stop, Allow,* and *Neutral* because that is exactly what they are. Beginning healers learn to push energy out their hands. They learn how to completely stop the flow of their energy and also to just allow it to flow naturally. They learn how to direct it where they wish. They learn to pull harmful energy out of the client's field with their energy hands. Don't worry; they learn to stop, clean, and release the harmful energy into the light before it gets stuck in their wrists or arms!

In time capsule healing, we use the first four energy-regulation techniques of push, pull, stop, and allow according to the field pulsations of the client, and according to what is needed for the healing technique. Students learn how to control the color of energy that comes out their hands and their field, and where to direct it into the field of the client.

During any healing, the HEF naturally pulsates through its four-phase cycle of expansion, stasis, contraction, and stasis. During a healing, the healer is always aware of what phase that four-phase cycle pulse is in, and regulates the healing accordingly. Doing this promotes a much more efficient healing. A long time ago, the second-year students named this technique "Following the Wave"! (Time capsule healing is taught in the second year of training at BBSH.)

As their training progresses into the third year, students become more efficient in matching the frequency of energy flowing from their hands to any part of, or anything in, the client's field, including any level of the field or any particular frequency of any organ in the body. Frequency matching is done in neutral mode and is very effective.

Healing Techniques Used in Time Capsule Healing

Chelation: After reading the field with HSP, the healer does a general clearing of the client's HEF; this healing is called a chelation. The healer does this powerful general clearing, charging, and balancing of the field by first charging and opening her field, and then "allowing" the healing energy from the universe to simply flow through her into the client. The healer carefully places her hands on the client's feet and works her way up the body from there.

The client's field goes through its normal expansion-stasis-contraction-stasis pulses as the healer works. The healer first holds each hand on each foot, *allowing healing energy to flow.* Then the healer (if right-handed) moves to the right side of the client. She puts her right hand on the

bottom of the client's right foot, and her left hand on the client's right ankle, to allow energy to flow through her into the client's right foot and up into the client's right ankle. The healer then reaches over the body to do the same on the other side. After this area is charged, the healer moves up to the client's right ankle and knee, and so on, till she reaches the chakras. Then she continues up through the chakras, allowing the energy to flow naturally through the client's body.

See Figure 14–2 for the hand positions for a chelation. (If the healer is left-handed, she usually works on the left side of the body, with the left hand lower on the body rather than the right hand.) In either position—right side or left side—the healer moves up the body in "allow mode," clearing and charging the field. The healer does this simply by keeping her field charged and in allow mode. In this way the energy flows from the universe into the healer and then into the client. The client's field accepts the healing energy according to its needs. It determines how, when, and where it receives the energy flowing from the healer. The client's field also moves the energy it receives along the client's field lines to the area most needed.

Overview of the Wave: The healer uses HSP as well as general and specialized Brennan Healing Science techniques to clear the time capsule waste material and release the client's original creative energy consciousness that is still caught in the time capsule. The healer focuses on and follows the unfolding and enfolding of the HEF with the creative pulse of life. The HEF expands from deep inside the body through all the levels of the field, through the fourth level (where the time capsules are), and then through the higher levels out to the outer levels of the field. It reaches stasis, pauses, and then contracts down deep into the lower levels, to again reach stasis deep inside the body.

The Rhythmic Process of Expansion and Contraction in Time Capsule Healing: During this process, the client goes through the expansions and contractions of the creative pulse as it moves through his HEF.

If the healer continues to concentrate enough healing energy into the time capsule (for example, in Time Capsule 9/T9 (NOW) as shown in Figure 14–1), it will open and release its captured energy consciousness. When this happens, the client will relive the event that caused this wound. This wound could be from an earlier time in this life or from a previous life.

With more energy consciousness flowing into the time capsule, the next time capsule (for example, T8) will open, depending on which one already opened and released. With each release of a time capsule, more energy consciousness is released into the creative pulse of life, which supports the opening of the next. This process will continue backward through this lifetime. As we continue backward in time, eventually something strange may happen. The client may suddenly experience himself in a different time era on Earth, perhaps on a different continent.

During a healing, the pulse of expansion-stasis-contraction-stasis is echoed in the vertical power current. When the creative wave expands, the stagnated energy is pushed up the vertical power current. When the creative wave contracts down through the levels, the stagnated energy may move back down the vertical power current to re-compact, unless the healer stops it. It is the healer's job to stop the recompaction of the stagnated energy and to remove it on the expansion phase of the pulse. The skill needed here is to know the difference between the recompacting stagnant energy consciousness and the natural healthy enfoldment of the creative energies on their way back down into the core. This is what takes both practice and clear HSP. Luckily, there is a big difference between the healing energy and the stagnant blocked energy that needs to be healed.

The stagnated energy is dark,
dense, low energy, and dualistic.

The creative energy is clear,
holistic, vibrant, alive, and healing.

This full-body wave continues throughout the healing process as more and more stagnated dualistic energy consciousness is released and becomes whole. The healer uses specific, more advanced healing techniques (see next section) to dissolve the time capsule, and to release and invigorate its original creative pulse. Each particular healing technique is performed by the healer in accordance with what the HEF needs in the moment. The HEF changes with each expansion as the old, stagnated, unneeded energy consciousness is cleared and released.

Advanced Techniques Used in Time Capsule Healing: The healer uses more advanced techniques to charge the stagnant, sometimes toxic, waste material that has accumulated around and inside the original wound within the time capsule. This helps loosen and release the toxic material. The healer then removes the waste by grasping it (in pull mode) with energetic fingers, lifting it out of the field and up into the light. As the healer lifts it up through the higher HEF levels and out of the field, she transforms it into clear light. This is done in both the expansion and expanded-static phase of the wave pulses. In the contracting portion of the wave, the healer goes into allow mode and simply follows the wave back down deep into the body to get more of the debris.

Understanding the Released Creative Energy: During a healing, a great deal of the trapped energy consciousness is cleaned and released from the blocks that are held in the field. Once released, the energy will be able to continue on the creative endeavor that it had originally started, perhaps a long time ago. This energy can now integrate back into the client's creative life pulse through all the levels of the HEF, as well as the four dimensions of the HEC.

Now, in the present, it will be a creation that is more appropriate to the present life. It will correspond to the client's needs in this life, needs that are similar to those in the client's past life. And now, in the present time period, the client will possibly be able to fulfill the creation that was originally blocked long ago. The client has the same needs now in this life as when the creative pulse was originally blocked.

*Once the creative energy consciousness
is strong enough,
the original creative intention
can be fulfilled!*

Since there are many similar wounds in each time capsule, in the same location of the body, from many similar types of experiences that are repeated in many different time frames, it takes many healings to remove them all. Each must be cleaned and the field completely restored in the areas of major, chronic blocks. Thus the wave process continues throughout many healings until the field is finished being cleansed of that particular issue that needed healing.

All the while the healer is doing this work, she is also being deeply, lovingly, supportively present and connected with her client, helping the client experience safety during the healing, even though the client may, at the same time, not experience it in the events that unfold out of the time capsule. (During the healing, the client's body reacts to these events as if they were occurring now.)

Beginning healers must learn to remain present during the full healing in order to support the client. If a healer gets scared, she may withdraw her presence of support. This will undermine the healing, and the client will experience being abandoned during a time of need. This will then abort the healing, and the healer must start again at the beginning—if the client is willing, and if the healer is ready.

If the client refuses, the healer must respect the client's wishes and create an appropriate healing closure for that unfinished healing. Without a healing closing, such a situation is very difficult for the client, who may carry the split trauma into his life circumstances until the next healing. If this happens, I recommend that the healer try to schedule another healing as soon as possible with the client. In addition, and very importantly, the healer must clear herself of fear, either through process work and/or receiving a healing before attempting to give another healing to that client.

*It is the responsibility of the healer
to remain clear and maintain integrity.*

When the client is finished going through all the waves of the healing, she is clean, clear, and usually feels younger.

*The energy consciousness
that is released during a healing
is the same age it was
when the wound was created.
Since then, it has been
held in suspended animation!
For example, if a wound happened
when you were five years old,
that is the age of the newly released
energy consciousness!*

*It needs a few weeks to grow up,
to become integrated within the client
at his present age.*

This is why the healing continues to work through the field for several weeks after each healing. Usually this takes two to three weeks. The newly released creative energies continue through the rest of the field and all so-called future lives unless it is once again stopped.

Results of Time Capsule Healing: Each time a wound inside a time capsule is healed, more creative energy is released into one's creative process. Thus the creative endeavors that one has not been able to complete once again spring into life to accomplish the remaining portion of their creation. This process releases tremendous creative energy forces in the HEF for the purpose of re-creating one's life the way one wants it to be. Of course, time capsule healing also changes one's concept of how one wants one's life to be. It opens greater opportunities and uncovers more passion for and enjoyment of life, because it opens one into one's deepest longings, which have been trapped in the past as undigested, unintegrated, and unutilized valuable experience.

My Experience with Time Capsule Healings

A Client with a Sprained Leg: A client came to my office for his first healing. He had just re-wounded himself by spraining his leg. The accident happened because he was once again preoccupied by his perennial problem with his boss and didn't notice the rut in the bicycle path. Now he is limping home on one foot, bracing himself with his bike, and pissed at himself for crashing. He is also worried about the upcoming marathon. So he schedules an extra healing. During the first part of the healing, he becomes deeply relaxed as I first clear and charge his field. He continues to relax as I concentrate the healing energy consciousness directly into his wound. As the energy builds in the wound, he begins to react as it releases the memory and the emotions that have been trapped inside the wound area for many years. I support him with loving, healing energy as he goes through his time capsule and reexperiences the painful events in which he split his energy consciousness, captured it, and froze it into that time capsule. The increased energy in the time capsule brings some of the split pieces of his time capsule back together to become whole and clear again.

Now my client is ready for the next wave. His experience deepens and all his senses become hyperalert, as his creative force begins its expansion phase from deep inside him. As the healer, I must push more energy right behind the wave. In this expansion, his body reacts as the past becomes alive in it once again. What was left in the field now activates that experience. Time is released from its encapsulation and once again flows through his system as the full experience that he stopped centuries ago is released from its encapsulated prison within. He is struck with disbelief! He feels, hears, and sees as if it were all happening now inside and around his body. His eyes are closed. What he sees is not the familiar. He sees an ancient world around him. He recognizes it as ancient Rome. His inner voice is silently screaming,

I'm on the ground. . . . I can't move. . . . My leg is broken. I was just trampled by a horse! I'm scared. It's war. . . .

I continue to pump as much healing energy into his system as it and the client can take without breaking the field or disengaging the client. The portion of the time capsule in the life that he experiences fully comes together in wholeness and is released up and out of the field.

Then there is a pause, and his creative force reaches its maximum expansion point and goes into stasis. I immediately stop sending energy into the wound and go into allow mode, still remaining fully present and maintaining the client's needed state of being that supports his healing. In this case the state of being that the client needs is acceptance and surrender in peace. All is quiet for a moment. Then, as the field begins its contraction inward, he relaxes deep into himself, beginning another period of deep peace. As the healer, I follow, confirming that peace by becoming it in the silence of gathering in, automatically centering. I stay with him in attendance—not moving, simply being there, my hands quietly loving.

Then once again the client's field automatically begins its expansive phase. I follow, going into push right behind the wave, once again running healing energy into the wound. I follow the flow of energy as it comes together in wholeness, is released, and flows up the vertical power current! Another aspect of the ancient experience is released as another portion of time is released. He once again sees, feels, hears, and fully experiences the event in and around his body. His body reacts in pain and contraction as if the event were happening now. Once again, his inner monologue is activated:

Oh, no! Oh my God! I just don't believe this. It can't be . . . I'm, ahhh . . . I'm, ahhh . . . I'm in a woman's body!

To summarize, the healer must stay with the client as the healer continues to remain completely present while working on the client's HEF time capsule. The healer continues to go through the cycles with the client, and the client purposefully regulates the flow of healing energy through each phase of the HEF healing pulses. The client doesn't need to speak out loud. The healer is watching and listening to the scene as it unfolds while following the pulsations of the client's creative wave through its four phases of expansion, stasis, contraction, and stasis. This continues through many complete cycles. Each cycle releases more of the trapped energy consciousness and time from inside the wound of that particular life experience. Most of the release takes place during the crescendo of the expansive part of the wave. In the beginning of the healing, each full cycle builds to an expressive crescendo, sometimes even a panic, as the client feels and expresses the painful event as it happened. Continuing on, the crescendo begins to level off in the middle of the healing. Then toward the end of the healing, the crescendos of feeling—even though very deep—calm down. As the healing progresses, the client gathers more wholeness, integration, light, and love. Then the waves of crescendos simply cease to be. The client lies in peace and harmony—"spent," as it were, in a good way. The body and HECS have reached a new state of harmony. The client is now capable of containing and wielding a greater amount of creative energy via his creative pulse of life. The client will remain in a vulnerable as well as deep contemplative state for some time after the healing, usually for hours, sometimes days. The healing continues to unfold for many weeks.

A Client Who Could Not Ask for Help: This client's presenting complaint was that she was unable to ask for help for anything in her life. She had no idea of what could have caused this fear. During the time capsule healing I gave her, she went back to the time of the great sailing ships. She reexperienced herself as a sailor in a storm at sea on the way to the Americas. Her body (his body, at the time) felt the entire experience. During the time capsule healing, her (his) physical body and HEF struggled with the rolling ship and the great waves washing over her. Then everything unfolded as it had then. She (he) was suddenly washed overboard. She (he) repeatedly called for help, but none of her (his) buddies could hear her. She (he) drowned, feeling that no matter

how much she (he) asked for help, it did no good. At the close of the healing, she was peaceful and calm, still integrating all that had happened. She went home in a deep contemplative state.

The next week, when she returned, I asked, "How are you doing with asking for help?"

"Great, so far. Every time I've wanted it, I've asked for it, and they've helped me! Oh, and by the way, I also got over my fear of drowning!"

"You hadn't mentioned that before."

"Yeah, I didn't know the two were related at all. I went in the pool and had a great time. I'm going to take swimming lessons."

A Client with Claustrophobia: This client came in with the presenting complaint of being very uncomfortable in small spaces. She could hardly tolerate them and wouldn't stay in them. During a time capsule healing, she reexperienced being a man chained to the wall in a prison during the Middle Ages in Europe where she eventually died. After the healing she did better in small spaces but still doesn't like them. She also commented that "now I know why I hate dark, badly lit rooms. Being outside at night in the dark is okay, but boy, do I hate dark rooms."

A Client with Poverty Consciousness: This client was very poor and died a number of times from poverty, so now he saves pennies. He is beginning to learn how to enjoy the money he earns.

A Client Who Had Weak Legs: During this time capsule healing, this man went facedown on the floor. He became pinned to the floor and couldn't move his legs. He experienced fire all around him and realized that a pillar had fallen, breaking both of his legs. He was also trapped under its great weight. He was in anguish because he was unable to rush home and help his wife and children survive the earthquake. After the time capsule healing, he was much more comfortable leaving home when he needed to for work. His legs also got stronger as he healed.

Important Points about the Many-Lives Theory of Human Existence and Time Capsule Healing

The talents we are born with can be seen as things we learned in other life experiences. Our innate core qualities are the higher principles by which we most naturally live. We have gone through the long process of developing them in other lives and have brought them into this lifetime. Our wounds can be seen as our unfinished creations that have fallen off our creative pulse of life. Time capsule healing is a way to reinstate our unfinished creations to bring them into fruition. We think we can avoid repeating our unresolved experiences from this and other lifetimes by avoiding experiencing our wounds. This is not true.

Avoiding our wounds is maintaining the duality that is held there. This simply leads to the creation of more duality, which causes more confusion, pain, suffering, low energy, blocked creativity, and wounding. We create entire lifestyles around our unexplained fears held in our time capsules.

Releasing our creative process requires that we go inside our wounds to complete the experience that we stopped. By being present in it—i.e., by feeling our emotions and allowing our thoughts that are locked inside to flow—we bring those two aspects of ourselves that were split from each other back together. In doing so, we free that creative energy consciousness, which then continues on its original creative wave to its completion.

This is how we re-create our lives the way we long for them to be.

Rather than considering karma as punishment for our "sins," it can be seen first as simply the reactions from our past creations. Taken a step further into understanding the implications of time capsules, karma can simply be the dualistic/unsatisfactory creations we continue to make because we have not yet brought the duality in our time capsules into wholeness, so they are still not part of our healthy creative process. Since they are still held in duality, they are still creating dualistically, thus the products of their creations are dualistic, not holistic, and therefore unhealthy and split into "good" and "bad."

Why Time Capsule Healing Is Better Than Past-Life Healing

Time capsule healing releases us from our fictitious unhealthy habit of victimhood. If there is no clear explanation to our situation that empowers us to change it, we easily fall into victimhood. We have the feelings of helpless victims because we don't know how to heal ourselves and our lives. Blaming our troubles on someone else's actions toward us, whether in this lifetime or a different one, doesn't help us *because it appears to give them power over our lives.* Actually, this is impossible, but when we act as if it were true, we remain victims. Why? Because we don't understand the processes that have been described in this chapter. Time capsule healing changes all this. It releases the blame we put on others for our state of inadequacy. Our problems that may have been initiated in relationship to another person do not depend on that other person.

Our problems, our wounds, are held in place by ourselves! They are held in our unfinished experiences inside our wounds. They are held in the duality maintained in our wounds. Our healing depends on bringing our inner duality together into wholeness, to regenerate our original creative endeavor that then joins our creative pulse of life. Once we have accomplished this, we have released our creative processes that will complete our original creative desires.

This creation is what we have longed for all our lives. It is our responsibility to focus on and complete our unfinished experiences that are still locked inside our wounds. This is what causes our problems in creating our lives, and not that someone somewhere in our close or distant past that has done something dreadful to us!

In this process we fulfill our longings, build our lives, and, in so doing, complete ourselves!

Understanding and living this gives us great freedom!

Welcome to your new life!

Chapter 14 Self-Review: Reinterpreting "Past Lives" as Time Capsules

1. Reinterpret your particular wounds and past-life experiences as time capsules. Give yourself time to write about this experience in your journal.

2. List the major time capsules in your field that need healing, and their original intent for creation.

3. What basic duality is held in the time capsule that prevents your creation from coming to fruition? This duality will most likely blame the other person. Under it lies a fear you had about your ability to create what you wanted. This prevented you from moving ahead with your creation. How can you do that now in your life? What form would it take? (It could be the same form, it could be a different one. There is always an opportunity waiting.)

Chapter 15

THE HEF OF DYING

You are not a slave to three dimensions
nor to the so-called arrow of time,
relentlessly moving forward
toward your so-called death.

Death is simply a change of form,
a letting go to
an expansion of being.

— HEYOAN

Here in the West, it appears that many of us want a fast, painless death to get it over with. We don't want to be present—for it or in it. We tend to think that we won't have to deal with it if we are not present and if we go fast. But, from my observations of the HEF during and after death, this is not true.

It is said that in the East, they pray for a slow death. Perhaps because that gives the person some time to adjust to the process. This makes sense. Yet there is more. Another reason for time to adjust to one's death is what happens in the field at death. I will describe that later. But first, here are some of my HSP experiences around death that have opened the way for me.

Post-Death Visits

One of my first experiences observing HEF events around someone's death occurred one day when working in the BBSH office in East Hampton,

NY. I was sitting at my desk doing paperwork. A woman who also worked in the office was sitting behind me at her desk. I will call her Carol. It was a perfectly normal office workday until Carol's recently deceased mother walked up the stairs and came into the room. I looked up to see her move toward her daughter. The mother was trying to get Carol's attention, but to no avail. I contemplated whether or not to tell Carol as I watched what might happen. I didn't want to cause Carol more pain in her mourning process. Then I saw that Carol's mom was trying to contact Carol through their relational cord connections. I noticed that her mom's intention was to send vital knowledge to Carol through their relational cords. It was a distilled form of knowledge that Carol's mom had learned in this most recent lifetime. Then I knew I had to tell Carol what was going on.

When I did, Carol quickly went into a state of gratitude, and meditated to stay completely present and reconnected to her mother. She opened herself to receive what her mother then gave her.

145

It looked like clear consciousness flowing through the heart cords from her mother to her heart. When she was finished, Carol's mom kissed her, bid her farewell, and left—down the stairs and out the door! I surmised that using the door and taking the stairs was from habit. Apparently she did not yet realize that she could have just floated into the room without need of doors or stairs.

We sat in reverence and gratitude: I for what I had witnessed, Carol for what she had received. We, in silent tears, continued to hold the sacred space. Love enveloped the whole office.

My Father's Last Good-Bye

Many years ago, my mother attended a workshop I was giving in Boston. It was her first time attending a workshop I was giving. The workshop went along its normal course. On Sunday morning, we did the normal goddess healing meditation. (Everyone asks me, but I do not know why this meditation became known as the "goddess healing." I did not name it.) During this healing, I walked through the meditating students, channeling high spiritual energies, somewhat like the Holy Spirit or Shekinah. I went around to each attendant, surrendering to the white light that flowed down over me and into the attendant. When I got to my mother, I noticed that my father was hanging on to her back for dear life. He had been sick with Alzheimer's for a long time, and she was getting exhausted. I released him from her back and then focused on the white light as it flowed through her.

At the next workshop, held shortly after in Long Island, NY, once again everything was going normally. At lunch on Saturday, I went up to my room in the hotel. There I received a phone call from my brother telling me that Dad had just died. I immediately went into a meditation in my room, thinking that I would help him if he became disoriented when he left his body. I had done it for others many times shortly after their death. But that is not what happened. Instead, my father came into the room and proceeded, in a very determined way, to fill me with the distilled wisdom he had learned in his life. At the end of it, he asked me to channel in the workshop instead of doing my normal lecture, because he had never seen me channel.

When I went back into the workshop after lunch, in tears I told the students,

"My dad just died. My sister, Sandy, and my brother, David, were with Mom in the hospital with Dad. They formed a circle holding hands around the bed. Mom held one of Dad's hands and Dave the other. They said it was a gentle death. Dave asked, 'How are you doing, Pop?' And on his last breath, Dad answered, 'Just fine.'"

A student responded, speaking for the group. "Well, don't you want to be alone for a while? We understand. You don't have to keep teaching."

"Oh no! I have just been talking to Dad, and he asked me a special favor. He wants me to channel because he never got a chance to see me do it."

"Oh! Are you sure? Well, okay!" the students said in amazement.

The Heyoan channeling was beautiful. It focused on how beautiful death, as well as life, can be, and how we always remain connected to our loved ones after death—perhaps, in some cases, even more strongly.

Then, shortly after the channeling started, I saw Dad come into the room. He was there with my aunt Grace, his sister who had died several years earlier, and I got a surprise. Dad had also brought his mother with him! It was a real treat for me. I had never known my grandmother, as she had died when father was only eight years old. He was so happy to see her again! (She is beautiful. Looks a bit like my cousin Jane.)

At first I was so caught up in my personal experience that I did not notice the rest of the room. Then, turning my attention to the students, I saw that the entire room was filled with many ancestors of all the workshop participants. Some participants were aware of the presence of their ancestors; others were not. I continued to channel Heyoan. He proceeded to tell everyone what was going on. Heyoan then led a healing that took place between each participant and their deceased relatives. This included healing and reconnecting the cords of relationship, as well as releasing ancestral roots between the relatives in the physical and in the spiritual. (See Chapters 17 and 18 for healing cords and roots.)

After the workshop was finished for that day everyone had quite a night, basking in the love of family. Years later, I found out that a woman who had had to cancel her participation in the Boston workshop did so because her mother had died. She was present for this one in Long Island. She saw her mother come into the room during this Heyoan channeling/healing. This enabled her to communicate with her mother. She decided to take the BBSH training as well, and ended up becoming a teacher at BBSH.

Mom Waits for Her Sisters to Come

My mother died slowly, from the feet up. Day after day, my sister and I sat with her. People came to give love, respect, and thanks. Or just to be there. Some watched while my sister and I attended; others kept their distance. All simply waited.

Mom was the youngest of seven sisters. She also had seven brothers. All had passed before her. She wanted to live to be 100, but was just two years short of her goal.

We waited. She endured the pain, remaining half here, half there, in and out of the body. Waking with a startle, looking at us now and then. Hospice came and went. Time passed more slowly each moment. My sister and I felt more honored each time we had the privilege of changing her diaper, remembering how she had done it for us. Her breath changed to Cheyne-Stokes respiration.

I kept asking, "Where are they? Why haven't her sisters come yet?" I had expected them to come and hover around the bedside. I was beginning to get very angry at them for delaying. Then I thought that since they all had passed so long ago, perhaps for some reason it took longer to gather together.

Then my mom turned her head toward us and looked at Sandy and me sitting there, our heads together ear to ear, our hands on her flowing with love, encouraging her to let go. As she looked deeply into our eyes, a tear rolled out of each of her eyes and down her face into her pillow. She turned her head toward the heavens and left as her sisters swooped down to help her away. As she began to leave her body, I worked with her HECS and pushed white light up her vertical power current to assist her clean departure.

Then came the deafening silence.

We sat there in silence, honoring and touching her body with love and gratitude. Later, we called hospice. They came and reverently took her body for cremation. As she had requested, my brother spread her ashes in the many lakes in north-central Wisconsin where he had done the same for my father. We all had spent many summers camping there together.

Marjorie

By the time Marjorie came to BBSH as a student, I had been channeling the goddess healing meditation alone for years. During the goddess meditation, a wall of white light comes into the room. It is always at least as big as the wall behind me, depending on the size of the wall behind me. The largest was about forty feet high and thirty feet wide. Many spiritual beings come into the room to participate in the goddess healings.

When Marjorie came the whole ceiling of the room would open above us. I would see tiers and tiers of angels, extending up through the hierarchy, to a blinding white light at the top. It was wonderful, and it was about to get even better!

Marjorie was trained at Juilliard, and had played with the Atlanta Symphony Orchestra. While still a student at BBSH, I convinced her to bring her harp to school. In those days, she was very shy about playing in front of her classmates. I had a secret plan to get her to channel the harp. I knew she could do it, but she didn't—that is, at first. She did play sheet music for her classmates. Then I tricked her. At the opening ceremony of the school one week, I asked her to play the four directions (an ancient Native American ceremony) as a student representing each direction called the direction in while holding a crystal. Finally Marjorie let herself be free and she channeled the four directions. It was beautiful.

After Marjorie played the four directions a few times, I asked her to play up on the stage with me for the goddess healing. We witnessed a beautiful miracle unfold. That miracle, luckily for us, lasted for years. From then on, Marjorie channeled her exquisite harp music for the goddess for many years. Each time she channeled the harp, it was as if the heavens opened up. *Actually, they did!* It was the music of the heart, the music of the spheres, the music of the spiritual worlds come to earth to bless us. I felt so blessed. I was living in heaven on earth every time I channeled with her! Each time we did the goddess together, more spiritual beings would come. My colleague Rosanne joined us on the stage to my left. She held a cylindrical light beam that grounded the whole, very sacred process.

Once Marjorie started channeling the harp, she and my colleagues Rosanne, Michael, and Levent traveled with me to do workshops. We did as many as twelve a year, all over the United States, in addition to the then six weeks of BBSH resident training. We had a ball and we all became great platonic buddies. We laughed and played together like kids in a candy shop. Marjorie sat on my right and Rosanne on my left during the goddess healings. After a while, Marjorie started complaining that she did not have enough notes on the harp. (By then, she was bringing the largest harp made to school.) Marjorie wanted more high notes. She said that her arms kept moving higher till they tried to play above the harp, but there were no strings there!

I begged Marjorie to record what she played, but she wouldn't. I begged her to put a mike inside her harp and give me permission to record it. Finally, and unfortunately after many years, she had a mic put inside her harp and she let me record her playing on the school's equipment. But unfortunately, it was toward the end and only a few recordings were done.[6]

After years of wonderful work together, Marjorie found a lump in her breast. It never had occurred to me to check her out with HSP. When I did, I knew immediately that it was cancer. Unfortunately, with HSP, I also knew that I couldn't stop it. I saw that it was already in the lymph nodes. The normal medical procedures took their course. Rosanne and I were there when the doctor told her. She continued to play for most of the next year. Then she decided to spend the rest of her time with her beloved Rob and his little daughter, whom she loved.

Her funeral was held in a large church in New Jersey just outside New York City. I sat on the aisle so I could see with HSP what Marjorie was going to do during it. They brought her coffin into the church covered with a purple cloth with a large golden cross. Here is what I witnessed with HSP:

Marjorie had a golden sphere in her left hand. She was wearing pure white robes. Her hair was as pure white as her robes. She had a golden halo around her head, and golden stars above that. Marjorie's lower half flowed together in robes of white, becoming narrower as she extended down into the coffin. There her spiritual body connected down into her physical body.

The architecture of the church itself is shaped like a cross. About three-quarters of the way into the church is the place where the architecture of the church makes the arms of the cross and the vertical shaft of the cross come together. The pallbearers set the coffin down in that place. The priest then walked down the aisle to where the coffin was. He chanted words in Latin and sprinkled holy water onto the coffin. When he did that, the spiritual body of Marjorie disconnected completely from her physical body. As she floated up toward the high ceiling of the church, she began to take on her more normal form but, of course, remained of spiritual consistency. (I have no idea why this happened. I did not

6   Downloads of Marjorie and Barbara's channeling are available on the school's website.

expect it to. It was as if something was left out of the prayers that were said in Latin.)

At first she watched the ceremony from the rafters, floating from one to the other, still in white robes, as she responded to what was being said. Then, when her younger brother was talking about her, she completely resumed her normal looks and clothes. She came down and stooped next to me in the aisle. I was glad I had an aisle seat—she had more room in the aisle. She kept telling me how proud she was of her brother, and how nervous she was for him because he had been so afraid to give a eulogy. Then she started giggling and joking about all that was happening. She was so excited to see everyone there, and surprised so many people had come. She also kept joking about how serious the priest was. She said, *"He is always pontificating like that! He just keeps going, nobody can keep up. But he means well. We all love him so."*

At the end of the funeral, she left with her family members.

Marjorie's Continued Presence

For many years, Marjorie still came and played at the goddess healings. She was very excited because, as she said,

Finally I have the high notes I have always wanted! Can you hear them?

For many classes, Marjorie moved up the levels of the hierarchy that appear above us during the goddess healing. I don't know what that movement meant. Each time I taught, I saw her getting higher toward the high ceiling of the lecture hall I was teaching in. I thought that she was preparing to leave. Then after several months, she told me that she would leave soon, and she did.

How Death Shows in the HEF

During my tunnel test,[7] I learned personally what it is like to leave the body. Later, during the time I was working with dying people, it was a good thing to know, because I was able to describe to them what it would be like.

During the tunnel test, I felt a strong force pulling me out of my body as my healing teacher and Sai Baba pulled me out. I went up the vertical power current. I could feel/hear the wind blowing inside me as I rushed out of my physical body. I felt it on the inside of my eardrums, but it was different from a normal wind, because

I was the wind
that was blowing on my eardrums
from my inside!

I also regularly channeled Heyoan to my clients who were going to die. Usually the conversation between the client and Heyoan would be about the dying experience they were about to have, as well as last-minute details about their love for their family and friends.[8]

The Silver Cord: Travel in the astral world is actually quite different from death, but it can help us get used to being outside the physical body, and learn to function in the fourth-level HEF reality without a physical body.[9] A "silver cord," as it is called, connects the fourth-level HEF reality and higher spiritual HEF levels to the physical body. In fourth-level HEF reality travel, the lower three levels of the HEF stay in their normal place as part of every aspect of the cellular structure of the physical body, while the fourth-level HEF reality body travels through the fourth-level HEF reality. The silver cord keeps the fourth-level HEF reality body connected to the physical body during fourth-level HEF reality travel. One might think of it as an umbilical cord between the physical body and the fourth-level HEF reality body and higher HEF-level-reality bodies. Since the silver cord does not exist in the physical

---

7   See Chapter 7.

8   At the time of this writing, I do not have a private healing practice. I closed my healing office many years ago. I do not give individual healings anymore. There are plenty of BBSH graduates who do. See the BBSH website to find a healer near you.

9   For a description of the fourth-level HEF reality, see Chapters 8 and 9.

dimension, you don't have to worry about it getting stretched too much in far distant travel through other HEF realities! The cord is very flexible and can stretch throughout the fourth-level HEF realities. In physical death, the silver cord disconnects from its insertions into the physical body.

When I first saw the silver cord, I was surprised to see that it bifurcates (splits into two cords) about a foot outside the skin. One cord of the bifurcated end inserts into the brain (at the center, where the tips of the seventh and sixth chakras come together in the third ventricle); the other into the center of the heart chakra in the upper posterior area of the heart, near the crux of the heart. Figure 15–1 shows the silver cord and its two insertions into the physical body.

The fourth, or astral, level of the HEF is commonly called the *astral body*. Our astral body is the body we have when we are awake and aware in the astral world. The astral world is more like the stuff of dreams. Our astral body is the body in which we experience our dreams. Our astral body experiences astral reality.

I noticed that during heart transplant surgery the cord is disconnected at the heart end only. One ought to have it properly reinserted by a healer after heart replacement surgery. (I have done this when it was needed. It shortened recovery time.) I am not sure what to do with a mechanical heart replacement. Oh—Heyoan just told me that,

What we would do is to rebuild the HEF of a normal heart in that place, insert the cord into it, and then synchronize the heartbeat of the HEF heart with the mechanical heart. There are a few other additional detailed procedures that would need to be followed to assure synchronization, but they are beyond the scope of this book.

The HEF Changes in Physical Death: In physical death, the lower three levels of the HEF dissolve and dissipate. When someone is experiencing a slow death from an illness, one can observe the three lower levels with HSP as they slowly waft off the body in a cloudy mist. This may take a few days to complete. The following is a description of the process that takes place in the HEF.

In the process of dying, the entire HEF circulates down around through the field and then all of its energy consciousness rushes up through the vertical power current and—hopefully, but not always—out the crown. Figure 15–2 shows the circulation of the HEF at death. This is very disorienting in a sudden death, because as the field circulates, all the blocks, wounds, misconceptions, and dualities that were not made whole in this life circulate through the vertical power current, and, of course, the psyche! In other words, all your defenses let go at once and you experience your fears and wounds as they flow up through your vertical power current. This is a lot to deal with in that moment, and can be very disorienting. By resisting it, one can easily get caught in negative thought-forms, ERs, or IRs, and have an agonizing death. As I mentioned in Chapter 11, this is certainly what happens to people who overdose on so-called recreational drugs. Many of them die in great disorientation, horror, and abject terror, which then leaves them caught in the lower fourth HEF level (or lower astral realms) after death. It is not a pretty sight to see.[10]

During the moment of death the silver cord completely disconnects from the physical body, and as far as I can tell from my few observations, it dissolves. The individual is then freed from that physical body, if s/he wishes to be. I could tell from my observations of both Marjorie and others at their funerals that they were no longer attached by the silver cord, but were somehow energetically hovering over and down into the solar plexus area of the physical body. I do not fully understand this yet. I need to make more observations of this particular phenomenon. It may be a way to stay

---

10   I have seen many individuals in great pain during my many trips into the nether hell worlds. During the full school goddess healing meditation, I regularly followed the angels down into those dark places called hell, to help the poor souls stuck there come up into higher realms where they could connect with their guides.

in contact with the physical world during the funeral as an opportunity for a last good-bye.

One of the reasons Eastern people pray for a slow death may be that during the process of slow death, as I have seen, the individual gets a chance to complete lagging issues, to tie up loose ends, and to say heartfelt good-byes. The process of long illness sometimes affords this opportunity; it offers time and space to deal with the leftover clearing of blocks for this lifetime that is ending. It's kind of like a last-minute house cleaning. I have seen this process while attending to people who are slowly dying of an incurable disease. Many friends and family come to give their love, pay their last respects, say their last appreciative words. This is very good for the dying person. But in the very last couple of days, it is important that just the closest loved ones—such as husband, wife, mother, father, siblings, and other very close relatives—be there.

I have witnessed their blocks dissolving and wafting off the field as the person urgently faces crucial, unresolved issues and sinks deeper into unconditional love with the significant members of their family and friends who come to say their last good-byes. Thus, in letting go of this life, they have time to receive help to be present, thereby letting go of the resistance to dying and to leaving the physical world in peace.

Preparing for Death the Eastern Way

Another reason Eastern people traditionally meditate to prepare for death is to learn how to regulate and clear the mind to become *luminous emptiness*, so that they can maintain *true clarity* at the moment of death and thereby avoid the pitfalls of the dying experience.[11] The *Tibetan Book of the Dead* is a guide that helps the dying person not get caught up in their duality as they go through the stages of death. It was written to be studied during physical life, and then read aloud during the dying process by an attendant at the bedside. Through listening, the dying person is directed to

higher levels of existence than the physical world. Even worlds of no duality, or at least, depending on the individual, to move into a better circumstance of reincarnation. The study called Poha is also a form of Tibetan Buddhist meditation to learn to bypass reentry into the physical world and go to a state of existence in higher spiritual realms.

All of this is now available to Westerners who wish to study it, thanks to the Dalai Lama and various Tibetan lamas.

How to Handle the Death of a Loved One for Their Benefit and Yours

1. Do not assume that you cannot contact them.

2. Believe it when they do contact you. Or just try pretending that it will happen, or is happening.

3. When you get the feeling of a presence, just calm down and act like it is your loved one, as it usually is. Calming yourself will help you sense their presence.

4. Open to what they want to tell you by sitting quietly open and receptive to them.

5. Let yourself be thankful for all they have given you in their life. Focus on them. If it seems appropriate, tell them what you are thankful for.

6. Honor their life. Let your gratitude for their presence flow through you, while you receive what they are giving you.

7. You may or may not feel it or know what it is. That is okay. You got it. *Remember it may be distilled wisdom rather than words.* You may suddenly know what it is some days later, when you are not even thinking about it. That is okay. Let it be what it is.

---

11   See *Luminous Emptiness: Understanding the Tibetan Book of the Dead,* by Francesca Fremantle, Shambhala, Boston, 2001.

Mourning the Death of a Loved One

There is simply nothing anyone can do to bring back your loved one. While we humans like to think we are more powerful than we actually are, sometimes we just have to admit we aren't. Mourning is an important and natural part of living. In mourning, simply be there in the pain and with your love for the one who has crossed over. At times you may feel the presence of your loved one in spirit form. Or, perhaps, you won't. Surrender to your process of mourning. It takes time. Let it be what it is. Give it to yourself, let yourself experience the gift of knowing this person—that gift will never go away. It is inside you forever.

It is good to be with one or two very good friends who can handle your pain by also simply being there in the pain with you in loving presence. There is nothing one can do to bring your loved one back into physical form.

A good Brennan Healing Practitioner who has graduated from one of my schools can give you a core star healing that would help a lot.

Essentially this type of healing would clear and charge your HEF, restructure your chakras, align and strengthen your hara, and upwell your core star throughout your cells and being, filling you with unconditional love. This would strengthen and relax you to help you handle your pain. Feel free to speak with your loved one at any time. Speak silently or out loud if you wish.

Chapter 15 Journaling/Self-Review: Getting Clear about Death

1. Remember your experiences of the death of your loved ones. What were your experiences?

2. How do you understand them better after reading this chapter?

3. How did you handle the mourning of your loved one?

4. Did you have any experiences where you felt your loved one tried to contact you?

Chapter 16

LIFE AFTER DEATH

What is your personal experience of so-called nothingness?
What is between the physical and the energetic?
Nothing. No-thing.

Humankind has defined nothing or no-thing as an empty Void and equated it with an absence of life.

Yet you have discovered that this so-called void
can be equated with the zero-point field
that is full of life and energy—
more life and energy than
all of the manifest universe together!

So that which is called no-thing, or nothing,
is actually teeming life.

Humanity's biggest problem or deepest issue is its belief in death.

Humanity believes that death actually exists!
And yet the void, Brahman, is all that there is:
the you, the knowledge, the wisdom,
the unified whole that underlies and is within all things
and is in all of the so-called space between all things.

— HEYOAN

After Marjorie's death, I decided to learn more about the processes that take place after death and how to help people going through that transition. I knew just where to go. I had already read a couple of Robert Monroe's books.[12] I checked out the Monroe Institute's literature. They had just what I wanted, and an opening right when I could get away, so I signed up. My main goal in doing this was to learn the system they had created and developed to travel into other realities (i.e., travel out of the body), and also, once one is proficient in that, to assist people to go to a way station after they leave their bodies at death.

---

12   *Journeys out of the Body, Far Journeys,* and several other books.

The Work of Robert Monroe

Robert Monroe did a great job clarifying how to get out of the body and how to travel in the nonphysical worlds. With the use of the Hemi-Sync sound system described in Chapter 7, Robert was able to teach people to enter deep states of meditation in a very short time. By entering deep states of meditation, people can then learn to travel the nonphysical worlds, as the Tibetans and shamans have done for centuries.

Robert found that certain brain states correspond to the experience of different nonphysical worlds. He delineated levels of the nonphysical world with numbers, each related to a different brain/mind state. Within some of these levels are what he called the *belief system territories*.[13] Robert also developed many techniques to help people during the dying process and to guide them to an after-death way station.

In the following four sections, I will describe my deep and personal learning experiences I had at the Monroe Institute.

Meditation Experience at the Monroe Institute: Several years ago, I attended two weeks of workshops at the Monroe Institute. What happened for me was amazing. I didn't expect it at all. It started with a simple group exercise. It was in the creative/intuitive drawing class. After a short meditation, we were asked to draw a picture of something significant to us. I drew a small dark spot, about the size of a dime. That was all there was on the paper. We were working in pairs. Our partners were supposed to help us understand our drawings. I asked my partner what it was.

He said, "Why, that's a bindu!"

"What's a bindu?" I asked.

"You go through it." That was all he would tell me.

So I meditated for a while focusing on the bindu and then went through it. What follows is my experience during that meditation:

I found myself floating among the clouds. They were tinged with pink and orange. Some angels flew by in a group. They were having a conversation, but I couldn't tell what they were saying.

"Where are you going?" I asked.

"We are going to the thunder to see creation. Would you like to come?"

"Yes!" With great curiosity, I joined them.

The thunder was deafening, like many H-bombs going off all at the same time. There were all the colors one could imagine and more. Yet it was all sweet, soft, and felt very safe. I had no idea what the angels were doing there. Were they just watching or were they up to something else?

The next thing I realized was that I was a boy of about ten to twelve years old in the Himalayas. My mother was taking me up the mountain to the monastery. I was scared. I didn't know what was about to happen. She left me there with them.

Time passed.

Now I was a bit older. The monks were walling me up in a cave. They were filling in the entrance to the cave with bricks made of mud, straw, and stones. It was a nice cave. I had gone there often. There was a trickle of water in the back of the cave, and a low ledge along one side. I could tell it had been used this way before. The buildings of the monastery were on both sides of the cave; they were about a quarter mile away. They were built into the cliff sides. I was both excited and terrified as the last brick went in. There was a narrow slit at the top of the bricks about five inches high. Each day, they put a bowl of porridge on the bricks that form the lower ledge of the slit.

Time passed.

I was still in the cave. I was writing information I had learned in meditation. There was a row of books along the wall that I had already written. My pen looked like it was a simple narrow piece of bamboo that had been cut at one end into a sharp point.

The ink seemed to be made of a black powder, some of which was made of soot from a wood fire that was mixed with a little ground black earth or coal and some sort of oil, ox blood, and a bit of water. Apparently the monks had provided me with this, as I did not have a knife or other tools. My outer robe-like clothes were dark orange with some brown garments under them. I had a blanket for the cold winter weather.

Time passed again.

I was an old man. I was still in the cave. I was now in the dying process. I was ready to leave my body. I took another look around. I wanted to remember how this beautiful cave looked when I returned. There were about fifteen books. They looked sort of like pages of a book, but were held inside larger sheets that were folded over. They were not rolled up. They were journals of my meditative experiences. In my early years in the cave I had learned how to get out of my body to travel the world. I had become very interested in the West, and had gone there many times. I easily passed out of my body as it died.

But the tradition was that I must remain there in the cave until my body decayed and turned to dust. I waited.

Time passed.

I had been waiting for years. I had been sitting there above the head of the skeleton that had no flesh. It was lying in the middle of the floor of the cave. Waiting.

Finally, I took my leave. Once out of the cave, I took my bearing as I always had from the two highest peaks on either side. I turned to the left and left for the West to find a new body.

I came upon a woman in a cottage that was originally an old goat shed. The woman was in labor and having a hard time. The baby was stuck in the birth canal. The cord was strangling the little girl. The little girl kept leaving her body to talk with her guides to figure out whether or not to let go of this birth opportunity and leave the little body that is suffocating.

In her previous life, she had died in a place called Ireland, at only ten or eleven years old. An ox cart full of straw had hit and run over her. The driver hadn't noticed at first. Orphaned, she had been in such despair, famished with nothing to eat. Too far gone to notice the cart coming. Her dress had been made of two gunnysacks, green with grass stain, and roughly hand-stitched together.

I approached the guides at the birth scene. This was an opportunity for healing and rebirth. I suggested that I go into the body with her, and be born with her. I could use the power I had from such long meditations to complete the birth. She could have her life for a number of years while I waited. I would then begin to merge with her. She would always know I was there inside, even though that would be confusing to her. Then I would emerge little by little to teach what I had written in my books, which were still in the cave. She thought about it and asked,

"You mean I will never be alone again?"

"Yes, that is the way it will be."

"Okay."

I rolled into her body with her. After birth we lay together in silence for three days. I became the quiet voice inside, the one that knows. She was the one who wanted to know—*everything*!

When I told my partner in the art class what I had experienced, his response was, "Okay, let's go get your books."

"You're kidding."

"No, I'm not kidding. Do you know where the cave is?"

"Yes. When I look with HSP, I can see Everest on the left and another mountain on the right. I see two rivers down below. The cave is on the slope of a smaller mountain below. I think my name was Nyang Tsang—or, actually I think I may not have had a name. Well, something had that name.

I'm confused. I always think that Everest is on the right, not the left. Do you have a map?"

"No."

"Oh! Wait a minute. I always picture the Himalayas looking down at India from the north, not up from the south. I bet the cave is facing north!"

"That makes more sense."

And that was only the first day of the workshop!

The workshop continued to progress and I continued to have experiences that were "out of this world."

Robert Monroe

One day, during the second week of the workshop, Robert Monroe came in. As we sat in a circle, he said he was having some physical problems, and asked if there was a healer in the room. Everyone turned to me. I said I would be glad to give him a healing, and asked if he had a healing table and a private room we could go to.

A healing table was produced in minutes. Robert was not interested in a private room, so I proceeded to give him a healing in the center of the circle. Rather than go into a deep state of relaxation with his eyes closed, he held his head up in his arms and watched me carefully. With HSP, I saw his recently deceased wife come into the room in fourth-level-reality form and stand on his left, opposite me.

Nodding my head toward her, I asked, "Do you see who is here?"

"Yes," he said.

I continued the healing. He communicated with her through telepathy. She was trying to comfort him. He was still in deep mourning for her.

Toward the end of the healing, he turned back to me and asked, "Do you know that you are five hundred thousand years old?"

"Yes!" I had known this for many years, but never mentioned it to anyone because it was so preposterous. He went on to ask, "Do you know that your name is Chiana?" (Pronounced "kee-aa-na.")

"Yes," I answered quietly, hoping that no one could hear us.

"I remember a life I lived five hundred thousand years ago. The place was also called Chiana. It was a beautiful island garden of peace and love. Flowers everywhere. I was a healer. But I don't understand that. There was nothing to heal! Thanks for the confirmation!"

Robert seemed very pleased to be telling me this. The healing continued without further conversation as he continued to intensely watch everything I did with great interest.

Robert was clearly contemplating his departure. He had a serious case of pneumonia. He told me that he no longer left his body to go traveling because he was afraid he would not come back. He was missing his wife so much.

Robert Monroe's Extraordinary Death: After the workshop ended, I stayed later to give Robert another healing. This time it took place in his living room. Robert's daughter Laurie Monroe and several other members of his family watched and took notes. His wife (in fourth-level HEF reality form) was there again. I channeled Heyoan in the healing. A lot of the healing was a long discussion between Heyoan and Robert about his work of building bridges between the physical and the spiritual worlds, and how the work would continue in the spiritual worlds. That was when I saw the Monroe Institute up in the spiritual world at what Robert called "level 27." I had seen the way station at level 27, but had not noticed that there was a Monroe Institute up there also. The institute at level 27 is much bigger than the one on the earth plane.

Robert's deceased wife was in the room again, standing at his left side. Robert got more and more excited as his discussion with Heyoan continued. I don't remember much of it because I was channeling. It was not recorded, and I never saw the notes that Laurie Monroe and the others were taking.

Later, toward the end of the healing, Heyoan told Robert about the big welcome party they had planned up in the Monroe Institute at level 27. With HSP, I saw them up there, with party hats, confetti, and a big chocolate cake.

Toward the end of the healing something happened that I had never seen before. It astounded me. Robert's wife, in fourth-level HEF reality, came close to his left side, and stretched out parallel to his body as if lying—but actually floating—next to him. Then, with a quick turn to her right, she rolled lengthwise into his body with him. I had never seen two people in one body together! I wondered if they had enough room in there, but then I saw how happy they both were to be in there together!

As I was leaving after the healing, he called out (in the physical-plane reality), "Good-bye, Chiana."

"See you later, Ashanee!" I answered, remembering his name from Chiana, where we had known each other 500,000 years ago. He liked that and smiled knowingly.

Our short reconnection in this life was great and very reconfirming. It had been a very long time—many lifetimes—since we had seen each other.

With a quick shift to the physical-plane reality, I realized I was late for my airplane. I rushed out the door and ran for the car that was waiting to take me to the airport. I just made it. On the plane home, I kept partially falling out of my body on my left side, and then, with great effort, pulling myself back in. I felt like I was dying. I had experienced this before after working with dying people. Each time they died I would partially leave with them. I would think that I was dying and get confused. But this time, I knew it wasn't me. This time I knew it was Robert.

By the time I got home, with HSP I could see the party going on at the Monroe Institute in the spiritual plane at level 27. Robert was celebrating with his wife. All was fine. Everyone up there was happy. As soon as I got to a phone, I called the Monroe Institute to confirm my HSP. Robert had transitioned while I was on the plane. They were all okay too, but, of course, in mourning for a great father who had done so much with his life.

Robert Monroe was a man with a lot of guts to stand up for and be open about his experiences. He helped many people. He has brought us all to a deeper, broader level of truth. I send my love and light to those who follow in the work at the Monroe Institute.

After Robert Monroe: After I had integrated the experiences with Robert, I looked for a map of the Himalayas in my National Geographic *World Atlas*. I was overwhelmed by the enormous size of the region I remembered living in. I couldn't find the names Nyang or Tsang anywhere on the map.

"Just forget it, Barbara," I said to myself. "This is ridiculous. You're not going to the Himalayas to look for some cave you once lived in!"

Several months later, I got a letter from the man who had been my partner for the work in the intuitive drawing class. He had found a very old map that showed Everest and another high mountain in the places I had seen them with HSP. It also showed two rivers right where I had seen them in meditation. They were named Tsangpo and Nyang-Chu. They were between two towns listed as Lhasa and Kathmandu. There where also two rivers named Nyang and Tsang. The correlation made me feel better. Who knows, perhaps some day I will be able to go to Tibet.

Letting Go of Death

Heyoan says that our concept of death comes out of our duality and that what we think about death is incorrect. This causes us tremendous fear, especially when we cannot perceive the worlds beyond the physical.

Your Erroneous Concept of Non-Life

There is no such thing as non-life.
Consider the possibility that everything
and every no-thing is alive.
Your existential fear is created by your persistent belief in death,
something you have drummed up out of your duality.

It simply isn't true.
It is only the duality within you that leads to the idea and the misconception of death.
The only thing that dies is duality when it comes together
into the unity of eternal life.

Life in the Timeline Doesn't Work

Your difficulty is that you have placed your-self on a timeline. Life is not at all like that, especially the life you experience from inside. Time is a tool that comes out of your observation of change. But most of that change is only from the physical perspective. Time is simply a tool you have created in your mind. In fact, it is not a very good tool at all when applied outside the mundane physical world.

Time is an attempt to explain flux. There are many illusions that arise out of your idea of time with which you attempt to explain the experience of constant change in yourself and all those around you, as well as in the entire world. Time is a handy tool of cooperation, perhaps a leveler of change, a way to communicate with another being who is also in constant flux.

Time is grounding from the outside.

*Your idea of time is your attempt
to create some kind of stability
based on a perspective from outside the self.*

*That is, you try to stabilize yourself
by something outside of you,
rather than stabilize yourself
from the center of your interior.*

Consider the possibility that you have always existed, that linear time is an illusion, and that you are in a phase of evolution of the human species that is beginning to develop the capabilities of understanding and directly experiencing this. Soon your scientists will show you that there is no such thing as linear time, or what physicists call "the arrow of time."

*Quite a concept: no time!
But it will take more work.*

*To the degree you hold yourselves in separation,
to that very degree you believe in, experience,
and are trapped in linear time.*

*As you bring these dualities together within you,
you will, perhaps slowly, but ever-so-surely
directly experience and move into nonlinear time.
In the so-called future that exists now,
you already do.*

Chapter 16 Self-Review: Your Experiences of Life after Death

1. What experiences have you had with life after death?

2. Do you consider them to be real? If not, why not? If yes, why?

3. How have they helped you deal with your own future death?

4. How have they helped you deal with your own future life in the spiritual worlds?

5. How have they helped you deal with your possibility of reincarnation if that is part of your belief system?

Chapter 17

HEALING OUR RELATIONAL CORDS

The life pulse that arises and radiates out from within you
and then comes into contraction
is in a certain degree of coherence and synchronicity
with your closest loved ones, be they family, friends, lovers, or partners.

They are involved in the most profound co-creation with you.
Your families are very significant in helping shape who you are.

Your personal choices of incarnation have been set very clearly with positive intention
so that you will be supported and challenged in many ways by your families.

Your families never go away
even if someone leaves this particular physical form,
or dies as you call it.
They are still very much present in your lives.

— HEYOAN

We now move to the fourth-level realities that involve our relationships. These interactions are created in the astral world and involve cords.

Our Cord Connections

We have all heard people referring to "our heartstrings" and "the cords that bind us." There are actually configurations in the HEF that correlate to these expressions. These configurations are involved in all the relationships we have. In both my books *Hands of Light* and *Light Emerging*, I have discussed our cord connections. I will briefly

review this information here and then go on to describe more information about cords that I have gathered since the writing of my two previous books. I will discuss cords, their healthy purpose in our life, as well as their unhealthy misuses that result in distortions in the HEF.

In *Hands of Light* and *Light Emerging*, I discussed three major ways we communicate with one another through the HEF. The first is harmonic induction, i.e., one HEF will harmonically induce its resonant frequency into another person's HEF (like striking a tuning fork that causes another to sound). The second type of communication is through streamers of bioplasma that flow through the air, and with which we exchange energy between us. The third is communication and energy exchange through our relational cords. Relational cords look like translucent soft blue, flexible, hollow hoses through which our energy consciousness flows. They are made of energy consciousness. **Relational cords transmit our energy consciousness. Emotional and mental energy flows through the cords that are connected between people who are in relationship. They transmit this energy consciousness directly into and through our seals of perception.** This flow of energy consciousness can occur no matter what the physical distance between two people is. Physical location does not matter; neither does the time of day or night nor even much longer times, such as years or centuries. It doesn't matter if the loved one is alive in a physical body or is no longer in the physical body after death. Communication through these cords can still take place. The longer and more intimate is the relationship, the stronger are the cord connections, and the more numerous are the cords. In the next section, I will describe the types of cords and how they function in the HECS.

The Five Types of Cords

After having worked with cords for some time, Heyoan informed me that there are five major types of cords. They are:

1. **Soul Cords** that the ongoing soul carries from its original God connection within the spiritual worlds.

2. **Past-Life Cords** from experiences on earth and elsewhere.

3. **Genetic Cords** that are gained by connecting to birth parents.

4. **Original Relational Cords** that grow with the primary caregivers, usually the parents or adopted parents.

5. **Relational Cords** that grow through relationship with others: humans, pets, and special objects with which people have personal connections. We continue to make these as we include more and more people in our relationships. Relational cords tend to be copies of our cords with our parents. If we have siblings, we make cord connections with them. We make them with anyone who is a member of our original family. If we have pets, we also make cord connections with them.

Healing Genetic and Relational Cords

Damaged Genetic and Relational Cords: There are many ways genetic and relational cords can be damaged. Small children tend to wrap their relational cords around their favorite toys. The child uses these toys as an attempt to make up for what is lacking in its relationship with its family. Forcefully taking a toy out of the child's hands is quite painful because it rips the cord connections between the toy and the child, thus destroying the child's feeling of safety in its surrogate relationship with the toy. Teddy bears and stuffed animals that the child sleeps with serve the purpose of helping the child feel safe in its feelings of isolation when it is forced to sleep alone, as most children are in our present modern societies.

When I was five years old my sister was born. I remember being very upset. My mother had been sick for the whole nine months of her pregnancy. At the same time, my father had just had a nervous breakdown from losing his job during an economic downturn. He was only thirty-two years old. He had three little kids and a wife to support. My older brother teased me all the time. Then on top of it all, my new baby sister got pneumonia. My mom kept her tightly wrapped up in the center of the dining room table. That way Mom could do housework and cook with the baby in sight. I couldn't figure out why my sister got to sleep on the table. Maybe that is why I always played under it! All I could feel was that nobody cared about me and they all loved my baby sister. So when she was given a little stuffed "doggie," I wanted it. I took it and pretended it was mine.

Probably it was a way to try to get the love I needed. Of course, that didn't work. My mother got angry, took the little "doggie" away from me, scolded me for stealing, and gave it back to my little sister. I was devastated. The entire experience actually did not have much if anything to do with how they cared about me in reality. But my child's mind did not understand that.

How Genetic Cords Are Created

Genetic cords are created between the heart chakra of the person wishing to be born and the mother-to-be. They must attach before the mother-to-be can conceive. This cord connection takes place outside of the seventh level of both the prospective mother and the child. See Figure 17–1. Once this has taken place, then the woman can conceive. I've worked with many women who wanted to become pregnant but could not succeed. These women had already gone to the medical profession for biological checkups that showed nothing wrong; yet, they still could not conceive. So they came to me.

From my HSP perspective, they were unable to conceive because they were unable to make the heart-cord connection between themselves and the individual that wanted to be born into the physical world. Unconsciously these women were afraid of pregnancy, and without knowing it, they prevented these cord connections. Once the cords were reconnected in a healing session, these women were able to achieve normal pregnancies just a few months later.[14]

Genetic cords also connect to the father. I am not sure exactly when this happens, since no men ever came to me with the issue of inability to conceive. However, reason suggests the cords between father and child would connect no later than conception.

Only a few men came to the healing sessions, primarily to be there to support their wives. Some came because their wives convinced them to come, since healing only the wives' heart cords had not achieved pregnancy. In these cases, I also worked on the husbands' heart cords. Once the husbands' heart cords were healed, pregnancy was achieved. Others simply came to support their wives' healing. Then I could actually work on their cords.

I also observed that some women (and men) were unable to allow genetic cord connections deep into their heart chakra from a soul that wished to be born. These women (and men) were unaware of their fear of pregnancy. By observing the energy fields of many women and men in this condition, I found a similar disfiguration in their heart chakras. Figure 17–2 shows a dense, dark block deep inside the heart chakra that prevents the cord connections from rooting deep into its center. This must happen to achieve pregnancy. To achieve this deep connection requires a deep spiritual and biological surrender to the will of God. Thus pregnancy requires a deep surrender to the will of God; that is, to the will of God as it is described by Heyoan below.

Many of us have very big misconceptions about what it means to follow God's will. We are influenced in negative ways both by our father's and other male authorities' discipline, as well as religious teachings—especially those teachings that include traditional information about the wrath of God. If you don't do what "he" orders, watch out! Inability to achieve conception is one of the many results of our misconceptions about God's will. This is why the following Heyoan teaching about divine precision with a light touch is so important:

Contemplation on Divine Will

*Practice contemplation on divine will
as an intricate, precise form,
rather than as a force that makes you do something*

---

14   See *Light Emerging*, pp. 187–202; *Hands of Light*, pp. 75–76.

or a force to rebel against.
As a result, your whole experience
of divine will changes.
Where then is the wrathful,
willful God that punishes you
if you do not follow his will?
It simply dissolves into the divine
precision of a beautiful form.
As you synchronize your lives with divine will
by practicing surrender to the divine
precision of this universe,
you will experience the joy and pleasure
of feeling completely safe in each moment of
the now that you surrender to.

God's will is the precise divine organization of life.
God's will is the template for divine precision.
It is the template for every shape of
everything and every being
that is manifest in the physical world.

God's will is divine precision with a light touch.
The physical laws of this universe
are tools of learning for you.
They exist within the intricate template
in divine precision.

God's will is a soft breeze upon your cheek.
God's will is a delicate unfolding
of the petals of a flower.
God's will can be seen every day in the
growth of a beautiful tree,
in the unfolding of a fetus in the womb.

God's will can be seen in the unfolding of your life.
God's will is a precise delicate
unfolding pattern of life
in the evolution of all species.
God's will is the music of the spheres.

God's will holds an open template for your free will
to choose each moment with your love,
to balance yourself and surrender
to the full experience of what is now:
what is coming to you,

what is moving through you,
and what is expanding and contracting in you,
unfolding your life most naturally, most beautifully.

What is the divine precision
that comes through your creative force of love?
Learn to recognize your unique perfect pattern.
The will of God has been portrayed to be
strict and severe from the perspective of the
human psyche.
It is not that at all.

God's will does not punish.
It is you who punish yourselves
because of your belief in duality and separation.
The divine template of will within you
and the universe is benign.

Once the genetic cords between the heart chakras of the person who wishes to be conceived and the two parents are connected, pregnancy can be achieved. The genetic cord connections of the other chakras between the parents and the child also happen very rapidly around conception. I have not had the opportunity to observe this for an obvious reason: once pregnancy was achieved and confirmed, the clients stopped coming. These genetic cord connections last forever.

If a child is given up for adoption, its genetic cords remain connected to its genetic parents forever. When damaged it is imperative that they be repaired and reconnected for the health and development of the soul. This will be made clearer in my discussion of ancestral root cords in the next chapter. Root cords are very different from cords of any type.

Of course, during my healing practice, genetic cord damage was not always the only cause of the inability to conceive. The other main causes I saw were that the combined pH of the sexual fluids of the man and woman did not allow a pregnancy to continue, and that problems in the husband's second chakra as well as weakness in the field of the womb caused miscarriages.

Relational Cord Development in the Womb

As the unborn fetus develops in the womb, its relational cord connections for the chakras grow between it and the parents. This growth also continues throughout the life of the child after it is born. The child's cord connections to its parents become the prototype for all other cord connections in relationships. The child develops cord connections between himself and others with whom he is in relationship (see Figure 17–3). These relational cords with others will be based on the primary ones developed with the parents or primary caregivers throughout childhood. In other words, the parents and primary caregivers build the prototype cords upon which all future relational cords will be based. The relationships we create with women are similar to those we created with our mother, or primary female caregiver. Likewise, the relationships we create with men are similar to those we created with our father, or primary male caregiver.

Summary Information about Our Cords

Healthy relational cords from the first chakra connect deep into the earth's core. The cords from the seventh chakra connect up into the higher spiritual worlds.

Relational cord connections are made between the remaining five chakras; i.e., second chakra to second chakra, third chakra to third chakra, fourth to fourth, etc. Thus healthy relational cords attach between two people and *like* chakras two through six. The energy consciousness is then transmitted between *like* chakras (two through six) of two people in a healthy relationship.

The relational cords from chakras two through six connecting from one's left side go to one's mother and to all female persons with whom one is or has been in relationship; the relational cords on the right side go to one's father and all

male persons with whom one is or has been in relationship.

Relational cords take on the character of the relationship. Thus, if the relationship is soft and soothing, the cords will be that way. If the relationship is harsh and difficult, the cords will be jagged and stiff, and transmit harsh energy consciousness.

Relational cords are hollow, flexible tubes, and look a bit like a soft water hose. They are blue in color. They carry information between the two people they connect together. The information that is transmitted can be seen as instinctual. It is not mental in nature. It is more like an innate sense of knowing, a basic way of being in life without knowing why.

Relational cord connections are used in all species for parents to connect to and teach their offspring. Relational (and genetic) cord connections last forever, beyond the grave.

Unhealthy cord connections have many different types of distortions. For example, they can be:

1. Torn out, entangled with other cords, and/or floating in space.

2. Deeply imbedded and entangled in oneself.

3. Shredded.

4. Connected to the wrong chakra.

5. Weak, stiff, heavy, polluted, sucking, demanding, controlling, dragging, etc.

6. Not connecting properly but wrapped around another person.

7. Imbedded and entangled in another person rather than connecting properly.

Once in relationship,
always in relationship.
Relational cords last forever!

✛ ✛ ✛

All unhealthy relational cords must be healed.
Until they are healed, the person creating them
will continue to create more unhealthy cords!

No matter how awful the relationship
and therefore its cords,
cord connections should never, ever be cut!
They need to be healed.

Every relationship,
no matter how painful or "bad,"
provides essential life lessons about the self!

I have heard that there are healers who cut cords.
This only results in more need for healing.
The cords that are cut must be restored.
Relational cords are forever.

Your original relational cords
start before birth and continue after death.

Healing Genetic and Relational Cords

There are some interesting and surprising things that occur in cord healing that one would not expect:

1. Cord healings take three people: the healer, the healing client, and the cooperation of the other person who was/is in relationship with the client.

2. The third person does not have to be physically present in the healing room, but of course can be if they happen to be physically present.

3. The third person must agree to the healing and come to it in the fourth-level HEF reality.

4. Relational cord healing can be done with long-distance techniques added to the cord healing techniques, the clients do not have to be present in the healing room.

5. This technique works with all five types of cords.

Healing Relational Cords between a Student and His Deceased Mother: A good example of a healing of relational cords occurred a few years ago during one of my classroom healing demos to students in their third year of training. The volunteer was a young 30-something-year-old man whom I will call Donald. Donald's mom had been rather controlling when he was young, and to gain his independence, he had torn away his third chakra relational cords to her and balled them up inside his third chakra.

During the healing, I first did the normal HEF preparation by clearing and charging the field. I carefully moved up the chakras from the feet, charging and repairing them till I reached Donald's third chakra. After clearing and charging his third chakra, I proceeded to untangle and clear the accumulated stagnant energy consciousness in his torn third chakra cords.

His mother appeared in spiritual form, ready and willing to receive the healing. She stood at a distance so that her seventh HEF level and Donald's seventh HEF level were not in contact (see Figure 17–4[a]). Once I cleared Donald's cords, I pulled them out beyond his seventh level and stabilized them so that they simply stayed there. Then I proceeded to do the same thing for his mother's cords. I cleared and charged them and also pulled them outside her seventh level.

The next step was to simply reconnect each cord, end to end, between Donald and his mother. This is done carefully and caringly. As each cord was reconnected, a burst of energy consciousness flowed again between the two of them. Their fields brightened and became joyful. Then I did a simple closing. The relief in both of them was obvious. See Figure 17–4(b).

Skills a Healer Must Have to Do Relational Cord Healing

The above healing may seem simple, and it is. However, the difficulty is in the skills necessary to accomplish this type of healing. They are as follows:

The healer must be able to hold all four dimensions (core, hara, HEF, and physical) steady and clear for the entire healing for all three people—the healer and the two clients.

The healer must be able to use HSP to perceive and work with the following aspects of all three fields at once:

1. the seven levels of the HEF
2. the hara
3. the cords
4. the chakras
5. the seals inside the chakras

The healer must also be able to hold a state of being of unconditional love during the healing.

Healthy Cords and Seals

The healthy anatomy of cords and seals is shown in Figure 17–5. Deep down inside the chakra are the seals of perception, as they are called. As described in Chapter 6, the seals of perception are part of the mechanism that detects energy consciousness in HEF frequency ranges. *Once again, I must emphasize that the only reason to call it energy consciousness is that in the HEF frequency range of live biological systems, **the component of consciousness has a large effect.***

As described in Chapter 6, the seals in the HEF dimension look a little like lenses, through which the incoming energy consciousness spirals down into the chakras (see black spiral arrow) to charge the HEF (see Figure 6–1). This energy consciousness can be detected, provided the "seals of perception" are functioning and the individual knows how to regulate one's own HEF. The cords, which look like long, flexible, hollow tubes, are HEF configurations. They are shown in their blue color. In Figure 17–5, notice that the cords go right into the seals.

One can perceive the HEF as energy consciousness in terms of color and form. It is similar to normal seeing in the physical. So what we can say of the information that is transmitted through the cords is that it is like the energy consciousness of the HEF. It is like a charged fluid or bioplasma. As it flows through the cords, it is carrying information that one can feel, see, hear, smell, taste, and know with HSP.

The Seals of Perception: Once inside the seal, the cord ceases to exist. The information flowing from the cord is transmuted as it moves into another dimension. Rather than a transmission of energy consciousness from the cord into the deeper dimensions, there is a *transmutation* of the information that is held in HEF as it moves down into the deeper levels of our being—the hara dimension (intentionality) and the core star dimension (essence). Therefore the nature of the energy consciousness will be transmuted into the nature of that dimension. To perceive deep into the seals and to follow this transmutation of information into the hara dimension and core is very difficult.

Once the information moves into the hara dimension, the information is transmuted into our intention. When our intention moves down into the core star, it is transmuted into our essence, our essential divine being. How does one perceive or experience essence, and what form of information does essence give? To me,

Experiencing another's essence is a full-bodied experience of their unique qualities of higher knowing and higher principles, embodied in love.

Thus it is through having relationships that we develop our essential divine being! These relationships are between ourselves and the people we know and care for, the ones we know and don't particularly care for, and all human beings we don't know. Our relationships with others include all living creatures—plants, animals, everything that is alive! This most likely includes more beings than we, at this stage of our human evolution, can imagine!

Chapter 17 Self-Review: Healing Your Relational Cords

1. What relationships in your birth family were the most difficult?

2. What relationships in your birth family were the easiest?

3. Given your answers to number one above, with whom in your birth family do you need to heal unhealthy cord connections?

4. Given your answers to number three above, with what type of people do you repeat the unhealthy cord connections in your relationships now?

5. What do you need to resolve in yourself in order to heal your relational cords in your present relationships? Describe three major issues you need to resolve within yourself that still negatively affect your present relationships.

6. Given your answer to number two above, which kind of relationships are easiest to form? What is it that you enjoy about them? What do you get from them?

Chapter 18

HEALING TRADITIONAL ANCESTRAL ROOTS

*You chose a family that has particular aspects of
intellect, interests, talents, environment, and monetary challenges.*

*Your physiologic and physical world were carefully
considered and determined
before any particular incarnation.*

*This includes those aspects of yourself
that you have already developed
as core essence through many generations.*

*You may also have been your own grandfather/mother
from many lifetimes ago.*

*That is, you may have lived the life of a
particular grandfather/mother
and then reincarnated many generations later, now.*

*Usually family members tend to skip several generations
when choosing this.*

*Thus, from this perspective, consider the possibility that:
You could be, or are indeed, your own guardian or guide.*

— H E Y O A N

Confusion about Our Roots

We have all heard stories about our ancestors. When I was a child growing up in the cold Wisconsin winters, my father told me stories about how his ancestors came to America on the *Mayflower* and braved the unknown. According to my family tree, two noted ancestors were the two Adams presidents. Probably most people have some noteworthy names in their family trees. They can be models for us when we need them.

My mother spoke of how her parents came over during the land rush. They lived in a covered wagon and claimed homestead land in Oklahoma.

167

They traded grain for buffalo meat with the Native Americans. Her brothers were wheat farmers in Oklahoma. Some of their sons still are.

Everyone looks for such things in their family history. They confirm our existence. They make us feel safe and that we too have the power inside us to create something we long to, no matter how hard it may be. All of these types of stories connect us to our roots. Our foundations are rooted to the earth and to the past with our ancestors who prepared a way for us to move into the future, to make it better for us as well as for the next generation. At least, that is what we try to do, but it doesn't always work!

We want to be rooted into the earth and to our ancestors. We feel connected to our ancestors when we speak of our roots. We hear stories about what our ancestors did that make us feel connected to them as well as proud of their courage to follow their dream!

So let us now explore the healthy configurations of our ancestral roots that exist in our Human Energy Consciousness System (HECS): what they do, how they affect our lives, how they are misused, how they become disfigured and very unhealthy, and how we heal them to re-create health for both ourselves and our relationships with them.

Our Roots

A healer can learn a lot about their clients' relationships with friends and family by simply observing both their relational cords and their ancestral roots. There are healthy and also unhealthy ancestral roots that exist in our HECS.

Ancestral roots are very different from our relational cords. There is a connection between our relational cords and our ancestral roots. This may cause some confusion at first, but upon looking more closely, they are easy to distinguish from one another.

In Chapter 17, I described how our relational cords function and the communication we have with our friends and loved ones through them. There is a big difference between relational cords

and ancestral roots. You will remember from Chapter 17 that the relational cords are hollow, long, flexible blue tubes, through which information flows between two people. This information is composed of colored energy consciousness. It contains a lot of information about the nature of each relationship between the two people connected by the cords. The cords serve as direct conduits through which this information flows almost instantly. The more interactions one has with a friend and the more information that is held between them, the more cords they will have created. That is one of the reasons it is painful to lose any relationship. The cords contain the flowing substance of our relational lives.

It is important to understand the differences between cords and roots. They function differently and there is a huge difference in the healing techniques used to heal cords and the healing techniques used to heal roots. Root healing is a set of the most difficult techniques for healing we teach at BBSH! Root healing challenges the healer to use all the healing techniques that are taught at the school.

Ancestral Roots: Ancestral roots are strong, solid black, and flexible. They are the ties that bind us to our birth families. They are more difficult to work with and require very focused concentration. They stretch from the inside aspect of the seals in our chakras down through the hara dimension and into the core of our being, the core star.

Traditional Ancestral Roots (TARs)

There is a great deal of confusion about our ancestral roots with regard to our HECS. To unravel this confusion, let's take a look at the anatomy of both our genetic cords and healthy ancestral roots. Then we can observe how imposed traditions can cause tremendous problems in the HECS! Traditions imposed from elders onto the next generation not only injure the new generation, but also freeze the progressive next step of development of that culture. The unhealthy entanglements of traditional ancestral roots are not necessary to save a culture; instead, they eventually kill it. Thus an understanding of how this happens is extremely important for all of us! First I will clarify the nature and function of our ancestral roots. Then I will show the damage that is done to the offspring of those who misuse traditional roots to control their young, and the damage done to humanity in general when these roots are misused in forced tradition.

Traditional ancestral roots, or TARs, are manipulated, distorted genetic cords. They have been distorted for the purpose of maintaining traditions by controlling the children of those traditions to insure that the traditions are carried on. Usually, the belief under the tradition is either for religious purposes or for survival purposes, or both.

There are a number of ways traditional ancestral roots can come about. The most common is simple. A parent—say, the father—who is perhaps not even particularly connected to a tradition, but who has not been able to create what he wanted to accomplish in his life, may do a lot to make his child accomplish it. Such a parent will tear his genetic cords away from his own chakra and insert them through the child's seals and into the child's chakras. Thus the child's healthy genetic cords, which are supposed to connect with his father, are replaced with the father's distorted, dark, solid, controlling, demanding, entangling, solidified cords; they actually look like black roots. These are not real roots. They are distorted genetic cords.[15]

Even though they are distorted genetic cords, I will call them *traditional ancestral roots* because they are the HEF mechanisms to maintain "our traditional roots" that control offspring from one generation to the next. Indeed, these traditional ancestral roots can do this for many generations into the future, since they are automatically handed down to each new generation until they are healed. Once a genetic cord is replaced with a traditional ancestral root, it continues down through the generations because the first child to become entangled has no healthy genetic cord with which to conceive a child. Instead, the child is conceived with an ancestral root. Thus a *traditional ancestral roots healing* must go all the way back to the original ancestral root that started the tradition. This is why it is so hard to heal.

Traditional ancestral roots are very unhealthy for a child. They interfere with his free will. These traditional ancestral roots actually look and feel like they are made of tar. They are usually entangled through the seals, causing disturbances in perceptions so that they can hold prejudices in place! The traditions and prejudices they spawn are blinding. They literally *create blind spots* in the HEF where the traditional ancestral roots damage the seals of perception!

Don't get me wrong here. I think the variety in humanity's cultures is wonderful. Each culture has something unique to contribute. Each has lessons for the others to learn. Each has developed different aspects of the HEF that result in gifts to humanity.

As Heyoan says,

> *Humanity*
> *is not meant to be homogenous.*
> *How boring!*

However, each culture also contains fears of and hatreds toward other cultures, many of which are based on past history and actually no longer have any grounds in reality. At one time in a culture's history, certain behavior was most likely necessary for survival. But that was long ago, and it is no longer applicable. Eventually, these fears and hatreds become solidified into prejudices, which become *unconscious stagnant belief systems* of the people who hold them. They probably don't think about it at all.

A Couple of Examples of Traditional Ancestral Roots: I once observed the unhealthy TARS of a person that I knew would be a good example of how much a rigid tradition can interfere with

---

15   Note: These are not the roots with which we root ourselves down into the earth. We do that through the relational cords we grow out of our first chakra.

an individual's free will. The case highlighted the difficulty for such a person to know what he wants and create the life he wants to have; unfortunately, I did not have an opportunity to do a healing on him.

In this example, the man had his genetic cords of the fourth chakra replaced by traditional ancestral roots from the male side of the family going back many generations. The roots penetrated the fourth chakra from the rear, curled through the back and front seal, then went down the vertical power current, where it continued to curl through the front and back aspects of the seals in chakras three, two, and one. This configuration means that the traditional ancestral roots controlled his balance of love and will function in his heart chakra! These TARs controlled who he was allowed to love and how he was to use his will. His will was oriented primarily toward making money for his birth family for their insured survival. As the root continued down the vertical power current, it also interfered with his free will and understanding of the function of each of his chakras! Essentially, he was controlled by *tradition*, by the TARs that were placed through his first, second, and third chakras!

He had been forced to behave in the following ways. In the fourth chakra, they controlled whom he was allowed to love and marry. In the third chakra, how he must take care of himself and specific members of his family, excluding all others who are not members of the family. In the second chakra, how and with whom he may express and enjoy his sensuality and sexuality, including whom he must marry. And in the first chakra, how and with whom he may enjoy and appreciate the physical pleasures of life.

On the front of his body, there is a traditional root coming from female ancestors. This particular TAR goes through the front of the fourth chakra only. It therefore affects only the front part of the fourth chakra and its seal of perception, whereas the many male ancestors exert much more pressure on him, since they have penetrated the seals of the fourth, third, second, and first chakras.

The next section discusses the blind spots caused by TAR penetration through the seals of perception.

The Blind Spots in the Seals of Perceptions That Result from TARs: Any time a TAR goes through a chakra, it most likely also penetrates through the seals of perception. When this happens, it creates a blind spot in perception at the point it penetrates the seal. An example of this type of damage from roots is shown in Figure 18–1(a). I observed this woman, but did not have the opportunity to give her a healing. I present it here to illustrate the blind spots that traditional ancestral roots cause. It is a drawing of the sixth chakra, the chakra of vision. The two adults are standing facing each other. The one who initiated the traditional root is on your left, and his adult daughter on your right. 6A is the front of the sixth chakra. 6B is the rear of the sixth chakra. The father has taken his genetic cords and pushed them first through his own seal at 6A, creating a blind spot in his visual perception. He then (later in life) pushed the root through the front of his daughter's sixth chakra three times and penetrated through her back seal at 6B three times, thus creating three blind spots in both the front and the back seals of her sixth chakra. See Figure 18–1(b). The blind spots look like dark spots on the seals. See Figure 18–1(c). They simply block a clear visual perception of reality that the seal would give her were it not blocked. Usually such blind spots are created in so-called taboos, or forbidden areas of life, that are not to be acknowledged. Thus the blind spot blocks the daughter's ability to see a particular area of life. She will simply not *see* the true reality of a particular aspect of life that the father does not want her to see. Notice how the TARs in Figure 18–1(a) stretch from the inside aspect of the seals in the sixth chakras down through the hara dimension and into the core star.

If any blind spot exists in any of the seals, that person will simply be blind to what a clear perception of that reality is. They simply will not be able to understand what you are trying to convey. They won't be able to see it until the blind spot is healed. This is one of the reasons it is so hard for traditions to communicate. They are blind to one another. Rival traditions create and promote blind spots in their peoples. This is why diplomacy between them is so hard! Even if everyone is aligned with the good of the greater whole—which, of course, is not usually the case—creating understanding and peace is difficult because of the blind spots that have been held for centuries. Instead of creating understanding, most focus on protecting their traditions, thus keeping the blind spots in place!

Trouble with Traditional Roots during the Dying Process

A short time after my experiences with Robert Monroe, an older friend of mine who was her 90s was in the hospital in the last stages of the dying process. I visited her in the hospital just before she died. I will call her Ruth. Ruth kept going in and out of her body, and became disoriented each time she "fell" out of her body. She kept saying that she was falling. I started using the techniques I had learned at the Monroe Institute. I grasped both of her hands and assured her that she was all right. Her family joined in to reassure her. Ruth died a short time after I left the hospital. I immediately went into meditation to offer to assist her to level 27 (see Chapter 16). It seemed to work. There I found a cottage her previously deceased husband had prepared for them to live in during their transition between lives.

Later, at her funeral, I watched the life energy fields as the rabbi said Kaddish and other prayers. He did each phrase of the various prayers in Hebrew and then in English. When he spoke in English, nothing at all happened in the life energy fields. When he chanted in Hebrew, a great deal happened. Here is the sequence of energy field changes that I witnessed when he said Kaddish and other prayers in Hebrew:

1. During the first chant, a protective energy dome was created over the area in which everyone was standing with the closed coffin containing her body. There were a few graves that, because they were so close, were also in this protective dome.

2. The relational cords from the family were disconnected.

3. The life energy field of the group of family members were separated from Ruth's life energy field and put into two separate protective domes: the family in one and Ruth in another.

4. Ruth's fourth level HEF body and higher spiritual bodies were separated from her physical body.

5. A long distant corridor opened to other deceased ancestors. They were reaching out in agony. They wanted her to join them and were sucking her to them. But she didn't want to go.

6. The next time the rabbi spoke in Hebrew, she was forced to go. She literally got sucked back into the place where the other deceased ancestors were.

7. The coffin was lowered into the ground while an energy seal closed around the body, preventing any more connection to it.

8. This same energy seal separates the family from the body in the coffin. The protective energy dome that was the first built around the coffin, grounds, and the people at the funeral was dissolved.

9. Kaddish ends and the family and others leave. The family is energetically disconnected from Ruth, who is with her ancestors.

10. As we are leaving, the ancestors are still intensely focused on the living, even though they are energetically separated from them. They seem

to desperately want life from the living. They appear to be victims of various pogroms, the latest being the Holocaust.

11. There was another aspect to this I haven't described earlier: the ancestors were connected to Ruth through traditional ancestral roots.

I didn't tell anyone about my HSP observations. I wasn't so sure how they would take it, and I didn't want to offend anyone. It was years before I saw the same phenomenon again. This time, it was in a different setting.

Healing a Woman with an Ancestor Problem Similar to Ruth's

Years later, when doing a healing demo in a workshop, an unusual thing happened that solved (at least for me) the ancestor issue I felt at the funeral described above, as well as for the person who volunteered to be a client for my healing demonstration. The woman in the workshop was associated with EST. She had progressed in her personal development through the EST training, and then had become a leader. Her presenting complaint was her constant nagging feeling of obligation. She felt caught in her large family matrix and could not extricate herself from it. It was as if energy was being sucked out of her. I will call her Hanna. Here is what I experienced in the healing:

As I demonstrated the healing on Hanna in front of the rest of the workshop participants, I saw that her energy was, in fact, being drained. I followed the flow energy as it exited from Hanna's field to find the source of the draining. Once again, I saw the hordes of deceased ancestors, all reaching to Hanna for life. They were in agony and were unable to clear themselves of the horror and terror they had experienced in the Holocaust, when they were tortured and killed.

I tried as hard as I could to disconnect the traditional ancestral roots and other attachments, but to no avail. They were completely locked into Hanna as if she were the only way out of their

agony. She was clearly one of their descendants. Finally, after a great deal of work trying everything I could think of, I let go. I surrendered and prayed for help. Then everything changed.

An alphabet appeared up in the air in an arch from Hanna's head to toe, and to the right of the table, between her and the ancestors. I assumed it was the Hebrew alphabet, but I wasn't sure, so I wrote the first two letters that I saw in the air on the board, and asked the students if it was. They told me that I had written the first two letters of the Hebrew alphabet on the board.

At that point, Heyoan told me to direct the ancestors into the arch that was the Hebrew alphabet. So I did. It is my understanding that the Hebrew alphabet represents God.

It took me a while to change the focus of the ancestors by contacting them psychically, but finally they were able to see the Hebrew alphabet and began to focus on it instead of Hanna. One by one, they focused on and went into the letters.

When they all were safely home, I returned to completing the healing with Hanna. I removed the traditional ancestral roots and her HEF brightened up. Then I finished the healing by repairing all the levels of her field and the hara, and helped her reconnect to her core essence.

It was over. After years of being dragged down as if someone were sucking her energy, Hanna had her precious energy back! She went on to continue her process of claiming her life for herself while, at the same time, honoring her ancestors.

Healing Debra's Traditional Ancestral Roots

Let's take a look at how healing traditional ancestral roots relates to the HEF and the results of traditional ancestral root entanglement. Figure 18–2(a) shows the beginning of a healing to remove a TAR between two people (for whom I did a healing in a class healing demonstration several years ago) and a few of their ancestors. This case is much simpler than the two I discussed before. The presenting complaint of the "client," whom I will call Debra, was her overwhelming caretaking of her younger brother and other members of her family. In looking at her field with HSP, I could see the black roots entangling inside her third chakra. While I prepared the field to remove the root by clearing, charging, and balancing the field, I saw her brother walk into the room in spiritual form. The roots ran through him and back through many generations of control. They held the energy consciousness of demanding caretaking in extreme quiet; i.e., Debra was supposed to be very quiet while she took care of people. I did not understand this till later in the healing, as you will see.

As I loosened, untangled, and removed the TARs from Debra's third chakra, I also had to concentrate on the ancestors' HEFs. As soon as a TAR was released from Debra's chakra, all the other fields that were connected through the generations went into deep terror. See Figure 18-2(b). I had to hold them all in unconditional love as I worked. This took a lot of concentration. As soon as the blind spot was healed in Debra, I could move on to the next in line, back through the generations, to heal the blind spot in that next person. To complete the healing, each person all the way back to the first TAR had to be cleared of the TARs!

I had to unwind and untangle the TAR and heal each blind spot back through each person, starting with her brother. The root was entangled in each of the ancestors' chakras and seals in the same way that Debra's was. Naturally, I asked permission from each person to proceed with the healing. Although frightened at first, each was happy to oblige. The healing continued through many more individuals than I expected. I traveled back through time to meet each one to untangle the root. As the healing continued back through the generations, I witnessed the circumstances that each had experienced in their lives and hadn't resolved as a result of the traditional ancestral root that had held them in bondage. One was in a fight using a bow and arrow for a weapon, one was freezing from cold weather, one

was frightened by lightning, one was chased by a large predatory bird, one was carrying a clay bowl with herbs, one was butchering an animal like a deer that he had just killed. The last was a caveman dressed in animal skins. His job was to keep everyone who lived in the cave very quiet, so that a cave bear that frequented the place would not hurt them. I had never witnessed so many generations connected together in this way before.

Once I untangled the unhealthy traditional root from the caveman, an unexpected thing happened. As soon as the solid black root was cleared, its original blue hollow relational cords were released from the caveman! The relational cords automatically jumped forward into the next generation, then into the next, and so on forward in time. Each individual was freed from the negative beliefs about their lack of freedom to choose to live his/her life as he/she wanted to. See Figure 18-2(c).

I watched in wonder as each person was freed from the bondage of the roots. Their spontaneous joy filled the room! As the beautiful blue hollow relational cords reconnected, communication flowed down into the next generation. The caring, loving energy consciousness of each generation was sent forward to the next. All the offspring were supported and loved for who they were.

Then, an amazing thing happened. Everyone in the healing classroom experienced it. As the genetic cords continued down through the generations, they came into the classroom. The feeling was wonderful. The entire room filled with the generational cords that were connected to the students! I didn't expect that! In fact, it was as if everyone were somehow genetically related since the original caveman. The feeling of brotherhood, sisterhood, and family was astounding. We personally experienced the actual genetic connectedness of everyone in the classroom. We were all descendants of that caveman! The instinctual wisdom of the generations flowed through the genetic cords that connected us all! Everyone there was in ecstasy the rest of the class week.

Results of Debra's Traditional Ancestral Root Healing

I waited a few days after the healing to interview Debra. I wanted to give her plenty of space to integrate what she had experienced. I was curious to find out how she experienced it. What she experienced was reiterated by many of the students in the classroom. While they witnessed Debra's healing, they also experienced the same healing processes occurring in their HECS during the healing demo I gave on Debra!

Their descriptions concurred with my experiences while I gave the healing. After a few days, during which Debra integrated the healing she received, I interviewed her to find out what she had experienced in the healing. I also interviewed Debra many years later to see how well the healing had held and how her life had changed as a result of the healing. She said that the healing initiated deep changes in herself and her life. The healing had held very well throughout the years since.

As you have seen in this chapter, cords last beyond this lifetime, and as you saw in Chapter 17, very interesting things happen with the cords shortly after death.

After all, it is your life!

Chapter 18 Self-Review: Finding the Unhealthy Traditions in Your Family Lineage

1. What are the unhealthy traditions that are handed down in your family lineage?

2. What are the unhealthy behaviors that result?

3. Which of your chakras and seals are affected by traditional ancestral roots? How?

4. Do you know your blind spots? What are you blind to?

5. Which side of the family do they come from? Notice the difference between the blind spots from your father's side of the family and those from your mother's. List three major blind spots for each side of the family. If you have trouble with this, think of the traditions of how you must behave in each side of the family. Do you behave that way or do you rebel?

6. How do your blind spots listed in number five above affect *your life?* What have you given up to behave according to your family's demands on each side?

7. What are the healthy relational cords that you need to establish instead of the roots? *This is your road to deep healing!* Feel your longing! What is the life you long to live? How do you want to re-create your life? What are your deepest longings for your life? How are you succeeding in creating their fulfillment? (Remember, clearing your unhealthy roots will also help free your family members of theirs! Even though they may be very upset with your choices in the beginning, you can help set them free just by being an example! It is up to you; there is no obligation other than to yourself for your life!)

Chapter 19

UNITIVE CORE CONCEPTS

I end this book with some of Heyoan's channelings about higher unitive principles to live by. I concentrate on the following concepts: world peace, life beyond death, healing our relationships and family heritage, and how that connects to global healing and our individual leadership roles. I conclude with a meditation for unity.

Creating World Peace

Align with your intention to be here now. Align with your intention to live in truth. In time before you, you will be challenged with the threat of terror. You have spent some time dealing with your internal terror; therefore you will be able to recognize the force of imagination as countries threaten each other and as these threats escalate. Remember that when you hear the threats over the airwaves, return to your center and note how such rhetoric evokes the terror within you. Note the reactions that you have, both the physiological reactions and the psychological/emotional reactions. Note the actions that you automatically do as a result of your fear. What do you choose to do in your life as a result of these threats? Are your actions based in unity or duality?

It is well noted that many of you are in the process of changing your value systems, and that many of you are on the way home to your true unified self. Homecoming includes the resurrection of families that have been split and the reuniting of relations that have been separated for quite some time, because as your value systems change you enter the sacred temple of the heart.

You will find many things there in your heart.
You will find a temple of love.
That temple embraces all aspects of life,
even so-called terrorism.

Notice how people in different nations, states, and various places of power use threatening rhetoric to induce a negative reaction on the astral level to get people to act negatively to "the opposition." Or, shall we say, "coagulate around one side of a negative dualistic archetype." Notice the dualistic creative process. The joining of forces in opposition begins with a lot of rhetoric, emotions, and lies that are all designed to evoke fear from your unevolved consciousness held in your time capsules. The underlying intent is to induce you to move into dualism and to choose a side of a fight or an impending war.

This challenge has faced humanity for millennia in your history. It is now in this century that we choose to educate you to the best of our ability, using all forms of communication to convince you that duality is an illusion and that all human needs are the same.

One of humanity's great fears is the fear of not having enough. It leads to overconsumption that then hurts Earth's ecosystem and depletes its natural resources. That ecosystem, by itself, without these exaggerations of humankind, easily maintains equilibrium.

Common images and fears are deeply held in people who are native to the same countries. Each country has its own dualism, its own fears, based on its history taught through verbal communication and action. These histories are written in dualistic form to create and hold dualistic images in the people in each country. Grouped together, these images form belief systems that dictate what one must do to remain safe. Thus the problems of humanity are the internal ones, and therefore, there are group reactions to internal group fears. For yourself, they are whatever fears are held inside you and your society. It is this history that is deeply ingrained in each individual in this room and in the world, in some form or another, that we seek to dissolve in order to solve humanity's issues, to retain Earth's natural resources, and to reinstate the natural balance of Earth.

Please remember that before anything is precipitated into the physical world, it must reach critical mass in the astral world. The international rhetoric that is occurring now, the expressions of various fears and the actions they seek to invoke that follow those fears, are primarily based on images and belief systems that are held in place nationally.

Take us with you, so that we might carry you and be with you in these times when fear will escalate as it has been. Understand that fear is simply separation from love. It is separation from your self. It is separation from the temple of love in your heart. When you feel that separation in you, know that you have removed yourself, to whatever degree your fear is, from the Community of the Sacred Human Heart.

It is in the Community of the Sacred Human Heart that is arising all over the earth that peace can be created. By facing the fears that are within you, seeing how easily they are evoked from within, and feeling how powerful they are, you can also see how dangerous they can become when you project them onto an imaginary enemy that you think wishes to destroy you. The enemy, however, is in your internal duality out of which you act in ways that are not compatible or synchronistic with the healing of humanity. There are no enemies other than your internalized imaginations, or, shall we say, misconceptions that form your dualistic belief systems.

Your so-called enemies are only people who are also experiencing and expressing great internal fear and acting upon it. World hunger can be looked at as an enemy, but it is not. It is a creation of humanity. World fear is a creation of humanity. Wars, of course, are, as you can see in this buildup. Notice that this dualistic creative buildup is in the psychonoetic forms. Certain individuals, out of their terror, are seeking to create a worldwide critical mass to precipitate war into the physical. They are following that step-by-step creative process. Others are seeking unity in a step-by-step creative process.

Consider the possibility that now, in this time of human history, we are challenged to continue this communication across the so-called veil and walk in both worlds. We are challenged to name the exaggerated emotions. We are challenged to name the process of purposefully exaggerating negative emotions—rage, anger, fear, terror—in order to control the emotional reactions and actions of those who are vulnerable. Vulnerable because these human beings have not had the privilege of this type of education. They are vulnerable because there is such a lack of knowledge of what is being said here. There is a great deal of knowledge of how to rev up negative emotions in order to get a particular reaction. However, there is a tremendous lack of knowledge about how to move from an emotional reaction to a centered feeling of light, love, and power.

Moving from an emotional reaction into love requires going into and through one's fear and the pain beneath it. This is exactly what history blocks. History turns the focus outward. Healing turns it inward. On the way into that pain at the very edge between an emotional reaction and pain, there is great suffering and great expression of that pain. Yet as you sink deeper into that pain, in communion with another human being, that pain becomes quiet and the light emerges in beautiful resonant communion. It means simply acknowledging each individual's human condition. The building up of emotional reactions in a political situation denies the simple truth and misuses humanity's denial of the true human condition, which is simply that all human needs are the same regardless of political or religious affiliation.

There is no question about this when sinking into your heart and joining the Community of the Sacred Human Heart. At this stage of evolution, human history is mostly based on emotional reactions and superego demands that one must deny one's true state of being and be better. This causes great strain on the internal system of any human being, no matter at what level of progress on the path. You are now given greater challenges to those places within you that are still held in shadow and confusion and that are also connected to the collective unconscious of humanity, some of which is rather split.

These things weaken humanity, primarily because you were taught you must be better, and that you must do things in a certain way. Yet the more you learn to sink into your spiritual longing, that you hold in your high heart, the more you are able to sink into this beautiful sacred human heart that you are, the more you will be able to face these things. They are quite simple. It is so relieving to make a simple statement of the truth of where you are right now, what you are feeling, what you are thinking, what the sum total of your life experiences is in this moment. It is so simple. When you find yourself able to do that, you will find that a great amount of the chaos or apparent chaos in your life dissolves. The chaos in yourself and in your

life is held there by denial of the simple truth of who you are.

Perfectionism of its own accord implies denial.

Yet by simply moving into the human condition, in truth, brings you into humility. Humility, what a wonderful word.

Humility means placing yourself in your perfect place in the divine plan of God. In fact, you don't need to place yourself there; you already have. It is simply allowing yourself to be in that place of divine precision with all of who you are.

You have great gifts. Each individual has many gifts to give. You also have great pain, some confusion, and undeveloped areas of your being that need development. So it might be confusing. Undoubtedly in your childhood as you were growing up, there were certain leaders that were held up before you who were considered to be great leaders. A certain degree of perfection was attached to them, as well as the idea that you would not have pain or that you would not have to struggle if only you were like that person.

Those teachings were based on duality. I assure you that every great leader, spiritual or otherwise, has great pain and personal transformation work to do. There are two major difficulties that were created by having been shown someone who was supposedly perfect: it induced an internal striving for perfection, and it generated self-judgment because you are not perfect in the way perfection was held out to you. Thus you have pain that is then followed by more self-judgments. You erroneously believe that if you become perfect, you will not be in pain. So every time you go into pain, you judge yourself. Judgment simply holds the pain in place. Learn to recognize judgment as the first level of defense; it hides your perfectionism. It hides your demand not to have pain. It hides your wanting to be better than others (just another way to avoid pain). Yet under judgment is your fear of pain. I am using *pain* in a general way here—any kind of pain: starvation, poverty, abuse, ridicule, being ostracized, etc.

You see, the power of the rhetoric that is flying around the world on either side of many sides of many fights is based on your fear of pain and your images of what you must do to avoid that pain. Your image says that if you have pain, it means there is something terribly wrong with you. After all, look how long you have lived, how much you have learned, and all the work you have done, etc.

The intent to war has a simple equation: first induce fear, then terror, then rage, followed by actions of war. You are the light bearers. You and many like you all over this planet are doing light work everywhere. Do not believe that because you are light workers, it won't happen to you. That's another version of "I did this work and now I don't have to have pain." Leaders who hold clear space, healers who give of themselves, light workers of all kinds, have pain and are not exempt. There are no exemptions in the human condition. There may appear to be some, for certain times of certain people's lives, but they are not exceptions.

Coming here means walking straight into your pain and fear. It means doing the work you have come into this incarnation to do and with this work you are blessed. The blessing is a blessing of humility. The blessing is one of the ability to walk into surrender and to simply be who you are, and that is enough. In being who you are, your cup runneth over. In being who you are, you can see through the dualistic rhetoric that is seeking to build up the dualistic creative psychonoetic consciousness energy forms into a critical mass to precipitate down into the physical world and explode into war.

With this self-knowledge, self-humility, and self-surrender comes a relaxation into divine precision, and with it you feel this eternal connection to the divine that says, "Take care of yourselves, initiate communion with the spiritual worlds of God, whatever that means to you in your life. With it you release and open the doors within you to the great surges of luminous awareness that come with the mystical life."

In this century there is the challenge to live the mystical life while living the mundane, to come out of the secret communities that are locked away somewhere in mountains or forests. Yes, of course we return to them for renewal, but live your life among humanity. Bring spirit to humanity.

Spirit moves through you in ways of divine precision that you most likely do not understand in the beginning. What at first appears to be chaos is in fact divine precision working through each individual on this planet, no matter what species. It is divine precision working through to bring synchronicity, love, and light.

When you are in your place that is just right, your mystical life unfolds to bring peace and love. When you choose not to engage in the escalation of fear; when you choose not to add to the duality of the collective unconscious that humanity is revving up in terror; when you choose to be in love, let the light flow through you, and follow it step by step; those dark clouds that are gathering will dissolve. Do it in communion with the light workers on this planet.

Allow the mystical to unfold from within you, to flood you from the spiritual worlds. What humanity calls power, many times is willful insistence on one's own ways, whether it is an individual, a small group, a nation, a religious sect, a religion, or parts of them.

Humanity has erroneously equated power with willful action, with acting against an individual's free will. True power is effortless.

This is, as you know, a distortion in the energy consciousness system. It is running a great deal of energy through the will centers and using a forcing current.

A lot is being done to convince one to go into that willful state. Yet here you have had the experience of true power. It is effortless. When your energy consciousness system is aligned, fully centered, balanced, and clear, it becomes more coherent. It is your vehicle to do your life task. It simply functions automatically with effortless intention because you have a balance of reason, will, and emotion, and because your purpose is solid and clear and grounded. When you have done that, you have entered into the sacred now in the space in the center of your heart chakra. The energy consciousness system is a great tool for doing this. It is most important to learn to do this.

If we wish to save humankind from self-destruction, this is one of the ways to accomplish it. Every individual can do this with your own individual precision, allowing your free will to flow in communion through the sacred center in your heart.

Out of chaos comes order. What appears to be chaos when you are in a dualistic state, when centered is seen for the truth that it is—divine precision.

Humanity is challenged to stay in truth.

The chaos in your life is challenging the areas of your being, the areas of your individuated self that are not yet developed because you have chosen this time to develop them.

If you have chaos in your life, you might need it to break your systematic control of how you run your life that brings you the pain and unfulfillment.

Because of the importance for each individual to learn now, to self-educate, your experience of chaos increases in order to break that unhealthy mold of behavior you have been in for perhaps many lifetimes.

Thank God for chaos; it is bringing you to truth.

Find how the chaos in your life is challenging the areas that you really want to change. It is breaking down the systems that hold those habits in place in your life. Utilize the international threats of war and terrorism. Utilize them to break down your unhealthy habits of how you run your life. They really work to do that. You see when some might be getting caught up in war, others can utilize that rhetoric, the speeches that

you hear on television, you can utilize it because it evokes fear within you and that fear is a direct line into your negative habits. It is precisely your negative habits that create your unfulfillment.

So now, let us come together as a great powerful force that emerges out of effortless intention, the intention to become whole, the intention to fill every need upon this planet. The need for clear loving communion; the need to create; the need to love and be loved; the need to be safe; the need to be comfortable, to have nourishment, to care for your body, to live in a community; the need to have freedom so that your free will can lead you through your creative endeavors; the need for your creations to be accepted; the need for recognition; the need to recognize each individual and that each individual's reality is different, that each individual's longing is specific to that individual, that each individual is sacred, that each individual's body is sacred, a holy temple to be cared for and honored; the need to be caressed and loved; the need to honor and love and care for yourself; the need to recognize self-judgments as a defense and splitting of your creative energies; the need to be here for yourself and thereby to honor others.

This is how one prevents war: to feed the hungry; to love the deserted; to hold love and clearing for those who are confused, whose pain is deep and who are lost in duality. Bring forth this love. Fill your body with it; fill your lives and your families with it. Let it radiate out over this planet. Send healing to the leaders of all the nations of the world for clarity, for love, for truth. Do your part in healing the collective unconscious held in duality by first clearing your own. When you do this, you also remove that which you help hold in place from the collective unconscious. You can also focus on clearing the psychic noise of the astral world that is held by others. This is your predilection for you are here and it is your privilege in being a human being.

☩ ☩ ☩

Radiance across the Veil

All who have supposedly been lost are here with us.
For all of those who have crossed the veil,
the veil now dissolves and all are here with us now,
without boundary, centered in the divine.

Without the veil, birth and death are in the
same breath.
It is simply transfiguration from one form
to another.
It is all life.
We are life and light on the wings of love.
Light and dark fuse into transparency.

We Will Never Leave You

We are here.
Our world does not exist
in the spatial framework that yours does.

Do not look far for us—we are here.
It is a matter of opening
to the truth and the love within you.
With it you traverse the universe.

Walking in Both Worlds

Walking in both the spiritual and material worlds can be a great pleasure. When we broaden our double-world experience to include other aspects of our lives, it becomes much more complicated and requires a great deal more clarity about ourselves. Until we can live our daily lives with clarity, walking in both worlds will be accompanied by a great deal of confusion between our projections and our perceptions. That is because walking in both worlds will immediately challenge our deepest issues. First our clarity is challenged, then our sanity. (What do we think about our own sanity when we hear, see, and feel folks "on the other side"?) Then our relationships are challenged and ultimately, our death.

We will need to sort out what we feel about death, what we believe and fear about death from our personal and traditional upbringing. It means facing our own upcoming death. It means facing the death of our most precious loved ones. No matter how much we may say we believe in the other world, when it really comes down to the experience of death we always face deep terror and pain, whether it be our own death or another's, no matter what our beliefs. This is partly because the physical body is designed to resist death. It will struggle against it, and so will our personality that has been created over this lifetime. The stages of death and dying that Dr. Elisabeth Kübler-Ross so clearly delineated several decades ago do occur, regardless of whether it is a slow or speedy death.

We are filled with defense mechanisms against entering that deep fear and pain. One of the simple mistakes people can make with high sense perception (HSP) is to project a fantasy like positive spiritual connection into the spiritual world in time of great fear or challenge. One of the main clues to such projection in the case of death-associated experience is the absence of feeling the profound loss, the deep pain, and the shock of losing a loved one. It is only through one's presence in the mourning experience that healing can take place. One feels great pain, and also at the same time may experience the immediate presence of that loved one through any of the high sense perceptions one has. The deceased person may indeed be at peace but also experience great loss because of the physical separation from loved ones. From all of my many years of observing people who have just crossed over, they are very much like they were a short time before they crossed.

The task of walking in both worlds is that of reframing birth, life, and death. Our fear of death keeps us from entering the spiritual. Yet to live wholly, we must integrate our spiritual existence with our physical one. Death is a great letting go. It is a great surrender. The key to integration is to surrender our defenses and face those parts of ourselves that cannot live in the moment of the now. This means experiencing the many small deaths of those parts of ourselves. This means surrendering to living each moment of our life in the now. It means surrendering to the human condition in all our vulnerability to a very large outer world.

The path of walking in both worlds is a long, deep one that will take many lifetimes in order to walk with peace, clarity, serenity, and wisdom. It is a path of honor, it is a path of surrender and it is a path that burns away some of our most firmly grasped beliefs and reality constructs. It is not a path to be taken lightly in one sense, and yet it is with lightness that we must walk. To walk in both worlds with grace and honor, we are challenged to speak the language of wholeness to ourselves and others, while respecting the other's framework of reality. It is not so important to convince another of one's perceptions as it is to hold the person in loving care during the mourning process. When in mourning, the experience of a spiritually present loved one may be confusing and rebuked with anger because the pain and shock are so great. Later, that spiritual presence may be very heartening.

In our challenge to find appropriate ways of living in both worlds that honor and respect both, we can use our knowledge of the human energy field, hara, and core star. The most difficult thing about HSP being the doorway into the other side is to remain clear. HSP can easily be influenced by fantasy arising out of fear. The main difference between fantasy and reality in the human energy field is the direction of spin of a chakra. If the chakra is counterclockwise, the individual is projecting. If the chakra spins clockwise, the individual is perceiving. Being in the now moment means having an aligned hara line, thus clarity of purpose and connection to the core of our being. HSP is clear if one is in the now. If one is not, then HSP is not clear. We do it in the healing room. The challenge is to do it in everyday life! Walk with Angels, dear friends.

✛ ✛ ✛

From Individual to Relational Healing

Your intimate relationship with another
is held by both individuals
and requires pure honesty with each other.

You will find the same aspects
of true pain and its relationship to fear,
emotional reactions and character defenses
in your relationships.

Your relationships have core essence.

Use the same process of healing
your relationships as you do to heal yourself.

Continue healing in ever larger groups
held by the honesty and integrity
of each member of the group,
in ever-expanding relationships
to cover the earth.

We heal in relationship.
It is essential.
As we expand our honesty,
we heal larger relational groups.

✛ ✛ ✛

You Are the Next Step

Your ancestors, the grandfathers and grandmothers,
have given you this great heritage
that you have been birthed into.
You also, in return, give the new learning,
the new evolutionary step to them
through your relational cords.

You are birthed into a foundation,
into a world of support.
You are birthed into a world
that needs to take the next step,
and it is you that take it.

Your growth, the song of your soul,
the love within you, expresses itself
in your beauty, in your song,
in every form of all the creations that you give forth
throughout your life.

This is the next step.

✛ ✛ ✛

The Teachings and Human Evolution

The processes of
transformation—exploring your inner landscape,
transcendence—expansion of self,
and transfiguration—direct transmutation

*of residuals
occur in all spiritual growth,
in all paths of awakening.*

*What is taught here
is simply another framework
in which we hold the teachings
for this time, for this century,
and for this group of individuating human beings.*

*With each stage in the evolution of humanity,
which is also the awakening process,
less rigid tradition is needed
and you evolve more than before.
With each step you let go, dissolve tradition,
and replace it with your own personal heritage
out of which you hold yourself
in alignment with the divine.*

*You no longer need the older traditions
that helped the generations before you.
With each new step into truth,
each generation releases all of the
generations before.*

✛ ✛ ✛

Prerequisites for Leadership in Global Healing

The more you align down deeply into the earth, the more you align with your individual life task, your purpose, and also with that of humanity. All hara lines meet in the center of the earth for the common purpose of humanity's evolution. And as you know, human evolution is no different from spiritual awakening. They cannot be, and never have been, separated.

Each of you is a lightning rod for your culture, for your country, for the resolution of international conflict, and for the healing of this planet. What then do you carry within your physical energy consciousness system that is a signature of your culture, your community, your nation, and your religion? Each of you carries that signature, both in the dualistic form and also in the unitive state, in those places within you that permeate your entire being, where separation has never occurred, time does not exist, and you are

in the blissful moment of the now, knowing that all of your being is, indeed, one with the divine.

We will look at Global Healing from both the perspective of individuation and that of awakening, i.e., fusing with the unitive divine. You carry a sacred longing that leads you every step of the way along this path of awakening that is also human evolution. Within this divine longing are the gifts that you have come to give to humanity, as well as your leadership from your individual perspective.

Let us talk about this leadership. Who are you within your family? What role have you taken in your birth family and in the family that you are building now? What role have you taken in your community? You have taken this role from the very beginning of this lifetime. The role in your community that you may aspire to is reflected in that which you have taken in your family structure. You are, shall we say, practicing within your family structure for your leadership in your community.

Depending upon your commitment and your following through with that, that role may increase from your community in ever greater circles around you. Or, shall we say, spheres of influence. How much you will expand this role of leadership is your choice. Each of you here is a leader in your particular personal way. You can expand this leadership beyond the family bounds, through your community, through your nation, internationally and globally, if you so choose.

First, it is very important to understand that every leader is also someone who follows. Before leadership of any magnitude can be taken on, it requires the ability to follow and support the leader in any area of your life. Especially in any area you wish to lead. This support of leadership, i.e., giving your energy and your wisdom to something you believe in that someone else happens to be leading at this moment, is very important because you will understand and learn—first of all, about your authority issues.

What frightens you about authority? Within that work you will find how leadership was misused in your distant past, as well as early life, and perhaps in your life now. You will learn to recognize that the fear you carry about authority is related to your own misunderstanding of authority that must be worked through as you progress in the expansion of your leadership.

And so, in your early childhood, how was leadership misused? And how has that affected you in terms of your own leadership? There are, then, blank areas that you have not learned about, i.e., aspects of leadership that were missing in your childhood. There may also be areas within your leadership where you have automatically followed the same pattern of misuse simply because you are not aware of that misuse.

So what is the flavor of leadership within you that you are developing? It is extremely important to individuate within your own leadership. Leadership can be firm and kind. Leadership can listen to the areas that need improvement. No one on this earth is perfect; that is, from the perspective of doing no harm, of doing no wrong, simply because of the state of human evolution. Imperfection exists within these physical bodies, within your personalities, because you are on a path of learning. Imperfection is part of, and actually is essential in, the incarnation process. Because when you choose to incarnate into the physical world, you have chosen, simply by the fact of incarnation, to focus upon areas of your being that are still learning and leave other areas behind so that your imperfections are more noticeable. From the greater perspective of unity that is also you, there is perfection. And yet, in this incarnation you are perfect in your imperfections because they bring about the learning, because they leave room for great creativity.

You live in a reciprocal universe that reflects and brings back to you what you have created, both pleasure and pain, success and the not yet successful. These are the keys to leadership. You get a direct response that lets you know whether or not you are on line with the powerful creative forces from your unitive creative principal coming down through the higher levels of the field into manifestation, into the physical.

Both following a leader and leading with followers require deep honesty with the self and deep personal process. And having said all of that, we, of course, also say that everyone is equal. Everyone is equally a leader and a follower. Everyone is equal as a human being. Each individual soul is precious. Each individual soul is held carefully, gently, in the arms of the divine, abundant, and benign universe. The basic foundation of your existence is divinity. You are permeated with the divine. The universe, manifest and un-manifest, is permeated with the divine. In bringing forth global healing, it is essential to begin with this foundation.

✝ ✝ ✝

Radiance over the Earth

All over the earth the boundaries dissolve.
Every individual is a child of the divine.
Include all peoples of the earth,
all peoples in all continents and nations.

See all tribes, all countries over the earth,
as one humanity,
birthing, living, relating,
transforming, transcending, transfiguring,
dying, and birthing again.

Include the four-footed ones,
the beings of the sea, of the air,
the plants, the animals,
the crystals, the earth, and other planets,
one universe of great diversity,
here in this sacred now.

We all exist in one great community of life
in constant creation,
changing microsecond after microsecond,
held here in this sacred now.

✝ ✝ ✝

Unity Meditation

Align with your purpose in being here. Feel the beautiful rope of colored light as it laces up and down the center of your body. Move ever so gently to the center of your heart. Hold your awareness in the very center of your heart. Allow your light to expand spherically. Maintain the connection to the center of your heart rooted in your love. Feel the radiant light descending upon you into every cell of your body, into every cell of your being, lifting you to higher worlds of light and consciousness. Feel the waves of love coming through yourselves and expanding out through the universe.

As your heart and your core star merge into one, recognize the sacred sphere that has formed carrying the ancient wisdom, enlightening the ancient wisdom within your own sphere of light as it arises out of your DNA, out of your own ancient memory, now being released into your conscious awareness, here, now, in this sacred moment of communion, of relationship, of love.

Send these waves of love out over the earth to your country, to your hometown. Help build this grid of life, light, love, and honor, by first anchoring into the places that you know on this earth.

As radiance builds from the center of the earth outward, watch the goddess emerge out of the center of the earth, bringing the gift of life, the gift of the material worlds, the gift of your sacred body, the gift of the mountains, of all sentient beings, the gift of life in the physical world, the gift of the sacred heart, of love, of humanity, the gift of your temple of love, your physical body. Melding the spiritual worlds of heaven with the physical temple of the body, melding them together as one in all of the great diversity, with no boundaries.

All who have supposedly been lost are here with us. For all of those who have crossed the veil, the veil now dissolves and all are here with us now, without boundary, centered in the divine.

All over the earth the boundaries dissolve. Light and dark fuse into transparency. Every individual is a child of the divine.

Include all peoples of the earth, all peoples. See all tribes all over the earth, in all countries, as one humanity—birthing, living, relating, transforming, transcending, transfiguring, dying, and birthing.

Birth and death are in the same breath without the veil. It is simply transfiguration from one form to another. It is all life. We are life and light on the wings of love, together with the four-footed ones, together with the earth, the crystals, the plants, the animals, the beings of the sea, of the air, on the other planets. One great loving universe of great diversity, with great change through creation, microsecond after microsecond, here in this sacred now of love. We all exist in one great community of life, in loving kindness and in light.

Let your individual radiance shine forth. Let your core qualities shine forth through your skin. Send your radiance to your loved ones. Expand spherically. Send your radiance and love to all those in need, all the people of the earth. The peoples that are experiencing hunger, pain, death, and violence lift their pain and the sorrow into the radiance and the unconditional love that is here. Spread it out all over the earth. Speak the power of the word in your heart. Speak the name of God in your language. Hold it in your heart.

✞ ✞ ✞

Come out, come out.
Uncover that beautiful self
and soar into the brilliance
that you are through your creativity.

It is time now to claim your freedom.

✞ ✞ ✞

Chapter 19 Self-Review: Heyoan's Unitive Concepts

1. Meditate on each concept or principle you are drawn to.

2. Journal if you wish.

APPENDIX

Investigating the HEF and HSP

Let your curiosity lead you.
It is one of your best learning tools.

— HEYOAN

This Appendix contains some of my personal experiences of measuring the HEF and using HSP over the course of many years. I thoroughly enjoyed meeting and working with such gifted people! With each experience, I learned many valuable lessons.

Darkroom Measurements of the HEF

I got into science again and became the head of the Energy Research Group at the Center for the Living Force (CLF). The group had been dormant for some time, and had not finished its experiments. Dr. Richard (Dick) Dobrin, Dr. John Pierrakos, and I started to do them again, and built another darkroom in the basement of one of the buildings at CLF. We did some experiments with the aura in a darkroom, using a photomultiplier tube that measured ultraviolet light at 400 nanometers. Dick and I also studied the previous data that was taken before I arrived at the Center for the Living Force, and included it in our results.

In doing the new experiments with Dick and John, we followed the same procedures as the old, in which each subject had to remove all clothing and completely clean the body of anything that would fluoresce. Each subject would stand about 16 inches from the front of the photomultiplier tube and try to energize his or her field. Since the signal-to-noise ratio was so low, we had to sum the signal over sixty seconds to get clear results. With this, and also with cooling the housing of the photomultiplier tube, we measured a 15 percent increase in most subjects when they tried to increase the energy in their HEF. A few subjects were able to increase the tube output by over 100 percent. One special subject, John P, always increased the signal by 15 percent just by walking into the darkroom, without even trying to increase his energy. When he did increase his energy he was able to consistently create the largest output, over 100 percent increase in the signal.[16]

An anomalous phenomenon, which was found repeatedly with the strong subjects, was that the signal did not completely disappear when

---

16   Barbara Brennan, Richard Dobrin, and John Pierrakos, *Historical Indications of the Existence and Function of the Human Energy Field* (New York: Institute for the New Age, 1978). Richard Dobrin, Barbara Brennan, John Pierrakos, *Instrumental Measurements of the Human Energy Field* (New York: Institute for the New Age, 1978).

the subject left the darkroom. It took fifteen to twenty minutes for the signal to completely decay. This "lag effect" has been observed by others and has led to the postulation that some form of energy has been left in the room by the subject.

Three subjects were able to increase the photomultiplier output from outside the room. They said that they were projecting their energy into the darkroom.

There were several subjects who decreased the observed signal below the darkroom signal after they entered the darkroom, even though they were trying to increase it. One such subject was extremely agitated at the time she was in the darkroom. The impression of the researchers was that she was "sucking energy" from people she came in contact with before and after the experimental run. This psychological impression seemed to have a physical analogue in our observations.

It was observed that there appears to be a relationship between the energy field intensity and mental and physical states. For example, hard thinking reduced the intensity of the subjects' signal while meditation in general increased it.

With the difficulties we were having, it became obvious that a different, more sensitive photomultiplier that peaked further into the ultraviolet was needed.

The next year, at the IEEE Electro '78 Conference in Boston, Dick and I presented a paper on ultraviolet darkroom measurements of the aura and another called "Demystifying the Aura," which included my high sense perception observations of the human energy field.

What the Darkroom Experiments Taught Me:

1. *It is very difficult to measure the HEF with a photomultiplier tube because most likely the stronger wavelengths of the HEF are in a higher spectral range. There are probably more sensitive instruments made now that will do a better job.*

2. *Even with the difficulty of low output, we did get data that supported the HSP*

observations of how the HEF behaves: the phenomenon of brighter energy output with someone who is exerting a lot of physical energy, the phenomenon of energy sucking of someone trying to take energy from another person, and the phenomenon of something being left in the room after everyone has left.

3. *Since so many different people could have some effect on the PM tube, it supports the HSP observation that the HEF phenomenon does exist for everyone.*

4. *I need another lab!*

Observing a Psychic Affect a Plant with Psi Energy

At the IEEE, I met scientists who invited me to go to Drexel University in Philadelphia to get involved in some measurements and to observe some others. We brought our aura experiment, and hoped to get better results.

There were several experiments going on at Drexel at the time. One was to mentally affect a plant enough to have the plant respond by changing the output of a polygraph that was attached to it. The polygraph output was sent to a recorder. Eugene Condor was the psychic working with the plant. The experimenters had asked him to focus on the plant and try to make the plant change the polygraph output every minute on the minute mark. I observed him with HSP. He held a wristwatch in his hand to know when the time came. It was very interesting to watch him shoot a narrow white bolt of light out of his third eye every minute, on the minute. He did it like clockwork. I saw him sit there for hours doing this successfully on the minute mark each time. I had never observed someone with such precise ability. Each time he did it, the aura of the plant would burst into light for a moment, then go back into its "normal" flow of energy.

What Observing Eugene Condor Confirmed for Me:

1. *This was most likely the first time I observed the white laser-like pulse of light coming out of someone's third eye.*

2. *It is possible to control the third eye to emit a laser-like burst of white light in a timed manner.*

3. *A strong burst of white light from the third eye can affect a plant's aura that then can affect the readout on the polygraph.*

Affecting the Measured Output of a Laser Beam with the HEF

There was another experiment going on at Drexel that was in trouble. I got involved with it because it involved communication between the scientists and the psychic. Karen Getsla, a well-known psychic who had worked with Dr. J. B. Rhine at Duke University on various experiments (such as waking up anesthetized mice), was having difficulty communicating with the physicists. They had set up a laser-bending experiment. The trouble was that when Karen entered the darkroom she immediately affected the laser. The physicists could not believe this. So they changed the experiment. She immediately affected it again. So they changed the experiment again. In fact, each time she was successful, the scientists would go into the darkroom and change things. Their skeptical energy included an expectation that there would be no change in the measured output of the laser. What the scientists didn't understand was that every time they went into the darkroom with their very skeptical energy, they would change the energy in the room, thus changing the entire experiment. So first Karen would have to clear all the "there shouldn't be any change in measurement" energy out of the darkroom, and only after that work was done could she start to affect a change in the light intensity measure from the laser beam. In other words, the skeptical energy made it more work to affect the measured output

from the laser. Each time the scientists added more skeptical energy, it was more work for Karen.

By the time I got there Karen was very upset and about to quit. She said that the scientists were lying to her, telling her that they had not gone into the room. As a psychic, she would know that they had. But to show them that she had a way of knowing that made sense to them, she finally put tape across the door and door frame that they would have to move when they entered. When she came back from a break, the tape had been pulled off the door and was left hanging on the door frame. The scientists still insisted they hadn't been in the room!

So I took on the job of communicating between Karen and the scientists. This helped a lot. Then I went into the darkroom with Karen. We sent positive loving energy to the laser, with the intent to bend it and have the output read less light intensity. It worked; that is, the measurements changed. As we added more energy, the readout showed the laser light measurement getting darker.

The question was, what was changing? The experiment was set up to measure the amount of light coming from the laser, which was firmly mounted on a railroad beam so that it couldn't move. The light from the laser was sent out from the darkroom, through a slit, and then into a photomultiplier tube that measured the light intensity. If the intensity of light changed, it meant the light put out by the laser was either bending or attenuating. The data was read out on a graph. Infrared cameras filmed the inside of the darkroom, so if one of us touched the laser it was recorded on camera. As Karen and I built up the positive intention and energy to bend the laser beam in the room, the output measured by the photomultiplier decreased. The scientists gave us feedback through microphones about the effect they were getting. The light measurements steadily decreased.

Then the scientists asked us to both increase and then decrease the measured light output. We practiced for a while to find out how to do it, and then became successful by withdrawing our energy and swaying back away from the laser, and then swaying forward and sending our energy. We never touched the laser. This worked well, and we could tell the scientists looking at the readout when the readout would get darker and when it would get brighter.

At first we used the words "Now, now!" to let them know when we were sending energy so that the readout would get brighter.

Each time we swayed toward the laser sending our positive energy, we became more elated and lifted into an ecstatic spiritual state.

Instead of saying *now*, we started saying, "Yes, Yes!"

The *yes* turned to a louder, "Love, Love!"

Then *love* shouted out into, "God, God!"

Suddenly I realized we were shouting "God" in the physics lab at Drexel University!

I will never forget this experience.

As I look back at this experiment, I realize that we were sending and then we were not sending energy to the laser. We were also rocking back and forth and thereby moving several different levels of our HEF into and out of contact with the laser. As we got closer, the laser was in our fourth level. As we rocked back, it was in our sixth and seventh HEF levels.

From the perspective of a physicist, we never really figured out what was causing the change in light intensity measured by the detector, a photo-multiplier tube. The light was emitted from the laser first. Then it went through a slit and into the detector that measured the intensity of light (brightness) that entered the detector. Thus, the change in light intensity could have been caused by a number of things. For example, it was not clear if we actually bent the laser light beam or if we affected a different part of the laser body, like the metal it was made of, that then caused the body of the laser to warp, throwing the laser beam off the slit. Or perhaps we had an effect on the crystal inside the laser. After all, we were concentrating on the whole laser, which was made of many parts.

Perhaps the light beam was being attenuated by some other phenomenon we don't understand.

Perhaps it wasn't the laser that was affected at all, but some other equipment that was part of the experiment, although common sense indicates not, since we were not concentrating on anything else. We did know that the laser was not physically moving, as it was bolted down onto a heavy railroad beam, and a sensitive seismometer was attached to it. Of course, we never touched the laser. The scientists knew that because they were carefully watching us via the camera that was recording us the whole time. So everyone is sure that the laser did not physically move.

What the Laser Experiment Taught Me:

1. *The laser bending experience taught me that there is a huge gulf between how healers and scientists think and act. That gulf needs to be bridged with acceptance of the differences between the two groups, and the common sense to set a clear, clean way to do research that allows for what we sensitives do know about how the worlds beyond the physical work and interface with the physical.*

2. *One of the problems is that many sensitives borrow words from science and then use them to refer to phenomena that clearly do not correspond with terms set through the scientific method. This is one of the worst things to do in trying to communicate with scientists who have put great effort into studying, defining, and confirming terms through experimentation.*

3. *On the other hand, the scientists, especially those who are not sensitive, make assumptions about experimentation without understanding how they are affecting the experiment just by the way it is done and their inability to regulate their own HEFs. At Drexel, the scientists did not know that they were running energy into the system they were experimenting with.*

They did not know they ought to include the effects of their energy as part of the experiment. They did not know how to control how they ran their energy into the system that was being experimented on. At times the lab was filled with fear, skepticism, and prideful skepticism, for one can have pride in being "skeptical," or just be skeptical without the pride. Both exist in the scientific community. Being skeptical or pridefully skeptical are very different types of energy consciousness in the HEF from being "openly curious" or "allowing what is to be or unfold." Since it is an experiment involving energy consciousness, their energy consciousness was having a negative effect on the experiment.

4. *I have found that one of the major tools of HSP is one's innate and individual curiosity. In using your curiosity, you also automatically compare the information you are getting against all the knowledge you have gained in your life. I consider this good science and one of the things that also drives good scientific investigation. It is very different from "skeptical." The history of science is filled with scientists ridiculing other scientists when they come up with new theories that challenge the belief systems underlying accepted scientific thought. Many times the new ideas are true and must wait to be accepted until the "old guard" has passed.*

5. *The energy I saw coming out of Karen Getsla's hands and body was clear and at the same time much denser than the energy around her.*

6. *Karen was also able to shoot energy out her chakras at will. (Please do not try this, as it is a special technique that utilizes the center of the chakra, not the vortices that spin clockwise (as seen from the outside) to take in energy to nourish the field as well as the body.)*

Videotaping the HEF in the United Nations Building

The next phase of our research was to determine if the HEF could be seen with a video camera and recorded on videotape. We connected with the United Nations Parapsychology Club. Using private studio facilities and with the cooperation of a group of television engineers from the United Nations, we were able to successfully record a signal associated with the HEF. Our method was to colorize a signal from a black-and-white TV camera and to display it on a color video monitor and record it. The "colorizer" used in this experiment divided the black-and-white television signal into 22 shades of gray and added a different color to each of these shades. Since the discrimination sensitivity was greater than that of the human eye, we hoped to see subtle differences in the TV picture that would be ignored in normal vision. We found that with proper adjustment of the "colorizer," given a medium-blue background, the TV monitor displayed a thin pulsating field around the human body. In addition to that, the TV monitor also showed several funnel-shaped forms in the areas of the chakras.

We tried a few movements during these measurements. If the fingers of a subject's hands were placed together and then slowly drawn apart, energy field lines were displayed joining the fingers together. This effect showed for all subjects tested, independent of the angle at which the hands were separated.

During this experiment, Dr. John Pierrakos and I observed the HEF with HSP, and described what we saw. Our descriptions were recorded on the videotape. We did not see the TV monitor when we did this. Later, we watched the videotape to determine how what we saw with HSP compared to what the camera recorded. We perceived about three times more HEF activity than the monitors and it was the correct color, i.e., not a virtual image in which the colors do not really correspond to the color of the HEF. At that time, I could see at least several levels of the field, as well as their color. My HSP vision has improved much more over the years since the late 1970s.

To us, these experiments clearly indicated the existence of a human energy field and they also agree with what we observe with HSP. It is apparent that the photomultiplier tube also records a small amount of the HEF. We hoped to do more experiments along these lines, but were never able to do more. Shortly after them, Dick and his wife moved to the Netherlands, and both John and I got so busy with the Pathwork, we never found the time.

What the HEF Videotaping Taught Me:

1. *That a simple black-and-white Sony video camera can pick up some of the energy of the lower levels of the HEF.*

2. *Using a colorizer (a standard technique used to depict satellite data) helps one see the different levels of the HEF.*

3. *The colors of the colorizer depict the different shades of gray and are not the colors of the HEF.*

4. *The equipment at that time could see perhaps one-tenth of what I could see then. It is insignificant compared to what I can perceive now in that it just shows large areas of different gray scales turned into color, whereas someone with good HSP can see details with a full range—from the macroscopic to the microscopic—including details of energy lines on each of the structured levels of the field, inside cells, and even, to a certain extent, the DNA.*

A Quick Little Test of Brennan Healing Science with the AMI Machine

While visiting a friend, Michael, in California, we stopped by the California Institute for Human Science, which was founded by Dr. Hiroshi Motoyama, to do a quick test to see if Brennan Healing Science could make a difference on Dr. Motoyama's AMI machine. Measurements were taken before and after a healing. Dr. Gaetan Chevalier put the electrodes on Michael's fingertips. First, he took measurements before I worked on Michael, and again after I did a fifteen-minute healing to balance and charge Michael's HEF. When Dr. Chevalier did the second measurements, he seemed surprised that they showed much more charge and balance in Michael's field after such a short healing. The results of the AMI machine are displayed in a circle. The more balanced and larger the circle, the stronger the meridians and the healthier the HEF, the healthier the energy state. It was easy to see the difference between the two readings. The first circle was smaller and imbalanced. It was late at night and Michael was tired. The second circle was much larger and more balanced. In general, the larger the diameter and more balanced the circle, the healthier the energy state. Dr. Motoyama's book *Measurement of Ki Energy, Diagnosis and Treatment* describes how the AMI machine works.

What the Quick BHS/AMI Test Taught Me:

1. *Since I worked on the lines of the HEF, and the AMI machine measures the meridians, it verified to me that the acupuncture meridians are larger aspects, say rivers of light, compared to the lines of light of the HEF, since the machine was affected so easily and quickly.*

2. *The energy in the system was improved very rapidly with simple healing techniques.*

3. *It was a great confirmation of what I did and saw in the HEF before, during, and after the work.*

Observing Marcel Vogel Charge a Crystal

Another great meeting I had in San Diego was with Marcel Vogel. I didn't know who he was at the time, but Bantam set up the visit. When I walked into Marcel's place, he had two glasses of water sitting on his coffee table. He asked me if I could see any difference between them. I immediately saw that the hydrogen bonding in one glass had been "opened," i.e., he had somehow made the angles of connection between the atoms wider, and that the surface tension was decreased. He liked my answer. He then proceeded to show me how he had taken newly bottled red wine and aged it to perfection by simply pouring it through a copper tube that was wrapped around one of his specially cut and programmed crystals. Marcel demonstrated how he programmed his specially cut crystal. He held the crystal in both his hands; the pointed end was in his left hand, and the rounded end was in his right hand. His hands did not touch each other. He then focused his mind, set his intention, took a deep breath, and then, with closed mouth, snorted his breath out his nose. At the same time, he zapped the crystal with a narrow burst of bright white light from his third eye (sixth chakra). I saw the crystal take on a geometric program overlay in its etheric field.

What Observing Marcel Vogel Taught Me:

1. *Marcel could create a dipole charge between his hands as he held the crystal.*

2. *Marcel shot the crystal with the same type of laser-like light from the center of his third eye that Eugene Condor used to affect the plant.*

3. *Marcel used a sharp, nasal "out breath" that rasped across the soft palate on the roof of his mouth like that mentioned in* Hands of Light, *similar to the breath of fire of yoga, but this was just one big breath. This breath charges the third eye, helps pull energy up into the third eye from the vertical power current.*

4. *Marcel used this breath to both charge his third eye center and discharge the collected charge there with another "out breath."*

5. *Marcel could charge his crystals for different purposes. The crystals Marcel charged could affect changes in things*

such as water and wine. Thus, he could probably imprint other objects for healing purposes.

6. *Marcel didn't show me how he changed the hydrogen bonding in the water and its surface tension, but he did tell me that he had run it through the copper tube that was wrapped around a charged crystal.*

7. *He charged water running through the tube around a charged crystal and gave me some to drink. It tasted exquisite.*

8. *He said that wine was cured into the perfect age by running it through the copper wire around the crystal. The person who escorted me said it was delicious.*

Observing a Black Belt Rabbi Use the Soft Touch

While I was on my book tour for *Hands of Light,* Bantam arranged for me to meet a rabbi who also was a black belt in karate. I found this to be a very interesting meeting. First the rabbi demonstrated putting on a prayer shawl and tefillin while he recited the appropriate sacred verses. During this ceremony his HEF intensified, became brilliant, and demonstrated two very unique colored streams of energy (peach and turquoise) that coiled up the spine. This coiling up is similar to what I see when the Ida and Pingala of the Kundalini coil up the spine, but are slightly different in color, in that the Ida is red and the Pingala blue.

Next the rabbi demonstrated what he called the soft touch. He placed two cinder blocks on top of each other onto two other cinder blocks that were placed on their ends on the ground. He then placed a small doily over the top cinder block. He stood back, centered himself, and did the kiai, the cry that usually accompanies a karate strike. However, he did not move when he did the kiai. Instead, using my HSP, I observed that during the kiai he drew energy from his tan tien up into his third eye, where it remained as a bright white light until his next move. He then told me to watch carefully. He gently raised his right arm, then lowered it slowly and softly, in a wave motion, onto the center of the top cinder block, barely touched it, and then slowly, in the reverse wave motion, raised his hand again to its original position. As he lowered his arm and touched the top of the cinder block, I saw a longitudinal wave of clear energy travel down the center hara line tube inside of his arm, exit the center of his right hand chakra, and move down into the middle of the two cinder blocks that were sitting on top of each other. That point of energy then expanded spherically with great force. It was not until his arm was back into its original position that the cinder block shattered from the inside out and fell onto the ground!

"Wow!" I exclaimed. "That was great!"

What Observing the Rabbi's Karate Taught Me:

1. *The "energy" that traveled through the rabbi's hara tube seemed to be a coherent longitudinal or compression wave with a lot of power. It was transparent but dense.*

2. *That "energy" can be directed with focused intention.*

3. *The energy can not only can be directed down the arm and into the center of the two blocks, but also, with intention, be focused into one intended small place.*

4. *I do not know if the rabbi intended the "energy" to expand spherically, or if it would automatically do that on its own.*

5. *This type of psi energy has very powerful effects on physical objects.*

Observing Psychic Surgeon-Healers from the Philippines

The first psychic surgeon I observed was Placido from Baguio City in the Philippines. I went with a client whom I shall call Betsy. Betsy had breast cancer that had metastasized into the liver. She had arranged for Placido to work on her, and invited me to come along to observe. At first Placido did not want me to observe, but then he allowed it. He was wearing short sleeves and had no pockets in his clothes. He asked me to stand on the opposite side of the table from him, upon which Betsy was lying awaiting treatment. This way, he said, I could get a good view as he worked. Before starting, he lifted his hands, and showed me the palms and the backs of his hands to let me be sure that nothing was in them. Next, he lifted them higher into the air, and then swooped them down, fingers first. They went right into Betsy's bare belly about two inches. Using HSP, I could see the fingers of both hands penetrating about three-quarters of an inch into Betsy's liver. They just barely reached into the place where I could perceive the cancer.

How is he going to pull all that cancer out when he can't reach it? I thought to myself.

Then to my amazement, he created a strong sucking energy at his fingertips, and began to suck the cancer tissue of the liver toward his fingertips that were still inside the body. I stood in awe. He looked up at me, and motioned for me to watch at the skin level. So I focused my attention there. He spread his fingers into a circle about three inches in diameter. His fingers were sitting on the skin; they were no longer sticking into the skin. He said, "Now watch!"

As I watched, the dark red smelly stuff that looked like tissue (not proved to be cancerous tissue) rose up out of Betsy's skin to a height of about one and one-half inches. It was a little less than half an inch in diameter. At that point Placido grabbed the stinky stuff with his fingers and put it into a bowl of water that was kept near the table for that purpose. Just a note: there was no stench in the room before the tissue rose out of the body.

Later, Betsy was completely exhausted. I also noticed some holes or tears in her HEF where Placido had worked. I sewed them shut with an advanced healing technique I had developed to repair the structured levels of the fields.

On another occasion, as I was traveling through Europe giving healing workshops, I noticed that a psychic surgeon by the name of Michaela was apparently taking a similar route as I, although just ahead of me. Many of the people in my workshops had received psychic surgery from her a week before coming to my workshop. I could tell where she had worked due to the holes or breaks in their HEFs. I sewed them all back up.

Later there was a large conference in London in which many psychic surgeons from the Phillipines were invited to demonstrate their work. Many members of the press were there. Each surgeon used the technique of entering the body with hands/fingers and creating suction to remove the diseased tissue, or whatever the dark red smelly stuff is. Most of them used very similar techniques to Placido's as described above. (Rumor has it that the dark red smelly stuff was tested, and it was not human cells.) I did notice that the stuff they pulled out of the liver smelled worse than the stuff from other parts of the body, such as muscle or ligament areas.

A woman psychic surgeon, who is also a nun, was giving a demo on a man who had lung cancer. There were so many TV cameras and bright lights around her that she was having a rough time. All that electronic equipment and skeptical curiosity of the newspeople was making it difficult to regulate the healing energy. I saw her repeatedly stick the whole length of her index finger down as deep as she could get it into the little notch at the bottom of his larynx, and then try to suck the cancer out. It just wasn't working well because of all the interference. Each time she pulled her finger out, it made the loud popping sound of a cork coming out of a wine bottle for the first time. This really upset the patient. She finally stopped, to try to do it without the news media the next day.

One healer used the same principles but did it differently. He made a small cut through the skin by sending a strong very narrow beam of light from the end of his finger that cut the skin. He never really touched the body. He then put a penny on the cut, and added a wad of cotton soaked in alcohol on top of the penny. He then lit the cotton with a match. Once it was burning he put a small shot glass over the burning cotton. This created a vacuum that then sucked out the stuff. He even, with permission, would use someone else's finger to create the cutting beam. After watching for a while, I let him use my index finger. He grabbed it with two fingers and his thumb. He then sucked a lot of energy out of my entire arm, gathered and compressed it into the area in my finger that was between his fingers and thumb. Next he shot the narrow beam out the tip of my index finger to make the cut in the patient's skin. My arm hurt for a while after that. I didn't let him do it again. Also, I just want to make it clear that I do not have any information about the healing effectiveness of the psychic surgeons.

What I Learned from Observing the Psychic Surgeons of the Philippines:

1. *Even though the techniques may look very different, all the psychic surgeons used roughly the same energy phenomena of entering the body with a laser-like longitudinal wave that came out the fingertips, and a sucking action to remove debris from inside the body.*

2. *I saw several spirit guides working with many of them.*

3. *The psychic surgeons use a lot of the client's energy to do their work.*

4. *The psychic surgeons do remove things from the body.*

5. *Work of the psychic surgeons leaves tears and holes in the HEF.*

Meeting Dr. Valerie Hunt

Some time in about 1992, after *Hands of Light* was published, I got a call from a Dr. Valerie Hunt. She said that she was going to do some research and was in the process of interviewing "the best healers in the country." I was very flattered. I knew that Dr. Hunt had done the famous Rolf Study with Rosalyn Bruyere and Emilie Conrad. Since I hadn't met Dr. Hunt before, at least in this life, I decided to investigate any previous connections we had had before this life. I did a couple of meditations to psychically read the past. What I received was very interesting. It was like watching a movie of a past life.

The first scene was in Atlantis. Valerie was the head of a large community of people who had protected the secret knowledge of the universe. Valerie, who was wearing a maroon robe with a large white collar, was conducting a ceremony for five departing boats. Since Atlantis was breaking up, my job was to carry the secret knowledge in two of the boats to what is now Egypt. The other three boats were to both protect and carry supplies. I saw myself and others leave on the boats for Egypt. The sacred secret knowledge was in the form of a giant radiating sphere composed of lines of energy consciousness of white and blue light. The sphere had many geometric figures within it. As my meditation continued, I "saw" that after arriving in Egypt we had trouble communicating with the culture of the people who lived there. A tragedy unfolded before my eyes. The sacred knowledge of the sphere was for everyone to understand and live with in communion with the presence of the "next world," or the "energy consciousness world" within and all around us now. I despaired as I saw our beautiful sacred knowledge of the energy worlds lose its vital essence. Then it was simplified down several levels and turned into stone pyramids to insure the powerful leaders' passage into the next world.

For several years after this meditation, I looked for this sphere everywhere. But instead, I kept seeing three crossed lines of white light in front of my third eye. All three crossed each other in the center, and were at equal angles of 60 degrees from each other, like a six-pointed star. I grew more frustrated with this every year, but it wouldn't stop. My rational mind kept saying that it must be an eight-pointed star, but each time I examined it with HSP, it was a six-pointed star. I had to wait. . . .

Now, back to the visit from Dr. Valerie Hunt:

Dr. Hunt walked into my office with the air of a complete confident authority, and said, "Tell me what you know!"

So I spent some time telling her about the HEF and healing. I was too shy to bring up anything else.

Finally, in frustration, she commanded, "Now tell me what you *really* know!"

"Well, I did do a meditation to see how we knew each other in the past."

"Now we're getting somewhere!" she proclaimed.

I shyly told her the story of the sphere of knowledge. She encouraged me to continue. So I did.

When I finished, she said, "Describe what I was wearing."

I described the robe and large white collar that looked like one huge ruffle.

"I remember designing that collar," she proclaimed!

We spent the rest of our day discussing research that I thought should be done with the HEF. Valerie had plans for a large lab to measure the field. By the end of the day, I was very happy and excited about possible future projects. But funding is very difficult in these areas.

What I Learned from My Meeting with Valerie Hunt:

1. *Valerie's confirmation of my HSP and my reading past-life experiences was very important support for me then.*

2. *Valerie gave me a lot of useful information about other people in the field.*

3. *Valerie did not mention what the sphere of knowledge was, but she didn't reject it at all. This helped me keep looking.*

4. *I no longer felt so alone with my HSP/ science combination.*

Comparing Long-Distance Viewing and HSP with Dr. Russell Targ

Several years later, after *Hands of Light* was published, I had lunch and a short meeting with Dr. Russell Targ and Dr. Jane Katra in New York City. During lunch I watched Dr. Targ do long-distance viewing of my house in Montauk, some 90 miles away. I saw a pseudopod of energy consciousness move out from his field and travel to and right through my house, which has lots of sliding glass doors.

He said, "I went right through it! Do you live in a glass house?"

"Yes."

Since that was so interesting, we decided to do another little distance viewing experiment, so we went upstairs to their room, where Jane put an unknown object into the bathtub while Russell and I waited in the living room. Then I watched Russell view the object in the tub with "distance viewing."

I would say, "Now you are looking at it on the north end, now you are looking at it from underneath, etc." Each time I reported on the object he was viewing, he confirmed that I was correct. I could tell how big it was, and that it was facing up in the tub, but I didn't know what the object was. This may be because for most of my work, I focused on live human beings or animals rather than inanimate objects.

Then, after viewing the object to his satisfaction, Dr. Targ concluded that it was a hairbrush. He was right!

So, from my point of view, distance viewing, whether it be long or short, is the same as using HSP to perceive things that are at a distance. The longest distance reading I gave was from New York to Tokyo. Another one was New York to Rome. In both cases, my reading of the two different individuals' HEF was correct.

What I Learned from My Meeting with Dr. Russell Targ:

1. *I was interested in the fact that I could not see the object, even when Dr. Targ was looking at it. Yet, I can easily look inside the human physical body to describe organs, bones, various tissues down into the microscopic level. I concluded that it must be a matter of learning to pick up the correct frequency of what one is looking at. After all, I have practiced the art of seeing inside the body for years but never tried viewing an object with HSP before.*

2. *In looking back at this now, I realize I most likely made one major mistake. I could see which side of it he was looking at by observing his pseudopod connection to the object. I realize now that I was tuning into him and his pseudopod frequency, rather than into the object being observed and looking for its frequency.*

3. *To me these psychic pseudopods look like the pseudopod of an amoeba, thus my label. (The psychic pseudopod is the fluid-like energy extension from your HEF body to the object you observe that connects the HSP to the thing one is observing. One can think of it as a wormhole through space that connects you with the subject of observation through which information travels.)*

Appendix Self-Review: Exploring Your Personal Investigations into the HEF and HSP

1. What experiences have you had in comparing your HSP with that of others?

2. Are you familiar with your pseudopod or wormhole? What is it like?

3. How has it helped your self-confidence in your HSP?

4. Compare your experiences of the HEF with your friends/fellow students. How do they confirm each other? How do they differ? What conclusion do you draw from the differences?

5. Have you noticed how you use all your background in discerning and making your information useful? Notice how someone else does the same thing, but utilizes their own life experiences to make the information useful in a different way. Explain what the differences are. How do these two sets of information form more complete information, rather than disagreeing with each other? Each carries a unique focus of the hologram!

BIBLIOGRAPHY

Research Publications—NASA Goddard Space Flight Center

Sparkman (Brennan), B. A. "A Method to Correct the Calibration Shift Observed in a Nimbus Medium Resolution Infrared Radiometer, on the NASA Convair-990." NASA X-622-67-37.

Sparkman (Brennan), B. A., and G. T. Cherrix. "Simultaneous Cloud ALBEDO Measurements Taken with Airborne Sol-A-Meters and Nimbus II Orbiting Medium Resolution Infrared Radiometer." NASA X-622-67-49.

Sparkman (Brennan), B. A., and G. T. Cherrix. "A Preliminary on Bidirectional Reflectance of Strato Cumulus Clouds Measured with an Airborne Medium Resolution Radiometer." NASA X-622-67-48.

Sparkman (Brennan), B. A., and G. T. Cherrix, and M. S. Tobin. "Preliminary Results from an Aircraft-Borne Medium Resolution Radiometer." NASA X-622-67-445.

Brennan, B. A. "Bidirectional Reflectance Measurements from an Aircraft over Natural Earth Surfaces." NASA X-622-68-216.

Research Publications—Other Organizations

Brennan, B., and W. R. Bandeen: "Anisotropic Reflectance Characteristics of Natural Earth Surfaces." *Applied Optics* 9, no. 2 (1970).

Conaway, J., B. Conrath, B. Brennan, and W. Nordberg: "Observations of Tropospheric Water Vapor Contrasts near the ITC from Aircraft and Nimbus III During BOMEX." Presented at the 51st Annual Meeting of the American Geophysical Union, April 20–24, 1970: Washington, D.C.

Dobrin, R., B. Brennan, and J. Pierrakos. *Instrumental Measurements of the Human Energy Field*. New York: Institute for the New Age, 1978. Presented at Electro '78, the IEEE annual conference: Boston, 1978.

Dobrin, R., B. Brennan, and J. Pierrakos. *New Methods for Medical Electronics Diagnosis and Treatments Using the Human Energy Field*. Presented at Electro '78, the IEEE annual conference: Boston, 1978.

Books

Brennan, Barbara Ann. Hands of Light: *A Guide to Healing Through the Human Energy Field*. New York: Bantam Books, 1988.

Brennan, Barbara Ann. Light Emerging: *The Journey of Personal Healing*. New York: Bantam Books, 1993.

Brennan, Barbara. Seeds of the Spirit. Boca Raton, FL: Barbara Brennan Inc., published each year, 1998–2009. Each year a Seeds was channeled by Barbara Brennan. The 2008 Seeds is translated into Japanese; the 1998 into Spanish, as *Semillas del Espiritu*.

INDEX

Hay House Titles of Related Interest

YOU CAN HEAL YOUR LIFE, the movie, starring Louise Hay & Friends
(available as a 1-DVD program, an expanded 2-DVD set, and an online streaming video)
Learn more at www.hayhouse.com/louise-movie

THE SHIFT, the movie,
starring Dr. Wayne W. Dyer
(available as a 1-DVD program, an expanded 2-DVD set, and an online streaming video)
Learn more at www.hayhouse.com/the-shift-movie

✢ ✢ ✢

*THE CHOICE FOR LOVE: Entering into a New, Enlightened Relationship
with Yourself, Others & the World,* by Dr. Barbara De Angelis

CO-CREATING AT ITS BEST: A Conversation between Master Teachers,
by Dr. Wayne Dyer and Esther Hicks

THE POWER OF LOVE: Connecting to the Oneness,
by James Van Praagh

YOUR LIFE IN COLOR: Empowering Your Soul with the Energy of Color,
by Dougall Fraser

All of the above are available at your local bookstore,
or may be ordered by contacting Hay House (see next page).

We hope you enjoyed this Hay House book. If you'd like to receive our online catalog featuring additional information on Hay House books and products, or if you'd like to find out more about the Hay Foundation, please contact:

Hay House, Inc., P.O. Box 5100, Carlsbad, CA 92018-5100
(760) 431-7695 or (800) 654-5126
(760) 431-6948 (fax) or (800) 650-5115 (fax)
www.hayhouse.com® • www.hayfoundation.org

✢ ✢ ✢

Published and distributed in Australia by:
Hay House Australia Pty. Ltd., 18/36 Ralph St., Alexandria NSW 2015
Phone: 612-9669-4299 • *Fax:* 612-9669-4144 • www.hayhouse.com.au

Published and distributed in the United Kingdom by:
Hay House UK, Ltd., Astley House, 33 Notting Hill Gate, London W11 3JQ
Phone: 44-20-3675-2450 • *Fax:* 44-20-3675-2451 • www.hayhouse.co.uk

Published and distributed in the Republic of South Africa by:
Hay House SA (Pty), Ltd., P.O. Box 990, Witkoppen 2068
info@hayhouse.co.za • www.hayhouse.co.za

Published in India by: Hay House Publishers India, Muskaan Complex,
Plot No. 3, B-2, Vasant Kunj, New Delhi 110 070 • *Phone:* 91-11-4176-1620
Fax: 91-11-4176-1630 • www.hayhouse.co.in

Distributed in Canada by:
Raincoast Books, 2440 Viking Way, Richmond, B.C. V6V 1N2
Phone: 1-800-663-5714 • *Fax:* 1-800-565-3770 • www.raincoast.com

✢ ✢ ✢

Access New Knowledge.
Anytime. Anywhere.

Learn and evolve at your own pace
with the world's leading experts.

www.hayhouseU.com